LEARN RUSSIAN

LEARN RUSSIAN

Ian Press

Duckworth

First published in 2000 by
Gerald Duckworth & Co. Ltd.
61 Frith Street
London W1V 5TA
Tel: 0171 434 4242
Fax: 0171 434 4420
Email: enquiries@duckworth-publishers.co.uk
www.duckw.com

A catalogue record for this book is available
from the British Library

ISBN 0 7156 2913 1

Typeset by Ian Press
Printed in Great Britain by
Redwood Books Ltd, Trowbridge

CONTENTS

FOREWORD

Peter Jones

Russian, like Russia, is not for sissies. To be thrown into the magnificent, seething, dark, heady stew of the language is a rich enough experience in itself. But language and culture are inseparable, and here, with the same enthusiasm and passion he brings to the teaching of the language, Ian Press explores the world of Russia — its people, history and literature. From their mixed origins, the first codification of Slavonic in the ninth century, their conversion to Christianity and volatile unification, the emergence of Moscow under Ivans the Great and Terrible and westernisation under Peter the Great (or Terrible?), we are plunged headfirst, no messing about, into the literature: Pushkin, Dostoevsky, Tolstoy, Chekhov — the real thing, in the real language.

As Ian Press emphasises, to learn Russian is a lifetime's work. *Learn Russian* sets you on the way by offering the firm basics of the most important grammar, but does not encourage you to plod religiously through everything, exercise by exercise. It offers, as it were, a map whose broad outlines are secure, and encourages the beginner to explore and enjoy the wonders of the landscape without becoming too worried about the details of the route.

So, if you are fascinated by the riddle of Russia ('wrapped in a mystery inside an enigma' — like its famous dolls), love the taste and smell of foreign languages, and like to take them, Russian fashion, in great, glorious draughts rather than pedantic little sips, this is the book for you. Hold tight.

INTRODUCTION

Why learn Russian? For a start, the Russians tend to learn English, and when they learn it they tend to learn it very well. Many people see no point. The point, perhaps, is that there's no directly utilitarian point. If your business can be done in English, with native speakers of Russian dealing with all the fiddly bits, fine. But that's short-sighted. Knowing some Russian in a 'real-life' situation is invariably extremely useful — it creates a different set of assumptions in the participants. And don't tell me business is done round a boardroom table and nowhere else. However, don't let's be too calculated about our motives.

Russian as Russian, in itself, is wonderful when you're dealing with Russians. And Russian is a puzzle, a very structured one — if you can get to grips with it, you've shown some real skill. Russia and Russian, and Russians, are 'soul' — they are in tune with essential things and, however chaotic you might think Russia is, are highly organized in their own terms. With a language like Russian, as you're about to see, how could they be otherwise? And the culture: you really are more in tune if you can talk about Russian painting and music in Russian. And then there's the literature. I'm sorry, but if you want to read any of the following, you simply do have to read them in Russian: Pushkin, Gogol', Turgenev, Dostoevsky, Tolstoy, Chekhov, Blok, Annenskii, Khodasevich, Akhmatova, Tsvetaeva, Mandel'shtam, Bulgakov, Olesha, Pasternak, Kharms, Venedikt Erofeev, Pelevin,...

And Russia is East and West, through the Tatar Yoke and perhaps choice for centuries isolated from our western Classical heritage, creating an identity through itself and its version of Christianity, but then seeking to recast its identity through the Schism in the Church in the seventeenth century and the adoption of Western values from the time of Peter the Great. There's a lot to be learnt from the nations on the margins of Europe, those that are 'not quite European' — Spain, Portugual, Russia, and the UK! And the confusion caused by the loss of Empire — Spanish and Portuguese, British, Tsarist and Soviet. Think about it.

When you learn a language, you learn something that is someone else's. Though people might feel delighted that you show an interest in their language, don't forget that the language remains theirs in a very real sense — respect is called for. Learning a language, then, isn't just the words and the constructions; it's the whole thing: the life, the culture, the appropriate ways of communicating with people — 'transferable skills'. Nothing, actually, new about this. Coming back full circle, the danger is that you might think you needn't work hard at the grammar. Well, generations of students have made it clear to me that you *have* to do the grammar, they've begged for tables and lots of 'irrelevant' exercises and drills. I believe in 'skills', but there are many ways of defining such things, and how you deal with the fashionable communicative ones very often has more to do with the sort of person you are.

Russian is a real challenge. In fact, it's a lifetime's work. One thing you can do, however, is quite quickly get together a good basic set of tools: the nuts and bolts of Russian grammar are straightforward. What is wonderful about it, too, is that much of it does seem to dovetail nicely with our attitudes to what we're saying, so learning Russian grammar may well deepen our knowledge of real-life skills, skills we already have. It's an enabling experience. If you can get through this book and get out of it, say, on the first couple of readings forty per cent of what I've put into it, then I reckon you'll have reached the top of a steep learning curve, after which Russian settles into a level, but immensely beautiful and worthwhile, plateau. In other words, I've brought the crunch in learning Russian forward a bit, and you should feel you're beginning to relax well before you get to Chapter 20. Do, too, wander around the book; once you're past the first couple of chapters it isn't really 'progressive'.

Let me make a few small points about using the book. First, on the whole, when I write Russian names and a few terms using *our* alphabet, I follow a system. But sometimes, when a name or word is well-known in a particular form, I stick to that spelling. I also depart from my system when a word put into our alphabet would end in an apostrophe; here I use the apostrophe only the first time we meet the word. Secondly, in the first two chapters I put quite a few words into a very informal phonetic form, to help you feel confident in the mental image you create of the sounds. Thirdly, with a very few exceptions, I give translations-glosses of texts, to help you get the gist and perceive the arguable structure of the words. I know people like word-lists, but they're wrong — get a dictionary, learn to use it, and make your own vocabulary lists.

Finally, a deep sense of gratitude to those native-speaker specialists who helped me: first, and indirectly, my teacher Valentina Coe and, until 1995, Lida Buravova and Anna Pilkington at London; more recently, and directly,Tania Filossofova at St Andrews and particularly Albina Ozieva at Edinburgh. And many thanks to Charles Drage for allowing me to use some of the exercises we produced together — there's no key, on purpose. The book has been typeset by me, with precious advice from Duckworth and kindly printed out by Alison Aiton at St Andrews, so I remain entirely responsible for errors both of content and of form.

CHAPTER 1
The Alphabet — Алфавит

1. Cyrillic

Russian is written in a different alphabet, called 'Cyrillic'. Why 'Cyrillic' when it's Russian? Well, Russian came later. But, actually, you can still ask the question. So, who was 'Cyril'? Well, he was a Greek, a linguist, from the area of Salonika, who devised an alphabet for the Slavs (from whom the Russians eventually emerged) in the ninth century. It was probably largely based on the small Greek letters, with lots of extra flourishes — as a result it looks quite bizarre and wonderful. Cyril's alphabet is called 'Glagolitic'. A century later, when the Slavs had developed a taste for writing, the big Greek letters were taken on instead and provided the basis for the modern Cyrillic alphabet, to be named after Cyril more as a tribute than as a declaration of origin.

So the first written Slavonic probably used a considerably, then a less considerably, adapted Greek alphabet (adapted partly because it had some weird and wonderful sounds, which needed extra letters). Since it was based on translations from Greek, mainly religious texts, this language was rather close to Greek in structure and so, in its artificiality and remoteness from spoken Slavonic, par for the course as written languages go — the great Russian poet Osip Mandel'shtam even reckoned Russian was the new Greek. In other words, this language was prestigious and not exactly the way to speak, unless you wanted to impress.

Over time the actual shapes of the letters changed — the decisive reform in Russian is down to Peter the Great. It made for rather 'square' letters, which seemed to dominate the Soviet period, but the computer age with lots of fonts, and the greater variety all along in handwriting, are now making their presence felt.

2. Russian

Here's the whole alphabet. It can be learnt in an evening. It's *using* the alphabet which requires time and practice. The actual order can be useful when using a dictionary, but don't toil over it. I want to leave the spelling system and pronunciation proper till Chapter 2, but have included a very rough and ready pronunciation guide in the third column and use it alongside some examples of Cyrillic in the first two chapters. It doesn't reflect changes in unstressed vowels (but I mark the *stressed* vowels with an acute accent) and certain changes in consonants. It may well help for the moment if you learn е, ё, ю, and я as each preceded by a *y*-sound, but please pronounce the *y* written before vowels which *immediately* follow a consonant as integrally to the consonant as possible. Then practise writing the words. Suggested pronunciations are as for British English.

Letters	Latin	Approximate pronunciation
А а	a	*a* — similar to *a* as in *hat* in the North.
Б б	b	*b*
В в	v	*v*
Г г	g	*g*, as in *get*.
Д д	d	*d*
Е е	e, ie	*ye*, with *e* basically as in *get* (*e* after *zh, ts, sh*).
Ё ё	ë, io	*yo*, like *ya* as in *yacht* (*o* after *zh, ts, sh*). See о.
Ж ж	zh	*zh* — similar to *s* as in *pleasure*. Something close will do — the same goes for ч, ш, щ.
З з	z	*z*
И и	i	*ee* — like *i* as in *machine*.
Й й	i	*y* as in *yacht*.
К к	k	*k*, without a puff of air, as after *s*, e.g. *skit*.
Л л	l	*l*. Don't ever join this letter immediately to a preceding letter — a little peak must come in front. This also goes for м and я.
М м	m	*m*. Look at the notes on л.
Н н	n	*n*
О о	o	*o*, as in *got*.
П п	p	*p*, without a puff of air, as after *s*, e.g. *spit*.
Р р	r	*r*, with one or two taps — no more.
С с	s	*s*
Т т	t	*t*, without a puff of air, as after *s*, e.g. *stop*.
У у	u	*oo* as in *look*.
Ф ф	f	*f*
Х х	kh	*kh* — *ch* as in *loch*, but don't damage your throat.
Ц ц	ts	*ts* as in *bits*.
Ч ч	ch	*ch* as in *chips*.
Ш ш	sh	*sh* as in *ship*.
Щ щ	shch	*shch* — a really long *shhh!* (hiss it evilly), or *shtch* as in *borshtch*.
Ъ ъ	"	*"* — the 'hard sign'. You don't pronounce it.

Ы ы	y	*i* as in *sin*, *bit*.
Ь ь	'	' — the 'soft sign'. No sound, but it affects most consonants which precede it — for the moment see it as a very weak *y*-sound integrated to the preceding consonant.
Э э	è	*e* again, but no *y* in front. A bit like RP *a* in *hat*.
Ю ю	iu	*yoo*
Я я	ia	*ya*

А	𝒜	П	𝒫	
а	a	п	n	
Б	𝒷	Р	𝒫	
б	б	р	p	
В	𝒱	С	𝒞	
в	в	с	c	
Г	𝒯	Т	𝒯	
г	г	т	m or ͞m or ͞т
Д	𝒟	У	𝒴	
д	д or д	у	у	
Е	𝓔	Ф	𝒻	
е	е	ф	ф	
Ж	𝒳	Х	𝒳	
ж	ж	х	x	
З	3	Ц	𝒰	
з	з	ц	ц	
И	𝒰	Ч	𝒴	
и	и	ч	ч	
Й	𝒰̆	Ш	𝒰	
й	й	ш	ш or ш̅
К	𝒦	Щ	𝒰ц	
к	к	щ	щ	
Л	𝓛	Ъ	ъ	
л	л	Ы	ы	
М	𝓜	Ь	ь	
м	м	Э	Э	
Н	𝒩	э	э	
н	н	Ю	𝒴о	
О	𝒪	ю	ю	
о	о	Я	𝒴	
		я	я	

3

Now here are a few lines of handwritten Russian. Russians don't all write like this. However, note that little peak before *л, м, я*. It's absolutely crucial, all the time. Don't force all the letters to join up — some just don't. And end *и, й, ш* in a downstroke — the last mustn't look like a *w*.

So here's what it's really about, one of the best moments in Pushkin's *Евгéний Онéгин Evgenii Onegin*, Tat'iana's final words to Onegin. Come back and say it aloud later, and listen to it in one of the great recordings of Tchaikovsky's opera:

А счáстье бы́ло так возмóжно,
Так блúзко! ... Но судьбá моя́
Уж решенá. Неосторóжно,
Быть мóжет, поступúла я:
Меня́ с слезáми заклинáний
Молúла мáть; для бéдной Тáни
Все бы́ли жрéбии равны́...
Я вы́шла зáмуж. Вы должны́,
Я вас прошу́, меня́ остáвить;
Я знáю: в вáшем сéрдце есть
И гóрдость и прямáя честь.
Я вас люблю́ (к чему́ лукáвить?),
Но я другóму отданá;
Я бýду век емý вернá.

And happiness was so possible, / so close! ... But my fate / [is] already decided. Carelessly, / perhaps, I acted: / me with tears of entreaties / [my] mother implored; for poor Tania all lots were equal ... / I married. You must, / I beg you, leave me; / I know: in your heart there is / both pride and real honour. / I love you (why pretend?), / but I am given in marriage to another; / I shall be true to him for ever.

A schyást'ye bílo tak vozmózhno, / Tak bléézko! ... No sood'bá moyá / Uzh ryeshená. Nyeostorózhno, / Bit' mózhet, postoopééla ya: / Myenyá s slyezámee zakleenáneey / Molééla mat'; dlya byédnoy Tánee / Vsye bílee zhryébeeee ravni... / Ya víshla zámoozh. Vi dolzhní, / Ya vas proshóó, myenyá ostáveet'; / Ya znáyoo: v váshem syérdtse yest' / Ee górdost' ee pryamáya chest'. / Ya vas lyooblyóó (k chyemóó lookáveet'?), / No ya droogómoo otdaná; / Ya bóódoo vyek yemóó vyerná.

Now work on the alphabet yourselves. There are various strategies, and I'll suggest a couple; but best if you work out your own (inevitable, actually). What is certain is that you will try out all sorts of approaches before it clicks, and some things may not click straight away. Keep yourself some pleasure for ten years from now.

One approach is if you know Greek — from A to X inclusive every letter, with the exception of Б, Ж, and partly Й and Ё, is straight from Greek. Do identify the differences of sound, but don't worry about slight differences of shape.

```
А АА АА АА АА АА АА АА АА АА АА АА АА АА АА АА
В ВВ ВВ ВВ ВВ ВВ ВВ ВВ ВВ ВВ ВВ ВВ ВВ ВВ ВВ ВВ ВВ
Г ГГ ГГ ГГ ГГ ГГ ГГ ГГ ГГ ГГ ГГ ГГ ГГ ГГ ГГ ГГ ГГ
Д ДД ДД ДД ДД ДД ДД ДД ДД ДД ДД ДД ДД ДД ДД ДД
Е ЕЕ ЕЕ ЕЕ ЕЕ ЕЕ ЕЕ ЕЕ ЕЕ ЕЕ ЕЕ ЕЕ ЕЕ ЕЕ ЕЕ ЕЕ ЕЕ ЕЕ
З Z3 Z3 Z3 Z3 Z3 Z3 Z3 Z3 Z3 Z3 Z3 Z3 Z3 Z3 Z3 Z3 Z3 Z3
И НИ НИ НИ НИ НИ НИ НИ НИ НИ НИ НИ НИ НИ НИ НИ НИ НИ
К КК КК КК КК КК КК КК КК КК КК КК КК КК КК КК КК
Л ΛΛ ΛΛ ΛΛ ΛΛ ΛΛ ΛΛ ΛΛ ΛΛ ΛΛ ΛΛ ΛΛ ΛΛ ΛΛ ΛΛ ΛΛ
М ММ ММ ММ ММ ММ ММ ММ ММ ММ ММ ММ ММ ММ ММ
Н NH NH NH NH NH NH NH NH NH NH NH NH NH NH NH NH NH
О 00 00 00 00 00 00 00 00 00 00 00 00 00 00 00 00
П ПП ПП ПП ПП ПП ПП ПП ПП ПП ПП ПП ПП ПП ПП П
Р РР РР РР РР РР РР РР РР РР РР РР РР РР РР РР РР
С ΣС ΣС ΣС ΣС ΣС ΣС ΣС ΣС ΣС ΣС ΣС ΣС ΣС ΣС ΣС ΣС
Т ТТ ТТ ТТ ТТ ТТ ТТ ТТ ТТ ТТ ТТ ТТ ТТ ТТ ТТ ТТ ТТ
У Υу Υу Υу Υу Υу Υу Υу Υу Υу Υу Υу Υу Υу Υу Υу Υу
Ф ФФ ФФ ФФ ФФ ФФ ФФ ФФ ФФ ФФ ФФ ФФ ФФ ФФ ФФ
Х ХХ ХХ ХХ ХХ ХХ ХХ ХХ ХХ ХХ ХХ ХХ ХХ ХХ ХХ ХХ
```

Another, very common, approach, is to start with those letters and sounds more or less identical in Russian and English, then those where the letter is the same or close but the sound different, then the others!

```
a a a a a a a a a a a a a a a a a a a a a a a a a a a a a a a a a a a
к к к к к к к к к к к к к к к к к к к к к к к к к к к к к к к к к к к
м м м м м м м м м м м м м м м м м м м м м м м м м м м м м
о о о о о о о о о о о о о о о о о о о о о о о о о о о о о о о о о
т т т т т т т т т т т т т т т т т т т т т т т т т т т т т т т т т т т

в v в v в v в v в v в v в v в v в v в v в v в v в v в v в v в v в
e ye e ye e ye e ye e ye e ye e ye e ye e ye e ye e ye e ye e ye e
ё yo ё yo ё yo ё yo ё yo ё yo ё yo ё yo ё yo ё yo ё yo ё yo ё yo ё
н н н н н н н н н н н н н н н н н н н н н н н н н н н н н н н н н
p r p r p r p r p r p r p r p r p r p r p r p r p r p r p r p r p r p
c s c s c s c s c s c s c s c s c s c s c s c s c s c s c s c s c s c
y oo y oo y oo y oo y oo y oo y oo y oo y oo y oo y oo y oo y oo y
x kh x kh x kh x kh x kh x kh x kh x kh x kh x kh x kh x kh x kh x
```

And here are the others. Some of them are no problem if you know Greek, and in their written form some come very close to English (but be careful with Д, *and* with the otherwise friendly Т). Perhaps group Ц Ч Ш Щ linking the first two with the nearby Т, seeing them as becoming 'bigger', and separating out the first, hissing, Ц from the following three, hushing, sounds. I think you just have to learn the others, but note that Ы seems to have our letter *i* (or rather Greek *iota*) as second component (unless you want to see it as '61'!), that Э looks like *e* anyway (its actual name is 'reverse *e*'), and that Я could be *A* with a tuck on the left (unless you really *have* to see it as a reversed *R*).

б b б b б b б b б b б b б b б b б b б b б b б b б b б b б b б b б b б b б
г г
д d д d д d д d д d д d д d д d д d д d д d д d д d д d д d д d д d д d
ж zh ж zh ж zh ж zh ж zh ж zh ж zh ж zh ж zh ж zh ж zh ж zh ж
з z з z з z з z з z з z з z з z з z з z з z з z з z з z з z з z з z з z з z
и ee и ee и ee и ee и ee и ee и ee и ee и ee и ee и ee и ee и
й у й у й у й у й у й у й у й у й у й у й у й у й у й у й у й у й у й у й у й
л л
п р п р п р п р п р п р п р п р п р п р п р п р п р п р п р п р п р п р п р п
ф f ф f ф f ф f ф f ф f ф f ф f ф f ф f ф f ф f ф f ф f ф f ф f ф f ф f ф
ц ts ц ts ц ts ц ts ц ts ц ts ц ts ц ts ц ts ц ts ц ts ц ts ц ts ц ts ц
ч ch ч ch ч ch ч ch ч ch ч ch ч ch ч ch ч ch ч ch ч ch ч ch ч
ш sh ш sh ш sh ш sh ш sh ш sh ш sh ш sh ш sh ш sh ш sh ш sh ш
щ shch щ shch щ shch щ shch щ shch щ shch щ shch щ shch щ shch щ
ъ " ъ " ъ " ъ " ъ " ъ " ъ " ъ " ъ " ъ " ъ " ъ " ъ " ъ " ъ " ъ
ы i ы i ы i ы i ы i ы i ы i ы i ы i ы i ы i ы i ы i ы i ы i ы i ы i ы
ь ' ь ' ь ' ь ' ь ' ь ' ь ' ь ' ь ' ь ' ь ' ь ' ь ' ь ' ь ' ь ' ь ' ь
э e э e э e э e э e э e э e э e э e э e э e э e э e э e э e э e э e э e э e э
ю yoo ю yoo ю yoo ю yoo ю yoo ю yoo ю yoo ю yoo ю yoo ю yoo ю
я ya я ya я ya я ya я ya я ya я ya я ya я ya я ya я ya я ya я

Here are a few lists to read or copy (the acute accent is there to tell you which vowel is stressed — the stress is rarely actually written, but *you* might use it as a way of learning the stress). Underneath some of them is the pronunciation — see if you can match them up. I start with places.

Москва́	Санкт-Петербу́рг	Псков	Ки́ев
Оде́сса	Минск	Ло́ндон	Пари́ж
Эдинбу́рг	Ду́блин	О́сло	Хе́льсинки
Стокго́льм	Копенга́ген	Нью-Йо́рк	Вашингто́н
Афи́ны	Пра́га	Братисла́ва	Со́фия
Lóndon	*N'yoo-Yórk*	*Brateesláva*	*Vasheengtón*
Paréézh	*Kopyengágyen*	*Pskov*	*Moskvá*
Stokgól'm	*Dóobleen*	*Prága*	*Óslo*
Afééni	*Méénsk*	*Sofééya*	*Odyéssa*
Edeenbóorg	*Sankt-Pyetyerbóorg*	*Kééyev*	*Khyél'seenkee*

Кана́да	Фра́нция	Голла́ндия	Ита́лия
А́нглия	Герма́ния	Да́ния	Норве́гия
Швейца́рия	Шве́ция	Испа́ния	Португа́лия
Финля́ндия	Соединённые Шта́ты	Кита́й	Япо́ния
Че́хия	Слова́кия	По́льша	Хорва́тия
Шотла́ндия	Исла́ндия	Румы́ния	Еги́пет
Литва́	Ла́твия	Эсто́ния	Ве́нгрия
Chyékheeya	*Eeslándeeya*	*Roomíneeya*	*Portoogáleeya*
Shvyéytsareeya	*Soyedeenyónniye Shtáti*	*Dáneeya*	*Yegéépyet*
Yapóneeya	*Feenlyándeeya*	*Gollándeeya*	*Kanáda*
Látveeya	*Leetvá*	*Germáneeya*	*Frántsiya*
Eetáleeya	*Ángleeya*	*Estóneeya*	*Eespáneeya*
Shvyétsiya	*Norvyégeeya*	*Vyéngreeya*	*Pól'sha*
Keetáy	*Khorváteeya*	*Slovákeeya*	*Shotlándeeya*

Just for reference, to come back to some other day, here are some names of peoples: male, female, adjective. For reasons of space I've had to make a few cuts here and there, but trust you will eventually be able to restore the full forms.

норве́жец, норве́жка, норве́жский
чех, че́шка, че́шский
бельги́ец, бельги́йка, бельги́йский
англича́нин, англича́нка, англи́йский
испа́нец, испа́нка, испа́нский
францу́з, францу́женка, францу́зский
белору́с белору́ска, белору́ский
слова́к, слова́чка, слова́цкий
ту́рок, турча́нка, туре́цкий
кита́ец, китая́нка, кита́йский
шотла́ндец, шотла́ндка, шотла́ндский
венгр, венге́рка, венге́рский
поля́к, по́лька, по́льский
латы́ш, латы́шка, латы́шский
швейца́рец, швейца́рка, швейца́рский
португа́лец, португа́лка, п-га́льский
кана́дец, кана́дка, кана́дский
америка́нец, америка́нка, -рика́нский
болга́рин, болга́рка, болга́рский
европе́ец, европе́йка, европе́йский

украи́нец, -и́нка, украи́нский
серб, се́рбка, се́рбский
швед, шве́дка, шве́дский
не́мец, не́мка, неме́цкий
датча́нин, датча́нка, да́тский
ру́сский, ру́сская, ру́сский
хорва́т, хорва́тка, хорва́тский
слове́нец, -е́нка, слове́нский
грек, греча́нка, гре́ческий
япо́нец, япо́нка, япо́нский
ирла́ндец, -дка, ирла́ндский
румы́н, румы́нка, румы́нский
эсто́нец, эсто́нка, эсто́нский
лито́вец, лито́вка, лито́вский
валли́ец, валли́йка, валли́йский
финн, фи́нка, фи́нский
исла́ндец, исла́ндка, исла́ндский
инди́ец, индиа́нка, инди́йский
египтя́нин, -тя́нка, еги́петский
африка́нец, африка́нка, -ка́нский

Each of the adjectives can be put, as it is, with the word язы́к *yazík* 'language', to mean the particular language (as appropriate), or it can be transformed into an adverb by following the pattern, for 'Finnish', по-фи́нски (note the last letter) *po-féénskee*. Then put it together with я говорю *ya govoryóó* 'I can speak' or я не говорю *ya nye govoryóó* 'I can't speak'. Thus: я говорю по-фински *ya govoryóó po-féénskee*.

People

Пу́шкин	Ле́рмонтов	Го́голь	Достое́вский
Турге́нев	Остро́вский	Толсто́й	Салтыко́в-Щедри́н
Че́хов	Блок	Мандельшта́м	Гумилёв
Хле́бников	Булга́ков	Ба́бель	Ахма́това
Пастерна́к	Солжени́цын	Цвета́ева	Замя́тин
Boolgákov	*Lyérmontov*	*Tolstóy*	*Saltikóv-Shchyedréén*
Dostoyévskeey	*Póóshkeen*	*Goomeelyóv*	*Khlyébneekov*
Toorgyényev	*Blok*	*Tsvyetáyeva*	*Pastyernák*
Bábyel'	*Akhmátova*	*Gógol'*	*Ostróvskeey*
Solzhenéétsin	*Zamyáteen*	*Mandyel'shtám*	*Chyékhov*

Чайко́вский	Му́соргский	Бороди́н	Гли́нка
Рахма́нинов	Страви́нский	Проко́фьев	Шостако́вич
Хачатуря́н	Бала́кирев	Скря́бин	Ри́мский-Ко́рсаков
Balákeeryev	*Stravéénskeey*	*Prokóf'yev*	*Shostakóveech*
Rakhmáneenov	*Khachyatooryán*	*Skryábeen*	*Chyaykóvskeey*
Móósorgskeey	*Borodéén*	*Gléénka*	*Réémskeey-Kórsakov*

Шага́л	Айвазо́вский	Гончаро́ва	Э́кстер
Левита́н	Ре́пин	Та́тлин	Су́риков
Эль Лиси́цкий	Удальцо́ва	Мале́вич	Канди́нский
Oodal'tsóva	*Malyéveech*	*Tátleen*	*Ayvazóvskeey*
Gonchyaróva	*Ryépeen*	*El' Lezséétskeey*	*Shagál*
Kandéénskeey	*Sóóreekov*	*Lyeveetán*	*Ékstyer*

Алекса́ндр	Никола́й	Екатери́на	Бори́с Годуно́в
Хрущёв	Ста́лин	Е́льцин	Горбачёв
Яросла́в	Ю́рий	И́горь	Бре́жнев
Yóóreey	*Éégor'*	*Alyeksándr*	*Yél'tsin*
Stáleen	*Bryézhnyev*	*Neekoláy*	*Yekatyerééna*
Gorbachyóv	*Boréés Godoonóv*	*Khrooshchyóv*	*Yaroslá́v*

Леони́д	Макси́м	Матве́й	Михаи́л
Па́вел	Пётр	Рома́н	Ростисла́в
Pyotr	*Meekhaéél*	*Rosteeslá́v*	*Pávyel*
Matvyéy	*Lyeonééd*	*Makséém*	*Román*

Алекса́ндра	А́лла	А́нна	Валенти́на
Да́рья	Евге́ния	Еле́на	Зинаи́да
Yevgyéneeya	*Ánna*	*Zeenaééda*	*Dár'ya*
Yelyéna	*Valyentééna*	*Álla*	*Alyeksándra*

Titles of works of literature

Пи́ковая да́ма	Ме́дный вса́дник
Ревизо́р	Мёртвые ду́ши
Отцы́ и де́ти	Обло́мов
Преступле́ние и наказа́ние	Бра́тья Карама́зовы
Война́ и мир	А́нна Каре́нина
Три сестры́	Вишнёвый сад
Ма́стер и Маргари́та	До́ктор Жива́го
Veeshnyóviy sad	*Ryeveezór*
Dóktor Zhivágo	*Péékovaya dáma*
Myédniy vsádneek	*Mástyer ee Margarééta*
Voyná ee meer	*Otsí ee dyétee*
Brát'ya Karamázovi	*Oblómov*
Myórtviye dóóshi	*Ánna Karyéneena*
Tree syestrí	*Pryestooplyéneeye i nakazáneeye*

Can you identify them? They are, for you to unjumble:

Oblomov, Crime and Punishment, The Government Inspector, Anna Karenina, The Bronze Horseman, The Brothers Karamazov, Three Sisters, Fathers and Children (perhaps better know as *Fathers and Sons*), *The Cherry Orchard, The Queen of Spades, War and Peace, Doctor Zhivago, Dead Souls, The Master and Margarita.*

Here are a few hints. First, you should be able to work out several without any problem, and that will also help you see what 'and' is in Russian. And secondly, think of a 'queen' as being a 'dame', note that *-(n)eek* most often refers to people doing things, and assume that 'crime' and 'punishment' are quite long words. I think that should do it. By the way, just in case you're really eagle-eyed, the pronunciation *Zhivágo, Yél'tsin,* and *dóóshi* (I'm thinking of the *i,* as if it was spelt ы) is correct — there's the same in two names of countries as well.

Don't hesitate to try and give an approximate sound to the words, as giving a sound helps make the words more real. More about this, but still just with the intention of giving you a *rough* idea, in Chapter 2, where I'll also give you the names of the letters.

CHAPTER 2
Spelling — Орфогра́фия

1. The Russians and their language

Who are the Russians? Well, as an ethnic group related to the Czechs, Poles, Ukrainians, etc., they are Slavs; and all these peoples originally shared a speech form. The ancestors of the Russians, the Ukrainians, and the Belarusians are the East Slavs, and just how long *their* shared dialect, 'Common East Slavonic', existed is one of those awkward questions. Note that the term 'Russian' is shared by all the East Slavs: 'Bela*rusians*' or 'White *Russians*', 'Ukrainians' or, formerly, 'Little *Russians*'.

Now, 'Russian' in Russian is ру́сский, but 'Russia' is Росси́я; the two words don't go together — the former is from an ancient word, Русь, while the latter is probably a sixteenth-century diplomatic term, from Greek or Latin. In modern Russian the adjective which is derived from Росси́я, росси́йский, is used more and more these days to refer to the inhabitants of Russia without regard to ethnic group.

Coming back to the usual word, ру́сский: the likely explanation of the origin of Русь/ру́сский turns out, helped by Finnish *Ruotsi* 'Sweden', to refer to the ancient Swedes or Norsemen from Roslagen, who as *róþsmenn* 'helmsmen, ruddermen' steered their boats over the seas. So the 'Russians' are one more instance of how the name of one group is grafted onto another community. So the Russians started off as Scandinavians, the *Rus'*, the name was extended to the East Slavs and probably members of Finno-Ugrian and Baltic tribes in the ethnic jumble that was north-eastern Europe at the time, and then was taken over by the ancestors of the actual Russians when political developments cut much of what would become Ukraine and Belarus' off from 'Kievan Rus' — more later.

The first written Russian (better 'East Slavonic' or 'Rus(ian)') was, like most written languages, artificial. It was a 'Russian' form of the first written Slavonic, 'Old Church Slavonic', which started off as something based on the Slavonic spoken around Salonika and on Byzantine Greek. Things began to move around 988, when Rus was 'christianized'. But we shouldn't get the impression that everything written was to do with the Church: there was a tradition of civil, business, legal writing, which was based on East Slavonic — a secular written culture, documented in such things as the Novgorod *birchbark documents* берестяны́е гра́моты. Over time the written language(s) adjusted to local linguistic circumstances (and *vice versa*), but a split between the written and the spoken languages did develop and coincided with a growth in influence from Western Europe — some of the people who could read and write wanted things other than religious texts. The situation was shaken up in the seventeenth century with the revision of the church books and emergence of the Old Believers, who saw themselves as the bearers of the true way, i.e. they wanted to keep the highly archaic texts, though they spoke and wrote down-to-earth Russian, as shown in the wonderful autobiography of the Archpriest Avvakum.

In the eighteenth century, under the impetus of changes set in motion by Peter the Great, the language question gained prominence in Russia, and was eventually 'solved' by the first thirty or so years of the nineteenth century — the writer most linked with this is the incomparable Pushkin, though if you want to cut him down to size (out of envy — that's the only possible reason) he was just the most outstanding of a mass of writers.

But it was still a language which was a hybrid of (at least) native (East Slavonic) Russian and Church Slavonic — actually, the socially fascinating enigma that is Russian is only now beginning to be unravelled. So, if we take together the introduced name, the introduced and then mixed-up language, the mix of languages and cultures but isolation from the classical heritage shared by most of the rest of Europe, and add to it the massive and rapid expansion of Muscovy with never a moment to sit back and work out its identity, we find ourselves with a community with an identity problem.

2. Now let's sort out the sounds and spelling

Russian is written in a very regular fashion, one which does the important thing of respecting the meaningful bits of words rather than how they actually sound — it's something you'll have call to be grateful for, notably because the vast majority of Russian words contain *one* vowel which is stressed. You have to learn the stress, as there's no one miraculous rule. The stress, by the way, isn't marked in the actual spelling, so here it'll be indicated by an acute accent. Somewhat like in English, in Russian the unstressed vowels of a word are made vaguer, but this doesn't affect the spelling (basically, *oo* and *i* just 'shorten'; *ee* and *ye* converge as a 'short' *ee*; *ya* and *yo* behave like *ee* and *ye* before the stress, but after it they *may* behave like *a* and *o*; *a* and *o* become like the *a* in *about* everywhere except at the very beginning of the word and immediately before the stress, when they become like a 'short' version of the *a* in Northern British

English *hat*). Anyway, if you pronounce everything clearly, you'll be understood, though you may have trouble understanding some people.

English has five vowels, *a, e, i, o, u*. But you will have noticed that Russian, which also has those five, has five *pairs of letters*: two *a*'s, two *e*'s, two *i*'s, *two o's*, and two *u*'s. Let's call the first of each pair 'Series 1' and the second 'Series 2'.

a = а/я	*e* = э/е	*i* = ы/и	*o* = о/ё	*u* = у/ю				

Series 1:	а	э	ы	о	у	—	Series 2:	я е и ё ю
Series 1:	*a*	*e*	*i*	*o*	*oo*	—	Series 2:	*ya ye ee yo yoo*

Now, Russian has *consonant* pairs too, but, first, as sounds, not as letters — to differentiate these we use the double helping of vowel letters. The consonants involved are:

б	в	д	з	л	м	н	п	р	с	т	ф
b	v	d	z	l	m	n	p	r	s	t	f

The difference is that before Series 2 vowels (я, е, и, ё, ю) and before the *soft sign* (ь) you must pronounce these consonants with the slightest *y*-sound actually integrated into them — so the 'soft' or 'palatalized' *d*, as one calls it, is a bit like the pronunciation of *d* in British English *dew*, and for many English speakers the soft *l* will be somewhat like the *l* in *leak*, and the hard one like that in *look*. One consolation: э is vanishingly rare. Let's have some examples of spellings:

бы — би	бу — бю	вы — ви	ву — вю
ды — ди	ду — дю	зы — зи	зу — зю
лы — ли	лу — лю	мы — ми	му — мю
ны — ни	ну — ню	пы — пи	пу — пю
ры — ри	ру — рю	сы — си	су — сю
ты — ти	ту — тю	фы — фи	фу — фю
bi — bee	*boo — byoo*	*vi — vee*	*voo — vyoo...*

Substitute а/я and о/ё after these consonants, and bring in е (try э too, if you like, but it *is* rare). Do bear in mind that, though the two *i*'s sound in themselves rather different, their relation to one another is exactly as with the other pairs.

Here are a few actual words: мáма 'mum' — мя́мля 'mumbler', стал 'became' — сталь 'steel', сáд 'garden' — ся́дем 'we'll sit down', бéдный 'poor' — си́ний 'blue', рад 'glad' — ряд 'row, series', толк 'sense, understanding' — то́лько 'only' (note especially this last pair).

The other consonants don't participate in this; they are subject to spelling rules. Let's just go through them.

К *k* г *g*, х *kh* (the 'velars') can only be followed by the vowel letters а, о, у and е, и — a mixture of the two types. This is the actual pronunciation — in other words, hard before а, о, and у, soft before е and и (very rarely, they may be followed by the soft sign, ь). Some examples:

ка	ко	ку	ке	ки
га	го	гу	ге	ги
ха	хо	ху	хе	хи
ka	*ko*	*ku*	*kye*	*kee...*

Ж *zh*, ч *ch*, ш *sh*, щ *shch* (the 'palatals', 'hushers') can only be followed by а, е, и, у, and о or ё (I'll spare you a lecture on which of these two when!). Another mixture, but this time historically based and only partly reflecting the pronunciation. Here just bear in mind that ж and ш are only-hard, while ч and щ are only-soft — since there's no hard-soft contrast, you can get away with a lazy pronunciation — don't be too tempted!

жа	же	жи	жо/жё	жу
ша	ше	ши	шо/шё	шу
zha	*zhe*	*zhi*	*zho*	*zhu...*

ча	че	чи	чо/чё	чу
ща	ще	щи	що/щё	щу
chya	*chye*	*chee*	*chyo*	*chyoo...*

Ц *ts* is followed by а, е, о, у, and и or (mainly confined to endings) ы. Yet another mixture, again historically based and only partly reflecting the pronunciation. And here note that ц is only-hard.

ца	це	ци/цы	цо	цу
tsa	*tse*	*tsi*	*tso*	*tsoo*

These rules are important because some endings seem unexpected until you realize it's just the rules. Remember, only *five* vowels in Russian.

I've left one consonant letter out: й *y*, which represents a full-blooded *y*-sound. This sound, as you must have noticed, also crops up when there is no й in sight. This is another rôle of the Series 2 vowel letters я, е, ё, ю, and sometimes и. When they come at the *very* beginning of a word, immediately after a vowel within a word, and immediately after a hard or a soft sign (ъ or ь), they are *one letter for two sounds*, a full *y* plus the vowel — one sometimes hears *y* before *ee* here.

я	е	и	ё	ю	but	а	э	ы	о	у
ya	*ye*	*ee*	*yo*	*yoo*	but	*a*	*e*	*i*	*o*	*oo*

моя́	ла́е	слои	твоё	хво́ю
moyá	*láye*	*sloéé*	*tvoyó*	*khvóyoo*

статья́	статье́	статьи́	статьёй	статью́
stat'yá	*stat'yé*	*stat'yéé*	*stat'yóy*	*stat'yóó*

объясни́ть	объе́хать	объём
ob"yasnéét'	*ob"yékhat'*	*ob"yóm*

Й itself is written before vowel letters only in foreign words (and then not always), e.g. райо́н *rayón* 'region', Нью-Йо́рк *N'yoo-Yórk* 'New York'. Most often we come across it after vowels: геро́й *gyeróy* 'hero'. And where й is the final consonant letter, if an ending is added, the й disappears and is replaced by the appropriate Series 2 vowel letter: дом - до́ма *dom* — *dóma* 'house (nominative and genitive, with an *a* ending)', but музе́й - музе́я *muzyey* — *muzyéya* 'museum (id.)'. For some reason, this penny can take a while to drop.

Now back to the hard and soft signs: ъ and ь. The soft sign softens softenable consonants. Sometimes you find it after the hushers, a position where it's superfluous since they're individually *either* hard *or* soft. Where it plays the same rôle as the rarer hard sign is when it comes between a consonant and a Series 2 vowel letter (this is the *only* position for a hard sign): here pronounce a clear *y* plus the vowel: статья́ *stat'yá* 'article' — you only find it before a Series 1 vowel in certain loanwords, e.g. павильо́н *paveel'ón* 'pavilion', where you might have expected павилён.

The hard sign does likewise, but indicates that the preceding consonant is hard,. Actually, consonant sounds that can go on and on, e.g. *s* and *z*, may well soften: съесть *s"yest'* 'to eat up'. For a hard consonant see the bottom line in the box above.

When a soft sign comes between two consonants, it softens the preceding consonant: то́лько 'only'.

And a word that ends in a soft sign, e.g. the noun тетра́дь *tyetrád'* 'exercise book' is a word that ends in a consonant! Vital information!

дал	даль		ел	ель
dal	*dal'*		*yel*	*yel'*

вес	весь		ос	ось
vyes	*vyes'*		*os*	*os'*

Differentiating hard and soft paired consonants is crucial. Context can certainly help a Russian sort out what you're trying to say if you're getting it wrong, but if you're coming to Russian because you like the sounds, aim to reproduce that beauty for yourself in your own pronunciation!

The second pairing of consonants is partly conveyed by the letters (there *are* some where it isn't) and is an opposition based on whether your vocal cords buzz or not during the pronunciation of the consonant:

б п	г к	д т	в ф	ж ш	з с
b p	g k	d t	v f	zh sh	z s

For each of those six pairs the consonant on the left is 'voiced', pronounced with buzzing of the vocal cords, and the one on the right is 'voiceless', pronounced without that buzzing — it's clearer in the last three pairs, which you can prolong: *zzzzz — sssss* (block up your ears or place a finger against your windpipe to appreciate the difference). I don't want to get into the details here; suffice it to say that voiced consonants are pronounced voiceless when final, e.g. род 'kin, sort' sounds just like рот 'mouth', and that changes occur in groups of consonants — in the most approximate terms a voiced first consonant becomes voiceless if immediately followed by a voiceless consonant, such that водка 'vodka' is pronounced as if written вотка. In other positions the difference can be important, e.g. дом 'house' — том 'tome, volume'. And some of these consonants can be hard and soft too, so the voice pairing is then doubled.

From now on, hardly any more guided pronunciation. You can do it.

Exercise 1

First of all, here are a few nouns with assorted grammatical endings — case forms, about which you'll learn soon enough. I give the patterns, and you can fill in the blanks (I leave the stress out here). It's primarily a writing exercise, just a question of copying and concentration, honest, so just go ahead and write! First, some masculine nouns (each pattern selects different case forms):

сад *garden*	сада	садом	сады	садов	садам
дом *house*					
дуб *oak*					
учитель *teacher*	учителя	учителю	учителе	учителей	учителям
гость *guest*					

бог *god*	бога	богом	боги	богов	богам
волк *wolf*					
верх *top*					
этаж *storey*	этажа	этаже	этажи	этажей	этажам
товарищ *comrade*					
нож *knife*					
отец *father*	отца	отцом	отцы	отцов	отцам
купец *merchant*	купца				

Now some neuter nouns:

окно *window*	окна	окну	окном	окне	окнам
болото *marsh*					
поле *field*	поля	полю	полем	полей	полями
море *sea*					
здание *building*	здания	зданию	здании	зданий	зданиях
знáние *knowledge*					

And now some feminine nouns:

картина *picture*	картины	картиной	картине	картин	картинам
квартира *flat*					
виза *visa*					
книга *book*	книгу	книги	книге	книг	книгам
рука *hand*					
нога *foot*					
душа *soul*	душу	души	душой	душ	душам
свеча *candle*					

Now some adjectives (I restore the stress; the slots are for the nominative case of the feminine and neuter singular, and for the nominative plural — gender disappears in the plural) — imagine they sound exactly as written:

masculine	*feminine*	*neuter*	*plural*
дóбрый *kind*	дóбрая	дóброе	дóбрые
уютный *cosy*			
нóвый *new*			
худóй *thin*	худáя	худóе	худы́е
злóй *evil*			

masculine	feminine	neuter	plural
ру́сский *Russian*	ру́сская	ру́сское	ру́сские
упру́гий *taut*			
ти́хий *calm*			
плохо́й *bad*	плоха́я	плохо́е	плохи́е
дорого́й *dear*			
лу́чший *better*	лу́чшая	лу́чшее	лу́чшие
све́жий *fresh*			
сидя́чий *sedentary*			
чужо́й *other's*	чужа́я	чужо́е	чужи́е
большо́й *big*			
зде́шний *local*	зде́шняя	зде́шнее	зде́шние
си́ний *blue*			
после́дний *last*			

3. The names of the letters

You've met the spelling system, so here are the names of the letters.

а	бэ	вэ	гэ	дэ
е	ё	же	зэ	и
и кра́ткое	ка	эль	эм	эн
о	пэ	эр	эс	тэ
у	эф	ха	це	че
ша	ща	твёрдый знак	ы	мя́гкий знак
э (оборо́тное)	ю	я		

What do you think about those names? Can you see any adjectives there? Look at the preceding exercise. If so, what gender do you think the names of the letters might be? And two names involve an adjective and what might well be a noun. Can you guess what those two names mean? What's the gender of the noun? The four adjectives, in order, mean 'short', 'hard', 'soft', and 'reverse', and the noun means 'sign'. The next section will, I hope, provide enlightenment!

4. What's important about Russian grammar

Russian has a great deal of 'visible' grammar; this allows its word order to be pretty flexible (note the positions of the adjectives in those letter names) — compare the rather strict word order of English.

17

'Correct' Russian has two fundamental principles: *agreement* (forms agree in gender, case, and number) and *government* (some words will require particular cases after them). Concentrate: Russian has three genders, six cases, two numbers. Where a group of words 'go together', e.g. 'big black dog', you must make them all agree, i.e. собáка *sobáka* 'dog' is a feminine noun; in its form собáка it is nominative and singular; so большóй *bol'shóy* 'big' and чёрный *chyórniy* 'black', if put with it, must go into their *nominative singular feminine* form. They are большáя *bol'sháya* and чёрная *chyórnaya*, and so: большáя чёрная собáка *bol'sháya chyórnaya sobáka* 'big black dog'.

Russian verbs have *person*: first person (I—we), second person (you), third person (he/she/it—they). There are six verb forms, two for each of the three persons. The good news is that this affects only the *non-past*, which does service for our present and future; the *only* other tense, the past, is quite different and very simple — more like an adjective.

Anxiety over agreement and government will fade. Here are functions of four of the six cases, adapting a table created by the late David Kilby:

	accusative	genitive	dative	instrumental
direct object	знáет Вáню knows Vanja	ищет покóя seeks peace	—	руковóдит óфисом runs the office
indirect object	—	—	дáл мнé gave (to) me	—
experiencer	—	—	мнé хóлодно I'm cold	—
time	сидéть цéлый дéнь sit a whole day	пéрвого мáя on May 1st	—	днём during the afternoon
measure	вéсит тóнну weighs a ton	—	—	двумя фýтами вы́ше 2 ft higher
possessive	—	дóм врачá doctor's house	—	—
partitive	—	заказáл винá ordered (some) wine	—	—
benefactive	—	—	стирáет емý рубáшки washes shirts for him	—

The instrumental is amazing — here are some of its other functions:

instrument	ре́жет *ножо́м* 'cuts *with a knife*'
agent	бы́л нака́зан *роди́телями* 'was punished *by (his) parents*'
location	идёт *ле́сом* 'goes *through the forest*'
manner	говори́т *гро́мким го́лосом* 'speaks *in a loud voic*e'
predicative	бы́л *учи́телем* 'was *a teacher*'
'essive'	рабо́тает *шофёром* 'works *as a driver*'
comparison	лети́т *стрело́й* 'flies *like an arrow*'
transport	е́дет *по́ездом* 'goes *by trai*n'
characteristic	сла́б *глаза́ми* 'weak *in the eyes*'

Wordplay — the bare bones of a chat

Here comes the communicative bit of this book.

'Hello!'
Здра́вствуй(те)! 'Hello!' — add -те if you're addressing more than one person or a single person formally. Basically it means 'be healthy!' — драв is related to oaks and strength (think of Welsh *derwen* 'oak-tree').

Приве́т! 'Greetings!' — A nice informal 'Hello!'

До́брый день! До́брое у́тро! До́брый ве́чер! — 'Good day!' 'Good morning!' 'Good evening!' — good, friendly, neutral greetings. Note how до́бр- has two different forms here; that's because it's agreeing with two masculine nouns and one neuter one. Remember?

О́чень ра́д(а) тебя́/вас ви́деть 'Very pleased to see you' — full marks if you see that the Russians believe in *video* — that's the verb 'to see'. О́чень is 'very' and рад and ра́да are 'glad' — the former if you're a man and the latter if you're a woman. Тебя́ and вас are one of the case forms (accusative, as direct object) of 'you', the former the singular and informal one, the latter the plural or formal singular one.

How are you?
Как пожива́ешь/пожива́ете? — the former is informal and singular; the latter is plural or formal singular. Как means 'how?'

Как дела́? — literally 'how are things/?' (дела́ is the plural of де́ло 'matter'). You can respond using Спаси́бо, хорошо́ / прекра́сно / норма́льно / ничего́ / так себе́ / пло́хо 'Thanks, fine / wonderful / OK / fine (all sorts of things!) / so-so / bad'. And then: А ты/вы? 'And you?' (guess which is which). And *then*: Спаси́бо, то́же хорошо́ 'Thanks, fine too'. Спаси́бо originally meant 'may God save you'.

Please tell me...
Скажи́(те), пожа́луйста,... 'Tell [me], please,...'
Не ска́жете/ска́жешь ли вы/ты, ... 'Won't you tell [me]...?'
Мо́жно тебя́/вас спроси́ть/попроси́ть,... 'May [I] ask you...?'
Бу́дь(те) добр/добра́ (до́бры),... 'Be [so] good [as to tell me]...'

You need to follow these up with a question — that'll have to come later, but two useful words here are где? 'where?' and когда́? 'when?' Пожа́луйста (you can drop the -уй- in pronunciation) means 'please; you're welcome; here you are' and a lot more — see Chapter 6.

It's time to...
Пора́ идти́ домо́й 'It's time to go home'. Пора́ за сто́л 'It's time [to sit] down to table'.

Пора́ is useful. In the first we have идти́ 'to go' expressed. It, or another verb, has been left out in the second, something that happens quite often — a real mercy, as you'll realize after Chapter 7.

The table and 'Help yourself!'
Прошу́ к столу́ 'Come to the table (lit. "I request to the table")'.
Прия́тного аппети́та! 'Bon appétit!'
Угоща́йся!/Угоща́йтесь! 'Help yourself/ves!' (a reflexive verb).

A meal will often be accompanied by во́дка 'vodka' and toasts. Everyone will be expected to propose a toast, so be ready: За (ва́ше) здоро́вье! 'To your health!, За дру́жбу! 'To friendship!', За Пу́шкина! 'To Pushkin!' If you *do* drink, but are worried what all this drinking will do to you, try to persuade your hosts that you never touch the stuff. Being a good guest is a part of politeness: Хоро́ший гость, хозя́ину ра́дость 'A good guest is a host's joy (lit. "Good guest, to the host joy")'. And, if you drink, remember (you'll be forgiven!) to down it in one, до дна́ 'to the bottom'.

Please pass me...
Переда́й(те), пожа́луйста, хлеб / соль / вино́ / шампа́нское / конья́к / икру́ / щи / борщ / торт / пирожки́ / пельме́ни / блины́...
'Pass, please, the bread / salt / wine / sparkling wine / cognac / caviar / shchi / borshch / cake (a large one) / pirozhki (small pies with various fillings) / pel'meni (sort of Siberian ravioli) / Russian pancakes.'

Or just stretch over the table — it's perfectly OK. Don't sit at the corner — superstitions are alive and well in Russia.

Sorry

Прости(те) / Извини(те), пожа́луйста 'Forgive / Excuse [me], please'. The first is more literary. Both are used to attract someone's attention too.

Ничего́ / Не беспоко́йся — Не беспоко́йтесь / Пустяки́ / Ничего́ стра́шного lit. 'Nothing / Don't worry / Rubbish ("trivialities") / Nothing terrible'.

Don't mention it

Пожа́луйста / Не́ за что / Не сто́ит.

Goodbye

До свида́ния! 'Au revoir!'.
Пока́! 'So long!' — very informal.
Счастли́во! 'Bye!'
Всего́ до́брого!, Всего́ хоро́шего! 'All the best!' (either adjective for 'good', using the genitive as in Прия́тного аппети́та!).
До (ско́рой) встре́чи! 'Till soon! (lit. "Until [our] 'soon' meeting!")'.

Don't say goodbye, or shake hands, over a threshold, and that includes a car door. And, once you've left, don't return, even if you've forgotten something — if you *do* return, look in the mirror before you leave the second time. And, before a departure, you will sit in silence at the table for a few moments; if you don't, your journey may be hampered in some way: Не бу́дет доро́ги 'There won't be a road'. The доро́га, the road, is an important Russian symbol.

Just accept some of these expressions as given — let the language flow over you.

You should be able to make up a few nonsense dialogues. Or would it be nonsense? After all, many a conversation says very little. Gestures will get you almost everywhere — don't take me *too* seriously, I did say 'almost'.

CHAPTER 3

1. Scandinavians, Slavs, and...

Imagine what much of Russia, Ukraine, and Belarus might have been like over fifteen hundred years ago: forests, bogs, rivers, plains. No high mountains, just spaces, impenetrable wildernesses, shallow valleys with rivers, each a world to itself.

The rivers — Oka, Volga, Dnieper, Don amongst many others, to some extent great thoroughfares, would have been subject to the seasons: low water, high water, and to cruelties of nature, such as rapids. The forests would have been barriers to movement, and the land thoroughfares would have been out of commission for long periods. Transport along the rivers would have been low-key, even local, with groups with small, manoeuvrable craft favoured so far as trade was concerned.

No real sense of ethnic groups, perhaps tribes is as far as you can go — nowadays we'd call them Balts and Finno-Ugrians. These and the many other names are attempts to put a name on something, to create order. In the south and south-west a great civilization would have been in place: the Greek and Roman world, Byzantium. And the Slavs?

The Slavs were ethnically closest to the Balts, and related, as an Indo-European people, to most of the peoples of Europe. They may have started out in the Pripet Marshes in north-western Ukraine, on the border with Belarus, an impenetrable area still, now most familiar as the site of Chernobyl'. Like the other peoples, they wandered slowly, settling in small valleys, on hilltops. They were pagan, and probably had some dreadful customs, but then other religions can be pretty bloodthirsty.

This was a time when the Norsemen were active thoughout Europe. They were in the east for trade and didn't always intend to settle for good. It was on the the whole a male society, though their own womenfolk might come along too, and over time communities with a more local allegiance and identity emerged. The Slavs of the area seem to have been the most numerous group, and the Rus emerged from a recipe of Norsemen, Slavs, Balts, Finno-Ugrians, Khazars,...

There was little need of writing in these small, almost certainly multilingual communities. The Norsemen may have brought elements of writing, but it needed the kick-start of some big factor. For this there was trade, and, perhaps crucially, there was Christianity, which was behind the first codified Slavonic 'language' in the ninth century.

Names to conjure with for this period include Riurik, the Varangian or Rus who according to legend came to bring order to the area. Then there is Igor', whose murder around 945 led to the interregnum of his wife Ol'ga and her three acts of revenge. Ol'ga was Christian. Her son, Sviatopolk, the first leader with a Slavonic rather than Norse name, disdained Christianity; he was a swashbuckling warrior prince. He was replaced by Vladimir the Great, who ruled till 1015 and during whose reign, probably in 998, Christianity was established in Rus and centred on Kiev.

After Vladimir a period of uncertainty ended with the rule of Iaroslav the Wise from 1036 until 1054, a period of stability during which the apparatus of state and the prestige of Kiev were established. This is the time of the schism between western and eastern Christianity and of the Metropolitan Ilarion's magnificent, state-shaping *Sermon on the Law and Grace*. Iaroslav was a northern prince, but he established himself in the south, on the middle Dnieper, in Kiev.

In this period Rus became more open to Western Europe, notably through marriage alliances. And between 1050 and 1113, the death of its main writer and compiler, the monk Nestor, the *Primary Chronicle* was put together. This first compilation of the history of Rus reflects how feelings of being different had taken root, and marks a turning away from the Greek heritage towards 'East Slav Christian'.

From 1113 to 1125 there is Vladimir Monomakh, the last great ruler of the period of princely strife, and the rise of the cities of the north-east, notably Vladimir and Suzdal'. Then there is Moscow, first mentioned in 1147. Lip service is paid to Kiev as 'Mother of all the cities of Rus'. The instability is reflected in the great Russian epic, the *Слóво о полкý Игорeве The Tale of Igor's Campaign*, recounting Igor's impetuous and failed campaign against the Polovtsians in 1187. The south is more and more threatened by the Tatars, and from 1240 to their defeat in 1380 at the Battle of Kulikovo we have the period of the Tatar Yoke. Novgorod was at first spared, and its independent history rendered glorious in the defeat of the Swedes on the ice of the River Невá *Neva* in 1240 by their leader Aleksandr Nevskii, later prince in Moscow. But constant pressure from the west caused it to seek the protection of the Tatars. Under the Yoke the Russians gradually unified; the Tatars were happy to receive their taxes, and Moscow won out as chief tax-gatherer.

2. Sex or gender?

Languages have 'gender'. One might say that some have sex. So English calls things which are things 'it' and things which are male and female 'he' and 'she'. But ships are 'she' and babies are 'it', which is where things get complicated. Russian tackles this by having gender, but sex does get in on the act in various ways. And remember, gender means 'agreement'.

Russian gender appears in three forms: *masculine, feminine, neuter*. Russian genders map onto to the ending of their dictionary-entry or citation form, and this helps you with the cases ('C' = consonant):

-consonant	=	-C	masculine;
	=	-Сь	feminine; some, but fewer, masculine;
-vowel	=	-а, -я	feminine; a few masculine, and some both;
	=	-о, -е	neuter;
special	=	-мя	ten neuter nouns.

Sex comes into it in that some nouns in -a and -я refer to males. They have *feminine* case forms, but *masculine* agreements. Nouns ending in a consonant may be considered to have a *zero ending*.

The only real bore is the nouns in a consonant followed by ь. Assume they're feminine unless they refer to a male, you've been told otherwise, seen them in the dictionary, or learnt a list!

Now for a few examples:

		masculine	*feminine*	*neuter*
I	(a)	слугá 'servant'	квартúра 'flat'	————
	(b)	дя́дя 'uncle'	земля́ 'earth'	————
II	(a)	дом 'house'	————	окнó 'window'
	(b)	учи́тель 'schoolteacher'	————	пóле 'field'
III		путь 'way'	часть 'part'	————
III + II		————	————	врéмя 'time'

Basically there are three declensions, two of them subdivided according to the hardness or softness of the consonant before the ending (this mainly just affects the spelling). The masculine noun in the third is all alone, differing from the feminine in one case form and in agreement. There are, too, a few indeclinable nouns (they simply don't change at all), but agreements will still be made: through, say, an accompanying adjective (you got a glimpse of a few of *them* in Chapter 2) you will reveal an indeclinable noun's underlying gender, number, and case: пальтó 'overcoat' is indeclinable and neuter, so 'a new overcoat' will be нóвое пальтó and 'new overcoats' will be нóвые пальтó. See the Reference Section for a few illustrative tables.

Just to add a bit of reality, here are some useful nouns, useful partly because you have them here on these pages. You can probably work out why they're split up into boxes — make use of them in the exercises.

24

автóбус	bus	буфéт	buffet, sideboard
дом	house	друг	friend
журнáл	magazine	словáрь	dictionary
карандáш	pencil	кинотеáтр	cinema
ковёр	carpet	магазúн	shop
мел	chalk	нóмер	number, hotel room
пол	floor	портфéль	briefcase
потолóк	ceiling	учúтель	teacher (school)
студéнт	student	стол	table
стул	chair	теáтр	theatre
телевúзор	television	фильм	film
чай	tea	этáж	floor, storey
трамвáй	tram	путь	way

библиотéка	library	газéта	newspaper
дверь	door	доскá	(black)board
истóрия	history, story	картúна	picture
кнúга	book	лаборатóрия	laboratory
лáмпа	lamp	пéсня	song
плóщадь	square	пóчта	post(-office)
рýчка	pen	стенá	wall
столóвая	dining room, café	студéнтка	student
кóмната	room	тетрáдь	exercise book
тря́пка	rag, duster	ýлица	street
аудитóрия	lecture room	дерéвня	countryside; village

задáние	task, exercise	письмó	letter, writing
окнó	window	здáние	building
пóле	field	врéмя	time

Let's add a few more masculine nouns in a soft sign: князь 'prince' (the same word as *king*), царь 'tsar' (*Caesar*), пáрень 'lad', some kinship terms, e.g. зять 'son-in-law' (the same word as French *gendre*), agent nouns in -тель and -арь, e.g. писáтель 'writer', преподавáтель 'university teacher', зрúтель 'spectator', вратáрь 'goalkeeper' (a Church Slavonic word!).

Feminines in a soft sign include those denoting women, e.g. мать 'mother', дочь 'daughter', abstract nouns in -ость and -есть , e.g. мóлодость 'youth', вéжливость 'politeness', глáсность 'openness', свéжесть 'freshness' (these often come from adjectives), and nouns where the soft sign is preceded by a husher, e.g. молодёжь 'young people', ночь 'night', чушь 'nonsense', and вещь 'thing'.

Masculine nouns in -a/-я, apart from nouns like мужчúна 'man', дéдушка 'grandfather', Никúта 'Nikita', are often the short or familiar forms of first names, e.g. Вáня for Ивáн, Тóля for Анатóлий, Жéня for

25

Евгéний, Сáша for Алексáндр (the last two also serve for the women's names Алексáндра and Евгéния). To these one must add the *epicene* nouns, masculine or feminine, depending on whether they're referring to a man or to a woman: пья́ница 'drunkard' (mainly men, I must say), левшá 'left-handed person' (amazing how many such people learn Russian), ýмница 'clever person', плáкса 'cry-baby', невéжда 'ignoramus', невéжа 'crude, impolite person', сóня 'dozy person', вы́скочка 'upstart'.

Things being how they are, nouns to refer to women are often created from the masculine ones, which may then end up generic. Here are some examples, so you can see a few patterns and what sometimes happens:

официáнт — официáнтка	waiter — waitress
нéмец — нéмка	German
англичáнин — англичáнка	Englishman — Englishwoman
актёр — актри́са	actor — actress
поэ́т — поэтéсса	poet
пóвар — повари́ха	cook
танцóвщик — танцóвщица	dancer
переводчик — перевóдчица	translator
писáтель — писáтельница	writer

Now, the nouns have been given in their citation form, the 'nominative'. It's what you use when you name something! 'This is (a/the) student' is э́то *студéнт* (э́то is an invariable word meaning 'this is, these are'). And so on, just slot in the nominative of any appropriate noun. You can do the same using the invaluable and invariable little word вот 'here is/are; there is/are': Вот *пóвар* 'Here's the cook'. And when you're talking about something, you simply name it, and this is often the 'subject'. So: '*John* is a student' is *Джон* — студéнт. Just in case, let's clear four things up:

(i)   э́то and вот never change;
(ii)   there's no word for 'is' here in Russian;
(iii)   what 'John' is identified with goes into the nominative too;
(iv)   Russian has no word for 'the' or 'a(n)'.

3. To be, most definitely 'To be'

Even 'am' and 'are' are missing too. Alas, this applies only to the present tense ('to be' in Russian has a separate future tense). Now, 'to be' in Russian is быть; do you think of English *be*? Actually, one present-tense form is encountered: есть — it's most useful as 'there is/are'. Do you think of English *is*? So here's the present tense of the verb 'to be' (you can replace 'he, she, it, they' with a noun) — it's just the personal pronouns!

я...	'I am'	мы...	'we are'
ты...	'you are'	вы...	'you are',
он/онá/онó...	'he/she/it is'	они...	'they are'

Exercise 1

The sentences Кто э́то? and Что э́то? mean 'Who's/What's this/that'?' Тут and здесь mean 'here', and там means 'there'; в and на mean 'in, on, at' and in those meanings require that the noun they govern take the prepositional case (given in the list below). Fill in the blanks on the basis of the patterns, using as many of the words and phrases listed above and below. Match the noun to the correct gender of the pronoun. You might also vary things, using вот.

Ктó э́то?   Э́то Ивáн.   Он студéнт.
Ктó э́то?   Э́то _____.   ___ _____.

Чтó э́то?   Э́то стул.   Он тут.
Чтó э́то?   Э́то _____.   ___ _____.

печь 'oven' (more modern is духóвка), жéнщина 'woman', дéвушка 'girl', мáльчик 'boy', артúст(ка) 'performing artist', студéнт(ка) 'student', врач 'doctor' (use for both male and female, and use sex to determine the personal pronoun, but address a doctor as дóктор), профéссор 'professor' (as for врач), журналúст(ка) 'journalist', турúст(ка) 'tourist', журнáл 'magazine', дивáн 'sofa', кровáть 'bed' (guess what a дивáн-кровáть is), сýмка 'bag' (another nice word for a bag, usually a string bag, is авóська, derived from авóсь, one of the indispensable words these days, both in Russian and in its approximate English equivalent, 'hopefully'), учéбник 'textbook'; and some locations: дóма 'at home', в дóме 'in the house', в музéе 'in the museum', в университéте 'in the university', в шкóле 'in the school', в óфисе 'in the office', на рабóте 'at work', на вокзáле 'at the railway station', на стáнции 'at the station', на урóке 'at the lesson', на лéкции 'at the lecture', в Москвé 'in Moscow', в Санкт-Петербýрге 'in St Petersburg', в/на кýхне 'in the kitchen', в спáльне 'in the bedroom', в столóвой 'in the dining-room', в вáнной 'in the bathroom', в кóмнате 'in the room', в квартúре 'in the flat/apartment', на стенé 'on the wall', на буфéте 'on the sideboard', на ýлице 'in the street, outside'. By the way, pronounce в together with the following word, without a pause (unless it's a natural one).

4. And now for a poem

One great Russian poet is Aleksandr Blok, Алексáндр Блок (1880-1921). Always personal, musical, and often a hint of existential bleakness. Learn it by heart — it's one of the best ways of getting to grips with Russian: learn and love their poetry is something Russians do!

Ночь, у́лица, фона́рь, апте́ка,
Бессмы́сленный и ту́склый свет.
Живи́ ещё хоть че́тверть ве́ка —
Всё бу́дет так. Исхо́да нет.

Умрёшь — начнёшь опя́ть снача́ла,
И повтори́тся всё, как встáрь:
Ночь, ледяна́я рябь кана́ла,
Апте́ка, у́лица, фона́рь.

1912

Night, street, lamp, chemist's, / Senseless and dim world/light. / Live yet at-least a-quarter of-a-century — / Everything will-be thus. A-way-out there-isn't. / You'll-die — you'll-start again from-the-beginning, / And will-repeat-itself everything, as of-old: / Night, the-icy ripples of-the-canal, / Chemist's, street, lamp.

From the 'translation' you'll see just how much information conveyed in English in several words Russian conveys in single ones. All the nouns but two are in the nominative; the exceptions are че́тверть 'quarter', which is accusative (identical in form with its nominative), and исхо́да 'way out', which is in the genitive case, something required with нет 'there isn't/aren't' (it may help to think of French *il n'y a pas de sortie — de sortie* is a sort of genitive). Note the adjectives, agreeing, of course: бессмы́сленный, ту́склый with masculine свет; ледяна́я with feminine рябь. The verb forms include an imperative, with an 'if' sense here, живи́ 'live', one form of the unique future of быть, бу́дет, and the non-pasts, with future sense, умрёшь, начнёшь, and повтори́тся, respectively 'you'll die, you'll begin, [it] will be repeated' — these all have non-past endings, which as you'll see also serve for the present. The -ся in повтори́тся is what makes a verb reflexive — really simple when you think of other languages. For the verb, more information is about to reach you!

5. What would we do without conjugations?

Indeed, it just wouldn't do. However, 'to be' might have suggested that the Russian verb is utterly easy. So then, how about verbs like 'to read' and 'to speak'? Well, Russian actually does remain wonderfully simple: it only really has two 'tenses', the *non-past* and the *past*, and they serve to convey almost everything English can throw at them.

Only the non-past conjugates, and pops up in two conjugations. Russian has hardly any 'irregular' verbs. To be convinced of this you must simply learn two forms of the non-past in addition to the infinitive — when your familiarity with Russian is greater, you'll be able to make do with just *one* non-past form.

So, here's the non-past of the two conjugations. Here it corresponds to 'I speak, do speak, am speaking', etc. Learn it all for now, but soon, as already said, you'll be able to deduce, *entirely confidently*, every form provided you know the first and any one of the last five forms.

	читáть	говорúть
	to read	*to speak*
я	читáю	говорю́
ты	читáешь	говорúшь
он/онá/онó	читáет	говорúт
мы	читáем	говорúм
вы	читáете	говорúте
онú	читáют	говоря́т

Stare at the table: е and и; 'I' and 'they'. Make connections. In the first conjugation (on the left) you have -ю(т) after a vowel; in a few verbs you also have -ю(т) after a consonant (otherwise, after a consonant, you have -у(т)). Bear this in mind when I give you more examples, and remember the spelling rules: you *have* to have y and a rather than ю and я after certain consonants (the ones that occur are к, г, ш, ж, ч, щ). And the stress: both these verbs have *fixed* stress, *not* on the ending in читáть and *on* the ending in говорúть. The only other pattern is: on ending in the 'I' form, not on the ending in the others.

And the personal pronouns: express them. Russian is like English here, though it does have much more scope for dropping them.

6. More verb patterns

Now a few more patterns — for now I give you *all* the forms:

	писáть	жить	вúдеть	звонúть	платúть	носúть	любúть
	to write	*to live*	*to see*	*to phone*	*to pay*	*to carry*	*to love*
я	пишу́	живу́	вúжу	звоню́	плачу́	ношу́	люблю́
ты	пúшешь	живёшь	вúдишь	звонúшь	плáтишь	нóсишь	лю́бишь
он...	пúшет	живёт	вúдит	звонúт	плáтит	нóсит	лю́бит
мы	пúшем	живём	вúдим	звонúм	плáтим	нóсим	лю́бим
вы	пúшете	живёте	вúдите	звонúте	плáтите	нóсите	лю́бите
онú	пúшут	живу́т	вúдят	звоня́т	плáтят	нóсят	лю́бят

Look carefully. Note four 'I' forms and one 'they' form which are down to the spelling rules (ш, ж, ч). Note that the whole non-past of one verb has a consonant different from that in the infinitive (ш). You see this too in the 'I' form of three (ш/ж/ч; and partly a fourth: бл) of the second-conjugation verbs. This is important — see Chapter 5 for a summary.

There are many second-conjugation verbs where these changes occur; but some of the first-conjugation verbs are important, and always have the stress pattern of писáть (many second-conjugation verbs have that too).

For жить (remember живи́ in the poem?), you need to know that this verb has a base жив- (there are quite a few verbs with a base ending in a surprise consonant). One verb that doesn't give you an unpleasant surprise is знать 'to know', which goes знáю, знáешь, etc. It's historically the same as English *know* (i.e. the *kn*) and reflects the *gn* as found in *gnosticism*, *recognize*, etc.

How about some more? Now *you* have to work. Don't worry! For the first five follow the pattern of жить (but note the stress of éхать).

	идти́	éхать	вести́	везти́	нести́	летéть
	to go/walk	*to go/drive*	*to lead*	*to convey*	*to carry*	*to fly*
я	иду́	éду	веду́	везу́	несу́	лечу́
ты	идёшь	éдешь	ведёшь	везёшь	несёшь	летишь
они́	иду́т	éдут	веду́т	везу́т	несу́т	летя́т

You'll recall носи́ть 'to carry'. Given нести́ 'to carry' here, and the fact that the two share н and с, you'll be wrinkling your brow! Well, Russian has 'verbs of motion' — masses of detail in Chapter 7.

Exercise 2

Give the Russian for: he sees, they see, I go, you (sing.) go, we phone, she phones, I pay, they pay, they write, I write, I convey, we convey, you (pl.) live, they live, I fly, they fly, you (sing.) read, they read.

7. Back to the past

Well, this form does everything else, including the conditional (and the subjunctive, if you want to show off). It's really child's play (well, so is every language, though once you're no longer a child,...), and is roughly the equivalent of English 'I done', 'she seen', which isn't at all 'ungrammatical', in spite of jokes of the sort: 'Mum, I done the letter to Dad' — 'What about your grammar?' — 'I written to 'er already'. Sorry about that. In other words, it's a participle, and a participle is a verbal *adjective*, so all it has is the forms you expect for agreement with the subject — three genders and one plural:

	masc sing я/ты/он + +	*fem sing* я/ты/она́ +	*neut sing* я/ты/оно́ +	*plural* мы/вы/они́
знать	знал	зна́ла	зна́ло	зна́ли
чита́ть	чита́л	чита́ла	чита́ло	чита́ли
говори́ть	говори́л	говори́ла	говори́ло	говори́ли
писа́ть	писа́л	писа́ла	писа́ло	писа́ли
носи́ть	носи́л	носи́ла	носи́ло	носи́ли
быть	был	была́	бы́ло	бы́ли

And that's it! Just link the singular subject to the right gender form, and for the plural it's just the one form — don't think in terms of 'I' and 'you' forms, etc. Form it by replacing the -ть of the infinitive with -л, etc. The only exceptions: verbs ending in a consonant + -ти́ or + -ть, the few verbs in -чь, and some verbs in -нуть, where the -ну- is lost. Just a few examples, so you can see for yourself:

infinitive	*masc.*	*fem.*	*neut.*	*pl.*
идти́ 'to go'	шёл	шла	шло	шли
нести́ 'to carry'	нёс	несла́	несло́	несли́
вести́ 'to lead (tr.)'	вёл	вела́	вело́	вели́
везти́ 'to convey'	вёз	везла́	везло́	везли́
красть 'to steal'	крал	кра́ла	кра́ло	кра́ли
мочь 'to be able'	мог	могла́	могло́	могли́
печь 'to bake'	пёк	пекла́	пекло́	пекли́
со́хнуть 'to dry (intr.)'	сох	со́хла	со́хло	со́хли

Вы 'you', even if 'you' is *one* person, goes with the plural form.

Exercise 3

Give the Russian for: he saw, they saw, I went, you (sing.) went, we phoned, she phoned, I paid, they paid, they wrote, I wrote, I conveyed, we conveyed, you (pl.) lived, they lived, I flew, they flew, you (sing.) read, they read.

8. Nothing like being negative

Some of the commonest words in Russian are, or in the recent past were, negative, e.g. нельзя́ 'You can't, it's not allowed', нет 'no'. The key form is не 'not'. Just put it in front of the verb and pronounce it together with the verb. If there's no verb, typically with the present tense of 'to be' or where the verb is understood, then you just use не on its own (don't use нет). You can also move it around the sentence, putting it in front of the word you want to negate. So:

Я рабо́таю в го́роде 'I work in the city'	— Я не рабо́таю в го́роде 'I don't work in the city'
Она́ рабо́тает не в го́роде, а до́ма 'She works at home, not in the city'	— Не она́ рабо́тает до́ма, а Ми́ша 'Misha works at home, not her'
Мари́на не студе́нтка 'Marina's not a student'	— Он не учи́тель 'He's not a teacher'

9. Nameplay

As any reader of Russian literature knows, Russians have a lot of names.

They have a first name (и́мя — one of the ten odd neuter nouns), a surname or family name (фами́лия — a false friend; 'family' is семья́), and in between they have a patronymic (о́тчество), a special form based on the father's first name. If you know someone well, use the first name on its own. If not, use the first name and patronymic. People are beginning to use господи́н 'Mr' and госпожа́ 'Mrs, Miss, Ms' with the surname more. There is also граждани́н 'citizen', for women гражда́нка — it is used in official documents and proceedings and can be the sort of term of address a suspicious policeman might use to you.

The first name may also occur in a 'short' form These can normally only be used either on their own or with a surname. Some examples:

Алёша for Алексе́й	Бо́ря for Бори́с	Ва́ся for Васи́лий
Ви́тя for Ви́ктор	Воло́дя for Влади́мир	Го́ша for И́горь
Йра for Ири́на	Ка́тя for Катери́на	Ко́ля for Никола́й
Ната́ша for Ната́лья	О́ля for О́льга	Пе́тя for Пётр
Све́та for Светла́на	Серёжа for Серге́й	Та́ня for Татья́на

One thing you get from the short form is a vocative — simply drop the ending: О́ль! Нин! Кать! — and Мам! from ма́ма — note the soft sign which replaces -я, otherwise the final consonant will be hard, and that won't do. Native speakers may reckon it to be very colloquial.

The patronymics typically end in -о́вич (males) and -о́вна (females) when stressed, otherwise -ович after hard consonants and -евич replacing -й and -ь, e.g. Петро́вич — Петро́вна, Ива́нович — Ива́новна, Серге́евич — Серге́евна, И́горевич — И́горевна — first names in -ий have -ьевич/-ьевна (-иевич/-иевна in a very few instances, and they may be optional), e.g. Васи́льевич — Васи́льевна, Дми́триевич — Дми́триевна.

If the first name ends in an unstressed -a, the -a is usually replaced by -ович/-овна, e.g. Кири́лович — Кири́ловна from Кири́ла ; but Ники́та has Ники́тич — Ники́тична. First names in stressed -a and -я have -и́ч for men and -и́нична for women: Луки́ч and Луки́нична for

Лука́, Фоми́ч and Фоми́нична for Фома́, and Ильи́ч and Ильи́нична for Илья́. Patronymics decline like nouns.

Now, family names. If it looks like an adjective (see the Reference Section), then it declines like an adjective: Достое́вский (the man), Достое́вская (the woman), Достое́вские (the plural). The other typically Russian surnames end in -ов and -ев, and in -ин and -ын, e.g. Ивано́в, Горбачёв, Митро́хин, Солжени́цын. For their declension see the Reference Section too. Others which look as if they could decline when referring to a man probably will do so for a man and in the plural (and will decline like a noun), but won't when referring to a woman; examples are Блок and, foreign but potentially confusing, Да́рвин 'Darwin'. Names in -енко tend not to be declined; the same goes for those in -го, -во, -их, -ых, e.g. Жива́го, Дурново́, Долги́х, and Черны́х.

How about getting to know someone? The basic, formal, question is Как вас зову́т? lit. 'How do-people-call you' — to a small child, a fellow student, or in a generally informal manner you'd use Как *тебя* зову́т? The answer might just be your name or Меня́ зову́т X — X marks a nominative spot! For 'him, her, them', the statements are Его́/Её/Их зову́т X (for the question it's Как его́/её/их зову́т?). Enjoy the following rather blasphemous (for a Russian) conversation:

Пу́шкин:	Дава́йте познако́мимся!
Го́голь:	С удово́льствием!
Пу́шкин:	Меня́ зову́т Пу́шкин, Алекса́ндр Серге́евич. А вас как зову́т?
Го́голь:	Меня́ зову́т Го́голь, Никола́й Васи́льевич!
Пу́шкин:	О́чень прия́тно.
Го́голь:	Вы вели́кий ру́сский поэ́т, не пра́вда ли?
Пу́шкин:	И́менно! Вы о́чень любе́зны. А вы, ка́жется, то́же пи́шете.
Го́голь:	Так то́чно. Но, к сожале́нию, я про́сто начина́ющий писа́ка.
Пу́шкин:	Всё равно́. Я зна́ю, что вы бу́дете писа́ть пье́су «Ревизо́р» и рома́н «Мёртвые ду́ши». Совсе́м непло́хо!
Го́голь:	Како́й вы симпати́чный молодо́й челове́к! Кста́ти, перейдём на ты!
Пу́шкин:	Ла́дно, договори́лись. Ты зна́ешь, я рабо́таю в ба́ре: пойдём вы́пьем на брудерша́фт!
Го́голь:	Это меня́ чрезвыча́йно устра́ивает. Я го́рький пья́ница.

P: Let's get to know each other!
G: With pleasure!
P: I'm called Pushkin, Aleksandr Sergeevich. And what are you called?
G: I'm called Gogol', Nikolai Vasil'evich!
P: Delighted.
G: You're a great Russian poet, aren't you? (lit. 'Isn't it true?')
P: Exactly. You're very kind. And you, it seems, also write.
G: Exactly. But unfortunately I'm only a débutant scribbler.
P: No matter. I know that you will write the play *The Government Inspector* and the novel *Dead Souls*. Not bad at all!
G: What a nice young man you are! Incidentally, let's go over to 'ty'.
P: OK, agreed. You know, I work in a bar: let's go drink to *brudershaft*!
G: That suits me exceedingly. I'm a hard drinker!

Lots of this is unfamiliar, so take it on trust for the moment. Try to decipher it: look out for pronouns you've met, for verb endings, etc. — on the basis of the grammatical bits you've encountered, you should be able to make some sense of it.

Note *a*, which is a very common entry into a statement, especially when the conversation has started. Не пра́вда ли? is a very useful tag in questions. И́менно means 'namely, exactly'. Note too the useful parenthetic remark ка́жется 'I think; it seems'. Another to bear in mind is коне́чно 'of course' (pronounce -чн- *shn*). And as for *brudershaft*, when they decide on informal address, men and women pour out a drink, link and cross arms, drink, then give each other one or more kisses.

The choice between ты and вы, the two words for 'you', is rather similar to that in French. Of course, the details are a matter of familiarity with how Russians do things. You can only really use ты without hesitation, from the very start, with a young person up to, say, the age of fifteen. After that, respect and recognition of autonomy have to be given. There's no problem using вы with a first name (perhaps not usually the 'short' ones, without a surname). And if there's to be a shift from вы to ты, and the two people concerned are a man and a woman, it's the woman who must be left to suggest it. And students are to be addressed as вы!

By the way, if you blunder and use ты before formalities have been dropped, you're likely to hear Вы мне не ты́кайте, мы с ва́ми на брудерша́фт не пи́ли 'Don't you *ты* me, you and I haven't drunk to *brudershaft*' (to express 'X and I' you normally use мы с + instrumental case, something you're about to encounter).

One small point: вы and all its forms, and those of its possessive ваш 'your, yours', are by convention written with a capital initial letter in correspondence; this is something which seems to be becoming a bit more generalized. Here, where there isn't any correspondence anyway, I keep to a small initial.

CHAPTER 4

1. From Kiev to Muscovy

By 1242 all the *рýсская земля* 'the land of Rus' except Novgorod and Pskov was under the Tatar yoke and the ancestors of Ukraine and Belarus had become linked to Poland-Lithuania.

Many separate principalities emerged, with polarization around the strongest: Moscow and Tver', and, from the fifteenth century, Moscow alone. Surrounded by marshes, it had been relatively untouched by the Tatar invasion, so many Russians moved there away from the Horde, and the town grew. Novgorod, near Tver, suspected Tver's intentions and so favoured the more distant Moscow. The boyars (the best-born of Kiev and Muscovy, the 'prince's men') too transferred their allegiance there. And in 1328 the Metropolitan of Russia moved there.

Dmitrii Ivanovich Donskoi reigned from 1359 to 1389, a period when cooperation between Church and State increased. Dmitrii initiated local resistance to the Tatars, resistance symbolized most vividly in the victory of the Battle of Kulikovo Pole — the Battle of the Snipe Field, in 1380, marking the end of one-and-a-half centuries of subservience to the Horde. The tide had turned.

In 1456 the ancient *liberties* of Novgorod were curbed. Thus far Crimea, Astrakhan' and Kazan' remained independent Tatar states – somewhat like pre-Conquista Spain.

1462-1505 marks the reign of Ивáн III Велúкий 'The Great'. Calling himself ruler of all the lands and Государь, he developed autocratic power, with Moscow or, better, Muscovy, as a centralized state. He added the Byzantine double-headed eagle to the royal arms and assumed the title of самодéржец 'autocrat'. Conservative, parochial, self-important.

The fifteenth century is characterized by spiritual struggles. Should the Church own land? At a Council of the Church in 1503 the Church split, with the hierarchy supporting those in favour of the ownership of land and a strong sense of ritual.

The tsar was more powerful than the Church, and the tsar, for that is what he now was, was Ivan the Terrible, the key figure of the sixteenth century. In 1552 he took Kazan and in 1556 annexed Astrakhan. One of his major aims was to gain access to the Baltic, but this achievement was left to Peter the Great. During Ivan's time contacts with the West grew.

Perhaps Ivan was unbalanced; perhaps he was progressive. Under him Muscovy became one whole. He targetted the power of the boyars, something which was probably already declining and disorganized. But he indulged in the insanity of civil massacre through his *Oprichnina*, his *private* realm, which controlled vast territory, much of it taken from the boyars. In 1572 Ivan abolished it, and in 1584 he died, having killed his son three years earlier in a fit of rage.

And so began the Смутное время 'Time of Troubles', with Boris Godunov and the beginning of the Romanov line. Before the eighteenth century there remains one fundamental development: the Раскол *Schism* of the seventeenth century. Apart from among the masses and the monastic clergy, there was a desire for revision of the Church books. But change was seen as heresy. In the 1640s the process of revision began. It was approved and those who did not accept it were seen as heretics. So there was a split. The dissenters, or *Old Believers* (Староверы) moved away from the centres of population. The Schism continued the Russian crisis of identity: a community with a foreign religion, to a large extent cut off from the intellectual mainstream, a mixture of very diverse peoples, subjugated to and intermarrying with the Tatars, leaning towards the West, but keeping its distance without knowing exactly why.

2. Nothing but questions

Let's start with questions where the answer is 'yes' or 'no'? You can leave the sentence just as it is (raise your voice on the bit you're questioning) — if you want to add a tag, i.e. 'isn't it, aren't you, innit,' etc., then just add не правда ли (lit. 'isn't it true?') or the very useful что ли, betraying uncertainty, 'how about it?': Это стол, что ли? 'This is a table, don't you think?' The little word ли can be used to mark a sentence as a question, but it mustn't come first: Дома ли он? 'Is it at home that he is?' (i.e. it comes 'second', after the word which is the 'core' of the question); many Russians would these days see it as poetic or restricted to indirect questions — see Chapter 18.

Here come a few question words — you often put them first, and you raise your voice on them. They mostly involve к or ч, reflected in кто? 'who?' and что? 'what? (pronounce что as *shto*) — I give you *all* the case forms of these, as an appetizer:

nominative	кто	что
accusative	кого	что
genitive	кого	чего
dative	кому	чему
instrumental	кем	чем
prepositional	ком	чём

They can also be used as 'who' and 'which', but mainly only preceded by a comma and forms of тот 'that (person/fact)', все 'everyone', and всё 'everything': Тот/Та, кто читáет 'That person (man/woman) who is reading', Все, кто жил здесь 'Everyone who lived here' (все is plural, but кто, as you can see from the verb, is singular and masculine), and Всё, что мы читáли 'Everything (that) we were reading' (as you'd expect, что is neuter and singular) — and check out Chapter 13.

когдá?	when?	как?	how?
где?	where (in what place)?	кудá?	where (to what place)?
откýда?	from where?	почемý?	why?

Full use of these ties in with knowing more forms and constructions, something not too far off. Here are some useful words for answers:

там	there	тут *or* здесь	here (no motion)
тудá	there (motion to)	сюдá	here (motion to)
оттýда	from there	отсюда	from here (motion from)
потомý что	because	такúм óбразом	in such a way

3. This and that

The main 'this, that' word is э́тот, one of the few native words beginning in э (э is much rarer inside or at the end of a word). Its three singular and one plural forms are: э́тот, э́та, э́то, and э́ти, and it means 'this' but may often cover for 'that'. If you want to insist on 'that', then it's тот, та, то, and те — the plural isn't a misprint. See Chapter 8 for more information, and recall that combining forms of тот with кто and что is a very important way of conveying 'he who', 'everything that', 'that which', 'she who', etc. respectively тот, кто — всё, что — то, что— та, кто, etc.

4. The case for case, just in case

Russian's cases make it an extremely powerful language: they permit a flexible order of words, as they give you clues, make links. Anyone who has learnt Russian, or Latin, or Ancient Greek, has shown skill in a lot more than learning a language: you've shown that you can deal with puzzles and create order out of, well, whatever. Russians don't need to be intellectual; they have a natural verbal input straight into how things are. No wonder there is so much respect for the word in Russia.

So, it's all very well saying я понимáю 'I understand' or я пишý 'I'm writing', but what about *who*, *what* you understand or write? In languages we make sense by forging relationships between words — English achieves this by having quite a strict order of words, while Russian uses the organizing power of cases. Look! In the pair of sentences below the word order is crucial in English, while in Russian one *could* have the same, but does not need to because, in this instance, the form of the word for 'politician' would tell us who is accusing whom.

The State accuses the politician — The politician accuses the State

The person you understand, the thing you write, the person you love, will normally go into the *accusative* case. For neuters, and for masculine nouns which don't refer to living things, this is identical with the nominative. Nouns in -а and -я change respectively to -у and -ю, and masculine nouns with a zero ending *and* referring to living things (animates) add -а to a hard paired consonant and to -ж, -ц, -ч, -ш, and -щ, and -я replaces -ь and -й.

'About/concerning' and 'where' involve the *prepositional* case, so called because it never occurs without a preposition. You might say it's a waste of time having *both* a preposition *and* a case form; surely just one or the other will do. Well, that does make sense, and often you can guess a meaning without scrutinizing the ending. But some prepositions can occur with various case endings, with different meanings, so...

Anyway, the prepositional case form is straightforward: most often it's -е, which is added to a final consonant letter and replaces -ь, -а, -я, -о, and -й (nominative -е after a consonant is kept). Feminines in -ь, and the single masculine путь, however, have -и instead of -ь (мать and дочь have мáтери and дóчери , where you can see they're related to the English words); and neuters in -мя are the same, except that they too have an extension, so имя 'first name' becomes имени . The big exception, however, applies to feminine and neuter nouns in -ия, -ие. These have -ии. Actually, this is a matter of spelling, as the pronunciation would be the same if their prepositional was spelt -ие.

Finally for now, c meaning '(together) with, accompanied by' takes the instrumental — pronounce it together with the following word, as with в. Basically, masculines and neuters are characterized by an -м here, and feminines (and masculines) in -а and -я by an -й, all preceded by -о- or -е- (-ё-) as a link vowel — neuters in -мя have the vowel after the extension: именем. Feminines in a soft sign add -ю to the soft sign (same for мать and дочь , but with their extension: мáтерью) — you'll occasionally come across poetic or old-fashioned -ию for -ью (note мыслию for мыслью 'thought' in Chapter 5). Regarding the vowel, after ж, ц, ч, ш, and щ this is spelt -о- if stressed and -е- if unstressed.

Now see it all happen:

I read	what?	about what?	with whom?	where?
	(что?)	(о чём?)	(с кём?)	(где? в/на чём)
	учéбник	о + литература	с + Ивáн	в + Москвá
	'textbook'	'about + literature'	'with + Ivan'	'in + Moscow'
	кни́га	о + футбóл	с + Мари́на	в + Петербýрг
	'book'	'about + football'	'with + Marina'	'in + St Petersburg'
becomes				
я читáю	учéбник	о литератýре	с Ивáном	в Москвé
	кни́гу	о футбóле	с Мари́ной	в Петербýрге

I see	what? who?	where?
I see	(что?, когó?)	(в/на чём)
	учéбник	кóмната
	кни́га	пóлка
	Ивáн	здáние
	гóрод	кáрта
	здáние	плóщадь
	чáшка	стол
becomes		
я ви́жу	учéбник	в кóмнате
	кни́гу	на пóлке
	Ивáна	во здáнии
	гóрод	на кáрте
	здáние	на плóщади
	чáшку	на столé

And now a table (the endings are italicized, with nothing where the ending is zero; just note the disappearing vowel in пáлец for now):

	accusative	instrumental	prepositional
кни́га	кни́гу	кни́гой	кни́ге
душá	дýшу	душóй	душé
дя́дя	дя́дю	дя́дей	дя́де
земля́	зéмлю	землéй	землé
фами́лия	фами́лию	фами́лией	фами́лии
учéбник	учéбник	учéбником	учéбнике
карандáш	карандáш	карандашóм	карандашé
пáлец	пáлец	пáльцем	пáльце
автомоби́ль	автомоби́ль	автомоби́лем	автомоби́ле
словáрь	словáрь	словарём	словарé
Ивáн	Ивáна	Ивáном	Ивáне
учи́тель	учи́теля	учи́телем	учи́теле
Евгéний	Евгéния	Евгéнием	Евгéнии

	accusative	instrumental	prepositional
окно́	окно́	окно́м	окне́
по́ле	по́ле	по́лем	по́ле
зда́ние	зда́ние	зда́нием	зда́нии
ча́сть	часть	ча́стью	ча́сти
мать	мать	ма́терью	ма́тери
путь	путь	путём	пути́
вре́мя	вре́мя	вре́менем	вре́мени

The ending -ой, -ей will occasionally be found as -ою, -ею.

5. The case for prepositions

Four prepositions occurred in the examples. All of them can be followed by more than one case. First, о + prepositional = 'about, concerning'; it becomes об when the next word begins with a vowel — in a couple of instances it expands to обо (обо мне́ 'about me', обо всём 'about everything'). В and на also take the prepositional. They mean respectively 'in' and 'on'. If there is *movement*, they take the accusative and converge as 'to' (or remain separate as 'into' and 'onto'). Use на for 'in' or 'at' in reference to activities, e.g. lessons, an opera or ballet (but not a theatre), points of the compass, surfaces (often geographical: peninsulas, islands, mountains, streets, squares), meteorological phenomena (air, frost, sun, dawn). Then there are oddities: на вокза́ле 'at the station' (from вокза́л *Vauxhall* — yes, it *is* from the English word), на по́чте 'at the post office' (from по́чта), на дворе́ 'outside' (from двор 'courtyard' — 'in the courtyard' is во дворе́), на Украи́не 'in Ukraine' — grammars will have lists. Though I'm unforgivably jumping ahead, note that в 'to' is paired with из 'from', and на 'to' with с 'from'. Из and с are constructed with the genitive case — see Chapter 7.

C is important. As we've seen, it's also used for 'in the company of', but 'with' in English can also mean 'by means of', and here the instrumental comes into its own: Ната́ша пи́шет письмо́ ру́чкой 'Natasha writes a letter *with a pen*' (from ру́чка) — yes, completely *on its own*.

Note regarding в and с that they are historically identical with English 'in' and 'co-, con-, com-, syn-, sym-'. In the latter case you can see they come from Latin and Greek in English. And those final consonants, *n* and *m* actually survive in Russian (as н) — more about that later. Note too that they, and the preposition к 'towards', enlarge to во, со, ко before awkward consonant groups (some others do too).

CHAPTER 4

Exercise 1

Here are a few really useful verbs:

писа́ть 'to write' — 'to be a writer' or 'to write a letter/about/to'. It's historically the same as the *pic* in *picture*, so it's not suprising that it also means 'to paint'.
жить 'to live'.
рабо́тать 'to work' — It *is* related to *robots* and German *die Arbeit*.
отдыха́ть 'to rest, be on holiday (lit. "to get one's breath back")', conjugates like рабо́тать and чита́ть 'to read'.
Печа́тать 'to print, type', де́лать 'to do, make', ду́мать 'to think'. No surprises.
Игра́ть 'to play' — no surprises, but use в + acc. for a game and на + prep. for an instrument: она́ так хорошо́ игра́ет в футбо́л 'she plays football so well', and он игра́ет на фле́йте 'he plays the flute'.
говори́ть 'to speak, talk, say, tell'. That's a mouthful! Note you've got two ideas here: speak/talk — say/tell. If you're talking *about* something, use о + prep. If you're *speaking to* (= 'with') someone, use с + instr. If you *say* something *to* someone, then no problem, but you need the dative — Chapter 7!
   Now work out the forms you need and make up your own sentences:

Ивано́в	сейча́с *now*	писа́ть	письмо́	о	мать
Мать	чита́ть	письмо́	об	Серге́й	Ивано́в
Ната́ша	игра́ть	на	бараба́н *drum*	на	у́лица
Оле́г	игра́ть	с	Вади́м	в	крике́т
Васи́лий	рабо́тать	с	Та́ня	в	теа́тр
Они́	отдыха́ть	с	Тама́ра	на	юг *south*
Ви́ктор	и	Викто́рия	жить	на	пло́щадь
Где	и	с	кто	она́	жить?
Что	вы	де́лать	сего́дня	в	о́фис?
О	что	ты	ду́мать	на	рабо́та?
С	кто	она́	говори́ть	на	ку́хня? *kitchen*
О	кто	вы	говори́ть	в	ко́мната?

6. Getting instrumental

We've seen that the instrumental is the case for when you use the preposition с 'with, accompanied by' and to express the instrument or means by which something is done.

   You also use the instrumental when you might expect the nominative. In the first place, the verb 'to be'. So far we've had the present tense (that was difficult, wasn't it?). 'To be' has two other tense forms (rather unusual, for the moment, for a Russian verb): the future and the past. The future looks just like a present tense, but it's exclusively future in meaning — see Chapter 6. Now, if you say 'I'm an actor', you just say я актёр. But the instrumental would practically be the rule if instead of the present you had the future, the imperative, the gerund, the infinitive, or the conditional mood — these are all somewhat more uncertain, and there the instrumental is a good idea! You could also do it with the past tense — here change comes in more: 'I *was* an actor', and now I'm an impresario! If there's something really permanent about the state (so it isn't really a past tense, or rather it's true of the past and still true), then you'll use the nominative.

Last, for 'it was', 'it will be', etc., you can use э́то plus the form of the verb appropriate to *what/who* 'was', 'will be', etc.: Э́то была́ Та́ня 'It was Tania'. It *is* possible to have an agreement between э́то and the verb, and then what follows will be instrumental, e.g. Э́то бы́ло после́дней ка́плей 'That was the last straw [lit. "drop"]'.

There are a few verbs which are similar to 'to be', e.g. 'to work' — what you work *as* will be instrumental. These *have* to be followed by the instrumental, and include (those verbs with -ся tacked on are reflexive; I'll only give non-past forms where you may still need to be told them):

рабо́тать 'to work (as)', служи́ть (служу́, слу́жишь) 'to serve, work (as)', выступа́ть 'to appear/give a performance / talk (as)'; and some reflexive verbs: ока́зываться 'to prove to be, turn out to be', станови́ться (становлю́сь, стано́вишься) 'to become', остава́ться (остаю́сь , остаёшься) 'to remain', счита́ться 'to be considered', явля́ться 'to be, appear'.

(Reflexives, with one exception, tack on -ся to a form ending in a consonant, and -сь to one ending in a vowel.)

Similar are verbs which seem to have two direct objects, e.g. 'I appointed him (1) chief clown (2)'. The second direct object must be instrumental (and the first must be accusative):

счита́ть 'to consider [someone *something*]', назнача́ть 'to appoint [someone *something*]', называ́ть 'to name, call [someone/something *something*]', and выбира́ть 'to choose, elect [someone *something*]'.

There are also verbs indicating some sort of control:

владе́ть (владе́ю, владе́ешь) 'to control, possess', управля́ть 'to manage', заве́довать (заве́дую, заве́дуешь) 'to be in charge of', по́льзоваться (по́льзуюсь, по́льзуешься) 'to make use of, use', злоупотребля́ть 'to abuse, misuse'.

And there are verbs where the subject is closely involved in the 'action':

занима́ться 'to study', интересова́ться (интересу́юсь, интересу́ешься) 'to be interested in', наслажда́ться 'to enjoy', любова́ться (любу́юсь, любу́ешься) 'to admire, like looking at', восхища́ться 'to admire, be enraptured by'.

CHAPTER 4

Exercise 2

After all that, some more exercise! First, here are a few job-names:

води́тель 'driver', учи́тель 'teacher', преподава́тель 'higher-education teacher', носи́льщик 'porter', ре́ктор 'vice-chancellor', президе́нт 'president', секрета́рь 'secretary', ме́неджер 'manager', худо́жник 'artist', престу́пник 'criminal', свяще́нник 'priest', медсестра́ 'nurse', судья́ 'judge', космона́вт 'cosmonaut', дире́ктор 'director', а́втор 'author', библиоте́карь 'librarian', инжене́р 'engineer', архите́ктор 'architect', компози́тор 'composer', режиссёр 'film director', корреспонде́нт 'correspondent', парикма́хер 'hairdresser', экскурсово́д 'tourist guide'.

Decline them as you'd expect; all the appropriate ones can refer to women as well as to men. And here are some other useful words:

дура́к 'idiot, fool' (ду́ра for a woman), пейза́ж 'landscape', архитекту́ра 'architecture', тури́зм 'tourism', домохозя́йка 'housewife', сестра́ 'sister', сын 'son', брат 'brother', тётя 'aunt', ба́бушка 'grandmother', де́душка 'grandfather', колле́га 'colleague', враг 'enemy', друг 'friend' (a woman friend is подру́га), помо́щник / помо́щница 'assistant', and the town names Тверь , Псков , Но́вгород, Оде́сса , Ирку́тск, Владивосто́к , Ряза́нь , Курск , Орёл, Ту́ла, Калу́га, Воро́неж, Калинингра́д.

Note that if you want to ask someone what he or she does, you can say either Кто вы?, to which the answer will be a simple Я ..., or Кем вы рабо́таете/слу́жите?, where you'll need an instrumental in your answer.

So, dream up answers to the following questions — have fun, don't bother too much about the meaning (and if it's a yes-no question, don't bother about giving a negative reply — it doesn't change a thing):

1. Где и кем вы рабо́таете?   _____
2. Интересу́ешься ли ты иску́сством?   _____
3. Где вы живёте?   _____
4. Чем вы занима́етесь?   _____
5. Кем мы его́ выбира́ем?   _____
6. Ты назнача́ешь его́ ре́ктором?   _____
7. Кем ты его́ счита́ешь?   _____
8. Кем он любу́ется?   _____
9. Где она́ слу́жит?   _____
10. Явля́ется ли она́ домохозя́йкой?   _____
11. Кем она́ рабо́тает в Пско́ве?   _____

Его́ here means 'him'; it's the accusative of он 'he'. Have you met it before?

Try changing the subjects and using the past tense.

CHAPTER 5

A welcome breather

Here are two extracts from East Slav literature, both in modernized Russian which I've intentionally left unstressed. We're often told that the early literature is unimpressive and that Russian only got going in the nineteenth century. Incorrect. Even modernized, much of the language is difficult — just enjoy the idea of it. The texts have been taken from I.P. Eremin and D.S. Likhachëv 1957 — here just concentrate on getting the gist.

1. The *Повесть временны́х лет Tale of the Years of Time* (The Primary Chronicle)

The years given in the Chronicle are from the creation of the world, i.e. 5508 B.C. So, just subtract that from the date given. Here's the legendary start of Rus.

В год 6370. Изгнали варяг за море, и не дали им дани, и начали сами собой владеть. И не было среди них правды, и встал род на род, и была у них усобица, и стали воевать сами с собой. И сказали себе: «Поищем себе князя, который бы владел нами и судил по праву». И пошли за море к варягам, к руси. Те варяги назывались русью подобно тому, как другие называются шведы, а иные норманны и англы, а еще иные готландцы, — вот так и эти прозывались. Сказали руси чудь, славяне, кривичи и весь: «Земля наша велика и обильна, а порядка в ней нет. Приходите княжить и владеть нами». И избрались трое братьев со своими родами, и взяли с собой всю русь, и пришли к славянам, и сел старший, Рюрик, в Новгороде, а другой, Синеус, — на Белоозере, а третий, Трувор, — в Изборске. И от тех варягов прозвалась Русская земля.

In the-year 862. They-chased-out the-Varangians beyond the-sea, and did not give to-them tribute, and themselves began to-rule themselves. And there-was not among them law, and kin rose against kin, and [there] was among them strife, and they-began to-wage-war with each other. And they-said to-themselves: 'Let-us-seek for-ourselves a-prince, who would rule us and judge [us] according-to law/rightness.' And they-went over the-sea to-the-Varangians, to-the-Rus. Those

Varangians were-called Rus similarly to-the-fact how others are-called Swedes, and others Normans and Angles, and yet others Goths — so thus also these were called. The-Chud', the Slavs, the-Krivichi, and the-Ves' said to-the-Rus: 'Our land [is] great and abundant, but there-isn't of-order in it. Come to-be-prince and rule us.' And three brothers were-chosen, with their kin, and they-took with them all the-Rus, and came to-the-Slavs, and the-eldest, Riurik, settled in Novgorod, and the second, Sineus, in Beloozero, and the third, Truvor, in Izborsk. And from those Varangians the-Rus land got-its-name.

2. The *Слóво о полкý Úгореве The Tale of Igor's Campaign*

Игорь спит, Игорь не спит, Игорь мыслию степь мерит от великого Дону до малого Донца. В полночь Овлур свистнул коня за рекою; велит князю не дремать. Кликнул; стукнула земля, зашумела трава, вежи половецкие задвигались. А Игорь князь поскакал горностаем к камышу, пал белым гоголем на воду. Кинулся на борзого коня и соскочил с него серым волком. И побежал к лугу Донца и полетел соколом под туманами, избивая гусей и лебедей к обеду и полднику и ужину.

Igor sleeps. Igor does not sleep. With-[his]-thought Igor measures the-steppe from the-great Don to the-little Donets. At midnight beyond the river Ovlur whistled [for] a-horse, ordered the-prince not to-doze. He-called. The-earth knocked, the-grass rustled, the-Polovtsian tents began-to-move. And Igor the-prince galloped like-an-ermine to-the-reeds, fell like-a-white duck onto the-water. He-threw-himself onto [his] swift horse and leapt from it like-a-grey wolf. And he-raced to the-meadow of the-Donets and flew like-a-falcon beneath the-mists, killing geese and swans for [his] morning-, midday-, and evening- meals.

That gives you a taste of the extraordinary poetic quality of the *Slovo*. The original manuscript was lost in the burning of Moscow of 1812, so we are at a loss as to its real origins, but it is more or less accepted that, though that manuscript may have been a late copy, the *Slovo* was probably put together around the time of the events. There are many references, notably Turkic ones, which an eighteenth-century forger could not possibly have known. And the *Slovo* does make it clear to us how ethnically mixed, and oriental, Rus was. And note those instrumentals!

3. Consonant alternations

What's going on in the final consonants before the non-past endings in verbs?

Conjugation 1:	писáть	— пишý, пúшешь, ... пúшут
Conjugation 2:	носúть	— ношý, нóсишь, ... нóсят

45

Do you see? If there's a change, this goes *all* through the non-past of the *first conjugation*, but only occurs in the 'I' form of the *second*. (In the second conjugation you'll also get it in certain other forms: past passive participles, deverbal nouns, and secondary or derived imperfectives — just in case you were going to ask.) The main letters and changes are:

First Conjugation	Second Conjugation	Effect
б в м п ф	б в м п ф	add a soft л
т д	т д	ч/щ and ж (жд in some forms you have yet to meet)
с з	с з	ш and ж
к г х	none	ч, ж, ш

Let's spell it out:

Conjugation 1	
дремáть — дремлю, дрéмлешь, ... дрéмлют	'to doze'
бормотáть — бормочу́, бормóчешь, ... бормóчут	'to mutter'
рéзать — рéжу, рéжешь, ... рéжут	'to cut'
плáкать — плáчу, плáчешь, ... плáчут	'to weep'
Conjugation 2:	
любить — люблю, любишь, ... любят	'to love'
спать — сплю, спишь, ... спят	'to sleep'
встрéтить — встрéчу, встрéтишь, ... встрéтят	'to meet'
возить — вожу́, вóзишь, ... вóзят	'to convey'

There's no change in the spelling of л, н, р, or of ж, ч, ш, щ (ц isn't affected). Й is there, but hidden by the Series 2 vowels. Look:

Conjugation 1	
колóть — колю, кóлешь, ... кóлют	'to break, chop'
борóться — борюсь, бóрешься, ... бóрются	'to struggle'
читáть — читáю, читáешь, ... читáют	'to read'
Conjugation 2	
валить — валю, вáлишь, ... вáлят	'to knock down, fell'
звонить — звоню, звонишь, ... звонят	'to phone'
говорить — говорю, говоришь, ... говорят	'to speak, say'
молчáть — молчу́, молчи́шь, ... молчáт	'to be silent'
слы́шать — слы́шу, слы́шишь, ... слы́шат	'to hear'
стоять — стою, стои́ть, ... стоя́т	'to be standing'

Through observation you'll note that there's overlap and therefore scope for confusion:

ч = т *and* к	ш = с *and* х	ж = з *and* д *and* г
	ч *and* щ = т	ж *and* жд = д

плачу́ goes with плати́ть 'to pay' — пла́чу goes with пла́кать 'to weep'
пишу́ goes with писа́ть 'to write' — пашу́ goes with паха́ть 'to plough'
вожу́ goes with води́ть 'to lead' — вожу́ goes with вози́ть 'to convey'
and дви́жу goes with дви́гать 'to move' (also дви́гаю)
посещу́ goes with посети́ть 'to visit' — встре́чу goes with встре́тить 'to meet'
сужу́ goes with суди́ть 'to judge' — стра́жду goes with страда́ть 'to suffer'
(стра́жду is archaic; modern страда́ю)

In other words, you must learn more than the infinitive, and for the time being that means more than one form of the non-past.

In the first conjugation the changes occur in a closed group of verbs, among which some are very important; if we take писа́ть as an example, see them as splittable as пис/а́ть; contrast this with рабо́тать, which will be рабо́та/ть — both have a *y*-sound coming before the slash, and where it immediately follows a consonant it causes an alternation: пишу́, пи́шешь, etc. In the second conjugation we can make this split before -ить, e.g. нос/и́ть, and this gives us the alternation in the 'I' form alone (this is because the *i* which characterizes the conjugation became a *y* sound there, but didn't in the other persons). Note how the 'I' form of second-conjugation verbs is -ю unless the spelling rules dictate -у (and this follows for the 'they' form: -ат for -ят). The only real bore is the ч/щ alternatives for т; the former is 'Native Russian' and the latter Church Slavonic. This is less of a problem for ж/жд for historical reasons (ж tended to do duty for both, at least early on). Жд appears in derived or secondary imperfectives (an joy in store in Chapter 6) and in the definitely bookish past passive participles and verbal nouns — Chapter 17.

Now for some exercises: fill in the gaps, and observe

	писа́ть	жить	ви́деть	звони́ть	плати́ть	носи́ть	люби́ть
я			ви́жу		плачу́		люблю́
ты	пи́шешь					но́сишь	
он...							
мы		живём					лю́бим
вы				звони́те			
они́			ви́дят				

	идти́	е́хать	вести́	везти́	нести́	лете́ть
я	иду́				несу́	
ты			ведёшь			
он...				везёт		
мы						лети́м
вы						
они́		е́дут				

	masc sing	fem sing	neut sing	plural
	я/ты/он	я/ты/она́	я/ты/оно́	мы/вы/они́
	+	+	+	+
знать	знал			
чита́ть		чита́ла		
говори́ть		говори́ло		
писа́ть				писа́ли
носи́ть				носи́ли
быть		была́		

I see	what? who?	where?
	уче́бник	ко́мната
	кни́га	по́лка
	Ива́н	зда́ние
	го́род	ка́рта
	зда́ние	пло́щадь
	ча́шка	стол
я ви́жу		в
		на
		во
		на
		на
		на

	accusative	instrumental	prepositional
кни́га	кни́г-	кни́г-	кни́г-
дя́дя	дя́д-	дя́д-	дя́д-
фами́лия	фами́ли-	фами́ли-	фами́ли-
уче́бник	уче́бник-	уче́бник-	уче́бник-
автомоби́ль	автомоби́л-	автомоби́л-	автомоби́л-
слова́рь	слова́р-	словар-	словар-
Ива́н	Ива́н-	Ива́н-	Ива́н-
учи́тель	учи́тел-	учи́тел-	учи́тел-

	accusative	instrumental	prepositional
окно́	окн-	окн	окн-
по́ле	по́л-	по́л	по́л-
зда́ние	зда́ни-	зда́ни	зда́ни-
ча́сть	част-	ча́ст-	ча́ст-
мать	мат-	ма́тер-	ма́тер-
вре́мя	вре́м-	вре́мен-	вре́мен-

CHAPTER 6

1. The arrival of the West

One extends to many periods of Russian history Bernard Pares's despairing reference to the eighteenth-century 'Palace Revolutions' after the reign of Peter the Great: 'Who would take this miserable record as the history of a people?' In literature the eighteenth century is at first sight unremarkable, but the intellectual foundations for the future are being laid by scholars such as Trediakovskii and Lomonosov. The language as we know it is taking shape, and works like Karamzin's sentimental novel *Бедная Лиза Poor Liza* (1792), Radishchev's angry, radical, and loving *Путешéствие из Петербýрга в Москвý A Journey from St Petersburg to Moscow* (1790), the works of the poet Derzhavin, and those of the fable-writer Krylov and the poet Zhukovskii, are accessible and rewarding. A nice contemporary quotation, from Kheraskov, is: Пётр Россúи дал тéло, Екатерúна дýшу 'Peter gave Russia a body, Ekaterina [gave Russia] a soul' (Discuss!). The politics of the century, the infatuation with things Western, especially things French from the middle of the century — perhaps not progress, but certainly change. Russia rushed headlong into the modern world, its language acquiring shape. And it was the writers, those dealing with fashionable genres, expressing radical thoughts inspired by the West, those bringing the language to life through satire and fables, who set the stage for Pushkin. Here we need a quotation from Pushkin — he too, after all, was a creature of the eighteenth century. There's nothing better than the beginning of one of the greatest of Russian poems.

На берегý пусты́нных волн	On the-shore of-desolate waves
Стоя́л *он*, дум велúких полн,	*he* stood, full of-great thoughts
И вдаль гляде́л. Пред ним широ́ко	and looked afar. Before him broadly
Рекá неслáся; бéдный чёлн	the-river rushed; a-poor craft
По ней стремúлся одинóко.	along it surged solitarily.
По мши́стым, тóпким берегáм	Over the-mossy, marshy banks
Черне́ли и́збы здесь и там,	showed-black huts here and there,
Приют убóгого чухóнца;	the-refuge of-the-miserable Finn;
И лес, неве́домый лучáм	and the-forest, unknown to-the-rays
В тумáне спря́танного сóлнца,	[of-the-]hidden sun in mist,
Кругóм шумéл.	around rustled.

'He', of course, is Peter the Great, and the poem is Pushkin's *Ме́дный всадник The Bronze Horseman* of 1833.

Much of the extract above looks alien (after all, you haven't 'done' adjectives yet), but if you use the translation and exploit what you already know, you will be amazed how much comes together. Finally, there *are* old-fashioned forms in Pushkin, but he is modern. In other words, his work is a vital part of what it means to know Russian.

Learning such poetry by heart is one of the surest ways both to learn Russian and to learn about Russian and Russia. Moreover, reading the best of a language, helped by a dictionary and a basic grammar or lots of tables, suits many as the way to learn a language.

2. Aspects of the future

I'll introduce verbal aspect and the future together, because this is the one area where aspect stands out as something different.

For all the verbs you've had *so far*, the future is conveyed *either* as in English, by using the present tense, e.g. 'I'm going to Manchester tomorrow', *or* by using a special structure using a form of the verb быть which you're about to see *plus* the infinitive — such a construction, i.e. an analytic one, using *two* words instead of one, is quite unusual in Russian. So, let's start with the future tense of быть, namely 'I'll be', etc.:

я	бу́ду	мы	бу́дем
ты	бу́дешь	вы	бу́дете
он/она́/оно́	бу́дет	они́	бу́дут

Add an infinitive, and hey presto!: я бу́ду рабо́тать 'I'll work', etc. Look! The endings of быть are the non-past endings we've met; and soon we'll meet lots of other verbs with a simple future just like that.

Now, think about what 'I'll *work*' actually means. 'Work' is an activity; it just goes on, it's a state of activity! No beginning, no end, no result — amazing how like real life this is getting. It simply states the activity, and that particular activity is either pure in itself, or it's habitual, frequent, ongoing. If you take писа́ть 'to write' you get something similar — its future, я бу́ду писа́ть, etc., can mean 'I'll be a writer'. Add an object: я бу́ду писа́ть письмо́ 'I'll write a letter'. The action is now more constrained, but it's still the activity without insistence on a change. You'll be writing a letter, and that's that. But what if you want to stress that the letter will be finished: 'I'll write *that* letter this evening' (and meaning *finish it this evening*)? In other words, a change. Well, you can't do that with я бу́ду писа́ть письмо́.

Писа́ть has a twin, and the twin does the business of conveying limitation. In the case of писа́ть, we just put something, a *prefix*, on at the beginning: написа́ть. Nothing else changes: я напишу́, ты напи́шешь, ... они́ напи́шут. Now, the present tense can't focus on a limitation, a change. So the 'present tense' of написа́ть is (nearly always) future: 'I *will* write', 'I *will* have written'. Think of English 'I'll have that letter written before you can say Jack Robinson'. It's the same. And here you have to say *what* you'll get written: письмо́, or it has to be 'understood', e.g. — Ты напи́шешь сего́дня письмо́? — Напишу́ '"Will you write that letter today?" "Yes, I will".'

Most Russian verbs seem to come in pairs, and the difference between them focusses on the one referring to the activity, and the other to some sort of change.

And the names for this? In English these are 'imperfective aspect', for verbs like писа́ть, and 'perfective aspect', for verbs like написа́ть.

Just one point: the infinitive used to form the imperfective, analytic, future (я бу́ду рабо́тать) *must* be the *imperfective* infinitive — this is one fence you can't sit on. Я бу́ду написа́ть simply doesn't happen.

Here are some hints regarding which aspect to select. Start with the meaning: 'forget', 'turn brown' *might* be likely candidates for perfective. Then, if still in doubt, a negated verb may be imperfective; or if there's an adverb hinting at repetition or frequency lurking, the verb will be imperfective, thus всегда́ 'always', ча́сто 'often', ре́дко 'seldom', не ра́з 'many a time', and expressions involving 'every'; but неме́дленно 'immediately', то́лько что 'just (used with the past to convey "have/had just")', уже́ 'already' will favour the perfective. And whenever the focus is on stressing the verb and the activity it refers to, use the imperfective; this also covers where a change occurs, but is then 'cancelled', like when you go somewhere and come back, a bit like 'he went to Moscow' when it means 'he was in Moscow', but is presumably now back, or where you say 'who opened the window?' when the window is clearly *not* open, i.e. you mean who opened it and then closed it again, because it's cold! We know it *was* open, but...

To some extent you have to treat every verb separately: aspect resides in meanings, in intentions. If you apply your wordly wisdom to Russian verbs, you may begin to get things right — trouble is, wordly wisdom is in-built. Anyway, take говори́ть 'to speak'. On the whole, 'speak' is like 'work' — it doesn't lend itself to being perfective. But Russian uses говори́ть also for 'to say', and there you *can* imagine moving from one finished action to another — there there's a twin, сказа́ть. Note by the way that some twins aren't all that similar to each other.

Think too about 'be', 'live', 'sit', 'stand', 'lie'. We *all* have aspect; in Russian it's real-world knowledge coming out in the grammar and something to discuss with Russians rather than to be a mistake you're terrified of making. So let's look at creating twins.

3. Playing around with bits and pieces

First of all, the basics as regards how these paired verbs actually pair for tense and aspect:

infinitive	non-past		past
	present	future	
писа́ть	пишу́	бу́ду писа́ть	писа́л
написа́ть	——	напишу́	написа́л

When you learn Russian you often start with pairs like писа́ть/написа́ть and де́лать/сде́лать 'to do, make'. A problem here can be that the prefix may change the meaning of the verb; exceptions are where the meaning of the prefix fits in nicely with the basic meaning of the verb: на- means 'on(to)', and that fits in with 'to write' — *onto* something. But one thing you can take as a general, but not exceptionless, rule is that a verb without a prefix becomes perfective when a prefix is added.

So, when you add a prefix to a simple verb, a verb that's the basic bit plus the infinitive ending, it usually makes the verb perfective, i.e., it limits the meaning of the verb, and that leans it towards 'perfective'. Some prefixes *may* be 'empty', i.e. they *may* have little effect on the basic meaning of the verb, e.g. по-, с-, на-, while others (including those three) change *both* the aspect *and* the meaning, e.g. пере- 'again, over', вы- 'out', в- 'in', про- 'past' — *they* form a larger group. Let's take писа́ть again for an example of how *real* aspect pairs are created:

imperfective		perfective
писа́ть	→	написа́ть
	↘→→→→→→↘	
		↘
подпи́сывать	←	подписа́ть
запи́сывать	←	записа́ть
опи́сывать	←	описа́ть

Now, perfective подписа́ть is писа́ть with the prefix под-, which is also a preposition meaning 'under', the difference of meaning is too great — it means 'to sign'. Without под , imperfective again, all you have is писа́ть, which *doesn't* mean 'to sign'. So, if you want an an imperfective meaning 'to sign', you have to keep под-, and one way to do this is by inserting -ыв-, immediately preceded by the stress; such *derived* or *secondary* imperfectives conjugate like чита́ть , i.e. are *really regular*.

And we have exactly the same for записа́ть 'to note down' and описа́ть 'to describe'. So far you only know a few prepositions, but you'll see soon enough that several prefixes and prepositions are identical.

Here are a few more examples, this time from second-conjugation verbs:

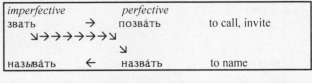

Note that -ыв- becomes -ив- preceded by a consonantal alternation (see Chapter 5). And note the change of -o- to -a- in the derived imperfective. I won't explain it now, but something essentially similar happens in other verbs, e.g.

Now note the following two patterns. The first is very common (all *these* derived imperfectives are like чита́ть too), and do note the consonant alternation. The second is restricted to the three basic verbs дать, стать, знать (the three derived imperfectives have the non-past (д)аю́, (д)аёшь,... (д)аю́т):

1.	*imperfective*		*perfective*	
	делить	→	поделить	to share
	↘→→→→→→→↘			
			↘	
	отделять	←	отделить	to separate
	посещать	←	посетить	to visit
	отвечать	←	ответить	to reply
	убеждать	←	убедить	to convince
2.	*imperfective*		*perfective*	
(i)	давать	←	дать	to give
			↓	
	отдавать	←	отдать	to give back
(ii)	(становиться)	←	стать	to become
			↓	
	вставать	←	встать	to get up
(iii)	знать	→	———	to know
	↘→→→→→→→↘			
	узнавать	←	узнать	to find out

There have to be a few oddities. I'll keep the number down here!

покупать	—	купить	to buy
кончать	—	кончить	to finish

And there are some verbs which look similar, e.g.

ложиться	—	лечь, лягу, ляжешь	to lie down
садиться	—	сесть, сяду, сядешь	to sit down
становиться	—	стать, стану, станешь	to become/go and stand

and there are some which look utterly different, e.g.

говорить	—	сказать	to say, tell
брать	—	взять	to take
класть	—	положить	to put
ловить	—	поймать	to catch

Exercise 1

Here's a passage from Daniil Kharms, one of the glories of Russian. I'll italicize the verbs in a tense form, give the usual 'translation', and add the aspect pairs you haven't encountered, listing the verb used in the text first — быть 'to be' has its one form, and сидéть is really on its own, but note perfective посидéть 'to sit for a while'. Play around, create different scenes. And relate the Russian verbs to their English equivalents and think about why this or that aspect appears in the Russian. You should be able to see that, while English has no *visible* aspect, it none the less *does have it.*

Ивáн Яковлевич Бобóв *проснýлся* в сáмом приятном расположéнии дýха. Он *выглянул* из-под одеяла и срáзу же *увидел* потолóк. Потолóк *был* укрáшен большим сéрым пятнóм с зеленовáтыми краями. Éсли смотрéть на пятнó пристально, одним глáзом, то пятнó *становилось* похóже на носорóга, запряжённого в тáчку, хотя другие *находили,* что онó бóльше *похóдит* на трамвáй, на котóром верхóм *сидит* великáн, — а впрóчем, в этом пятнé мóжно *было* усмотрéть очертáния какóго-то гóрода. Ивáн Яковлевич *посмотрéл* в потолóк, но не в то мéсто, где *было* пятнó, а так, неизвéстно кудá; при этом он *улыбнýлся* и *сощýрил* глазá.

'Ivan Iakovlevich Bobov woke-up in the-most pleasant disposition of-spirit. He looked-out from-under the-blanket and at-once [emph.] saw the-ceiling. The-ceiling was adorned by-a-large grey spot with-greenish edges. If to-look at-the-spot fixedly, with-one eye, then the-spot became similar to-a-rhinoceros, harnessed to a-wheelbarrow, although others found that it more resembled [lit. "resembles"] to a-tram, on which mounted sits a-giant, — and moreover, in this spot it-possible was to make-out the-lines of-some city. Ivan Iakovlevich looked into-the-ceiling, but not into that place, where was the-spot, but just-so, unknown whither; alongside this he smiled and screwed-up [his] eyes.'

проснýться, проснýсь, проснёшься , imperf. просыпáться 'to wake up';
выглянуть, выгляну, выглянешь, imperf. выглядывать 'to look out';
находить, -хожý, -хóдишь, perf. найти, -йдý, -йдёшь, -шёл/-шл- 'to find';
походить, похожý, похóдишь (imperf. only) 'to resemble';
улыбнýться, улыбнýсь, улыбнёшься, imperf. улыбáться 'to smile';
сощýрить, сощýрю, сощýришь, imperf. щýрить or сощýривать 'to screw up'.

---

4. Yet more patterns

Remember they're 'patterns'. Gaps again — you guess what's there! But let me explain the notation accompanying the past tense: '(á)' indicates that the feminine form is stressed on the ending, and '(-)' and '(л-)' indicate that *all* the endings are stressed. And note that the third person plural of мочь is мóгут; in verbs in -чь, all of which have underlying г

56

(as here) or к, г and к become ж and ч respectively before the -e- of the middle four persons.

брать	взять	мочь	начáть	торговáть
to take	to take (perf.)	can	to start (perf.)	to trade
берý	возьмý	могý	начнý	торгýю
берёшь	возьмёшь	мóжешь	начнёшь	торгýешь
брал(á)	взял(á)	мог(л́-)	нáчал(á)	торговáл

сказáть	слышать	послáть	смотрéть	слушать
to say (perf.)	to hear	to send (perf.)	(на + acc.) to look (at)	(+ acc.) to listen (to)
скажý	слышу	пошлю	смотрю	слушаю
скáжешь	слышите	пошлёте	смóтрите	слушаете
сказáл	слышал	послáл	смотрéл	слушал

Note торговáть (+ instr.) 'to trade (in)', an example of an *extremely* common type of verb, that of those in -ов/ать and -ев/ать. No problem here with the past, but in the non-past -ов- and -ев- become -у- and -ю- respectively (subject to the spelling rules for ц and the hushers), followed by -ю-, -е-. So танцевáть 'to dance' becomes танцýю, танцýешь, etc., and плевáть 'to spit' becomes плюю, плюёшь, etc.

Exercise 2

Here's an extract from a text in Glazunova 1997:29 about пожáлуйста. As usual, there are forms you don't know: *use* the gloss. Every finite verb, barring the impersonal кáжется 'it seems' and the conditional следúл бы, I've put into the infinitive in brackets, with extra information as necessary. Get the meaning from the translation. Get the gist of the text. The original has non-past imperfectives (= present tense), except for four verbs in the past and one in the imperfective future. Use your dictionary and build up your vocabulary.

You will come across mystery forms, e.g. after the preposition к 'towards' — this is the dative case (Chapter 7). And there's the strange verbal form побледнéв meaning 'having become pale' — this is a perfective gerund (Chapter 16). And just one small thing, which you'll already have noticed: in my gloss I often attach words to adjectives, e.g. 'the-first man'; you might feel that 'the' really goes with 'man' — well, I'm just trying not to complicate the order of words, and in any case I only insert such words as 'the' to make the text more accessible.

Don't worry — I want you to *get the feel*; I'm surrounding you by grammar and know it could crush you — give it, and yourself, time, and be happy to get that gist. It does take time, always.

[Америка́нец] (ви́деть — уви́деть), как како́й-то взволно́ванный ру́сский (стара́ться — постара́ться) проби́ться к око́шку. Челове́к я́вно (спеши́ть, спешу́, спеши́шь — поспеши́ть), он (говори́ть — сказа́ть, скажу́, ска́жешь) умоля́юще: «Пожа́луйста!». Америка́нец (запи́сывать — записа́ть) в блокно́т: «Пожа́луйста — плиз».

Но лю́ди в о́череди то́же (говори́ть — сказа́ть, скажу́, ска́жешь): «Пожа́луйста». Америка́нец (вздра́гивать — вздро́гнуть, вздрогну́, вздрогнёшь), (вычёркивать — вы́черкнуть, вы́черкну, вы́черкнешь) «плиз» и (запи́сывать — записа́ть): «Пожа́луйста — не стесня́йтесь, проходи́те пе́рвым». Спеша́щий челове́к (протя́гивать — протяну́ть, протяну́, протя́нешь) че́рез око́шко ру́ку к телегра́фному бла́нку. Телеграфи́стка (пододвига́ть — пододви́нуть, пододви́ну, пододви́нешь) бланк побли́же к нему́ и (говори́ть — сказа́ть, скажу́, ска́жешь): «Пожа́луйста!». Америка́нец серди́то (вычёркивать — вы́черкнуть, вы́черкну, вы́черкнешь) пре́жнее обозначе́ние сло́ва и (впи́сывать — вписа́ть): «Вот то, что вам ну́жно».

Челове́к (брать, беру́, берёшь — взять, возьму́, возьмёшь) бланк и вдруг расте́рянно (начина́ть — нача́ть, начну́, начнёшь) ощу́пывать карма́ны: ему́ не́чем писа́ть. Сосе́д по о́череди (протя́гивать — протяну́ть, протяну́, протя́нешь) ему́ ру́ку и — о у́жас! — (говори́ть — сказа́ть, скажу́, ска́жешь): «Пожа́луйста!» Америка́нец расте́рянно (запи́сывать — записа́ть) ещё одно́ значе́ние сло́ва: «Охо́тно гото́в услужи́ть вам».

Челове́к торопли́во (писа́ть — написа́ть) текст телегра́ммы, телеграфи́стка (счита́ть — сосчита́ть) слова́. Она́ (улыба́ться — улыбну́ться) и (говори́ть — сказа́ть, скажу́, ска́жешь): «Мо́жно приписа́ть ещё три сло́ва». Он (хвата́ть — схвати́ть, схвачу́, схва́тишь) бланк и поко́рно (произноси́ть — произнести́): «Пожа́луйста!». И (впи́сывать — вписа́ть) три сло́ва: «Люблю́, люблю́, люблю́». Америка́нец, уже́ заме́тно вспоте́вший, (ста́вить, ста́влю, ста́вишь — поста́вить) во́зле напи́санного ра́нее жи́рный восклица́тельный знак. Пото́м (де́лать — сде́лать) тако́е примеча́ние: «Тут, ви́димо, бесконе́чное мно́жество ра́зных значе́ний».

В э́тот моме́нт у двере́й телегра́фа (остана́вливаться — останови́ться, остановлю́сь, остано́вишься) такси́, и америка́нец слы́шит, как шофёр (открыва́ть — откры́ть, откро́ю, откро́ешь) дверь и (говори́ть — сказа́ть): «Пожа́луйста!». Из маши́ны (выска́кивать — вы́скочить) же́нщина, она́ (подбега́ть — подбежа́ть, подбегу́(т), подбежи́шь) к телегра́фному око́шку, (хвата́ть — схвати́ть) а́втора телегра́ммы за рука́в и (устра́ивать — устро́ить, устро́ю, устро́ишь) ему́ сце́ну. Она́ (заявля́ть — заяви́ть, заявлю́, зая́вишь), что всегда́ (ненави́деть — rough perf. возненави́деть) его́, да́же тогда́, когда́ (люби́ть), а тепе́рь (ненави́деть — rough perf. возненави́деть) до конца́ свое́й жи́зни, она́ (обеща́ть — perf. and imperf.) ему́ э́то! Челове́к (пожима́ть — пожа́ть, пожму́, пожмёшь) плеча́ми и говори́т: «Пожа́луйста!». Америка́нский фило́лог су́дорожно (писа́ть — написа́ть) что́-то в блокно́те, (вычёркивать — вы́черкнуть, вы́черкну, вы́черкнешь), сно́ва (впи́сывать — вписа́ть) и, наконе́ц, побледне́в, (па́дать — упа́сть, упаду́, упадёшь) на́ пол. Над ним (склоня́ться — склони́ться, склоню́сь, скло́нишься) це́лая толпа́ ру́сских.

— Вам ду́рно? Мо́жет быть, посла́ть за врачо́м? — (спра́шивать — спроси́ть, спрошу́, спро́сишь) они́ фило́лога.

— Пожа́луйста! — (говори́ть — сказа́ть) он дрожа́щими губа́ми по-ру́сски.

[The-American] sees how some anxious Russian [a man] tries to-get-through to the-window. The-person clearly is-rushing, he says entreatingly: 'Pozhaluista!' The-American writes-down into [his] pad: 'Pozhaluista = please'.

But the-people in the-queue also say: 'Pozhaluista'. The-American shudders, crosses-out 'please' and notes-down: 'Pozhaluista = Don't be shy [= "worry"], go first'. The-rushing person stretches through the-window [his] hand to a-telegraph form. The-telegraph-woman moves-up a-form closer to him and says: 'Pozhaluista!' The-American crossly crosses-out the-former designation of-the-word and writes-in: "Here's that which is-necessary to-you".

The-person takes a-form and suddenly confusedly begins to-feel [in] [his] pockets: he's nothing to write with [to-him there's-not with-which to-write]. [His] neighbour in [according-to] the-queue stretches to-him a-pen and — oh, horror! — says: 'Pozhaluista!' The-American confusedly notes-down still one meaning of-the-word: "willingly/desirously ready to-serve you".

The-person hastily writes the-text of-the-telegram, the-telegraph-woman counts the-words. She smiles and says: 'It's-possible to-add-in-writing still three words'. He seizes the-form and submissively pronounces: 'Pozhaluista!'. And writes-in three words: 'I-love, I-love, I-love'. The-American, [who has] already perceptibly come-into-a-sweat, puts next-to what-was-written earlier a-bold exclamation mark. Then he-makes such-a [= "the following"] remark/note: 'Here, apparently, an-infinite multitude of-different meanings.'

At this moment at the-doors of-the-telegraph-office stops a-taxi, and the-American hears how the-driver opens the-door and says: 'Pozhaluista!' Out-of-the-car jumps a-woman, she runs-up to-the-telegraph window, seizes the-author of-the-telegram by the-sleeve and arranges for-him a-scene. She declares that always [she]-hated him, even then, when she-loved him, and now will hate him to the-end of-her life, she promises to-him this! The-person shrugs [with]-[his]-shoulders and says: 'Pozhaluista!' The-American linguist convulsively writes something in the-pad, crosses-out, again writes-in and, finally, having-become-pale, falls onto the-floor. Over him leans a-whole crowd of-Russians.

'Is-it bad to-you [= "do you feel bad"]? Perhaps, to-send for the-doctor?', they ask the-linguist.

'Pozhaluista,' says he with-trembling lips in-Russian.

Present tenses (imperfective, of course) except for убеди́лся, вы́брал in the first paragraph, and ненави́дела, люби́ла, and the future бу́дет ненави́деть in the fifth paragraph. With this last one think of the meaning: you'll only get a perfective of such a verb if it has the sense 'to conceive (perhaps suddenly) a hatred for someone'. Try telling it all in the past — it'll be good practice.

CHAPTER 7

1. Almost a Dead Poets' Society

Well, two of them, Pushkin (1799-1837) and Lermontov (1814-1841), died in duels, and Gogol', who called his *magnum opus*, Мёртвые души *Dead Souls*, a поэма 'long, narrative poem', starved himself to death.

While rooted in Classicism, Pushkin wrote works which are a triumph of Romanticism and more than anything else are simply 'Pushkin' — probably no other writer in the world has such a devoted following. Well, there *is* Byron — and he has a tremendous following in Russia too.

Lermontov wrote both rebellious and intensely lyrical poetry. Though Nabokov hated it, Lermontov also wrote one of the prose classics of the nineteenth century, Герой нашего времени *A Hero of our Time* (1840). Some of his verses might make one cringe, but at other times they are just right, and certainly very Russian.

If you read only one work by Gogol, it has to be the first volume of Мёртвые души *Dead Souls*, which has the best of everything he wrote; but you really must try his stories Записки сумасшедшего *Diary of a Madman* (1835), Нос *The Nose* (1836), and Шинёль *The Overcoat* (1842); not to forget his play Ревизор *The Government Inspector* (1836). The products of an intensely tortured mind — misunderstood, dissatisfied, imperfect, in the grip of пошлость 'vulgarity', Gogol's is a static portrayal of existence, into which he felt ever more acutely a need to put some dynamism — and this was ultimately his downfall.

We'll leave Pushkin out here. But try his prose, and once you can read Пиковая дама *The Queen of Spades* in an evening, you've made it.

From Lermontov let's have one of his best-loved poems — you may be expected to recite poetry in Russia, so it's worth getting this one behind your belt, even if you're in 'business'. Here it is: Ангел *The Angel* (1831):

> По нёбу полуночи ангел летёл,
>   И тихую песню он пел;
> И месяц, и звёзды, и тучи толпой
>   Внимали той песне святой.

Он пел о блаже́нстве безгре́шных духо́в
  Под ку́щами ра́йских садо́в;
О бо́ге вели́ком он пел, и хвала́
  Его́ непритво́рна была́.

Он ду́шу младу́ю в объя́тиях нёс
  Для ми́ра печа́ли и слёз;
И звук его́ пе́сни в душе́ молодо́й
  Оста́лся — без слёз, но живо́й.

И до́лго на све́те томи́лась она́,
  Жела́нием чу́дным полна́;
И зву́ков небе́с замени́ть не могли́
  Ей ску́чные пе́сни земли́.

Through the-sky of-midnight an-angel was-flying, / and he was-singing a-soft song; / and the-moon, and the-stars, and the-clouds in-a-throng / listened to that holy song. / He sang of the-bliss of-the-sinless spirits / under the-shades of-the-paradise (adj.) gardens; / about the-great God he sang, and praise / his was unfeigned. / He carried a-young soul in [his] embrace / for the-world of-sadness and tears; / and the-sound of-his song in the-young soul / remained — without tears, but alive. / And long on-the-world it languished / filled with-a-wondrous desire; / and the-sounds of-heaven to-replace couldn't / for-it [= the soul] the-tedious songs of-earth.

In the last two lines, where's the subject? There's only one possibility: it's a plural, ску́чные пе́сни 'the tedious songs'. See Chapter 8.

As for Gogol, one of the choice moments is the very beginning of *Мёртвые ду́ши Dead Souls* (Vol.1, 1842):

В воро́та гости́ницы губе́рнского го́рода NN въе́хала дово́льно краси́вая рессо́рная небольша́я бри́чка, в како́й е́здят холостяки́: отставны́е подполко́вники, штабс-капита́ны, поме́щики, име́ющие о́коло со́тни душ крестья́н, — сло́вом, все те, кото́рых называ́ют господа́ми сре́дней руки́. В бри́чке сиде́л господи́н, не краса́вец, но и не дурно́й нару́жности, ни сли́шком толст, ни сли́шком то́нок; нельзя́ сказа́ть, чтобы стар, одна́ко ж и не та́к, чтобы сли́шком мо́лод. Въезд его́ не произвёл в го́роде соверше́нно никако́го шу́ма и не́ был сопровождён ниче́м осо́бенным; то́лько два ру́сские мужика́, стоя́вшие у двере́й кабака́ про́тив гости́ницы, сде́лали ко́е-каки́е замеча́ния, относи́вшиеся, впро́чем, бо́лее к экипа́жу, чем к сиде́вшему в нём. «Вишь ты, — сказа́л оди́н друго́му, — вон како́е колесо́! что́ ты ду́маешь, дое́дет то колесо́, е́сли б случи́лось, в Москву́ и́ли не дое́дет?» — «Дое́дет», — отвеча́л другóй. «А в Казáнь-то, я дýмаю, не доéдет?» — «В Казáнь не доéдет», — отвечáл другóй. Этим разговóр и кóнчился. Да ещё, когдá брúчка подъéхала к гостúнице, встрéтился молодóй человéк в бéлых канифáсовых панталóнах, весьмá ýзких и корóтких, во фрáке с покушéньями на мóду, из-под котóрого виднá былá манúшка, застёгнутая тýльскою булáвкою с брóнзовым пистолéтом. Молодóй человéк оборотúлся назáд, посмотрéл экипáж, придержáл рукóю картýз, чуть не слетéвший от вéтра, и пошёл своéй дорóгой.

Into the-gates of-the-hotel of-the-provincial town NN entered a rather pretty sprung small-britzka, of-the-sort-in-which bachelors ride: retired lieutenant-colonels, majors, landowners, having around a hundred peasant souls, — in-a-word, all those, whom [people]-call gentlemen of-an-average station [lit. 'hand']. In the-britzka sat a-gentleman, not a-handsome-fellow, but also not of-an-ugly appearance, and-not too fat, and-not too thin; it-is-impossible to-say that [he was] old, but also and not so that [he was] too young. His entry did not produce in the-town any stir at all and was not accompanied by-anything special; only two Russian peasants, standing by the-doors of-the-hostelry opposite the-hotel, made certain remarks, relating, moreover, more to the-carriage than to-him-who-was-sitting in it. 'Just look!' said one to-the-other. 'What-a wheel there! What do you think, that wheel will-get, if [it]-happened, to Moscow or it-won't-get?' 'It'll-get.' answered the-other. 'But to Kazan, I think, it-won't-get?' 'To Kazan it-won't-get.' answered the-other. With-that the-conversation ended. And moreover, when the-britzka drove-up to the-hotel, there encountered a-young man in white canvas trousers, exceedingly narrow and short, in a-tail-coat with attempts on fashion ['pretensions to fashionability'], from-under which was visible a dicky, fastened with-a-Tula safety pin with a-bronze pistol. The young man turned-round back, looked-at the-carriage, held-on with-[his]-hand [to] [his] top-hat, scarcely not [which-had]-flown-off from-the-wind, and went-off on-his way.

Just what became of that young man, never mentioned again?

2. Getting even more of a move on

Let's get you moving with the verbs of motion. This is not *all* verbs referring to motion. Listed below, they occur in pairs even *before* we get to aspect: one for a single direction, even a repeated route, so long as it's intended to be seen as one-way, and the other with no single direction, overlapping with habit/frequency/round-trip and natural ability. Here we go, with the most frequent ones marked with an asterisk:

one-direction	many-direction	approximate meaning
бежа́ть, бегу́(т), бежи́шь...	бе́гать	to run*
везти́, всзу́; вёз/везла́...	вози́ть (з/ж)	to convey by transport*
вести́, веду́; вёл/вела́...	води́ть (д/ж)	to lead*
гна́ть, гоню́, го́нишь...	гоня́ть	to chase, lead animals
гна́ться (see гнать)	гоня́ться	to pursue (за + instr.)
е́хать, е́ду, е́дешь	е́здить (зд/зж)	to go by transport*
идти́, иду́; шёл/шла	ходи́ть (д/ж)	to go, walk*
кати́ть (т/ч)	ката́ть	to roll, drive (something)
кати́ться (т/ч)	ката́ться	to roll, go for a drive
лезть, ле́зу; лез/ле́зла	ла́зить (з/ж)	to 'climb' using hands*
лете́ть, лечу́, лети́шь...	лета́ть	to fly, go by air*
нести́, несу́; нёс/несла́...	носи́ть (с/ш)	to carry on foot*
нести́сь (see нести́)	носи́ться (с/ш)	to rush, go fast*
плыть, плыву́; плыл/плыла́	пла́вать	to swim, sail, float*
ползти́, ползу́; полз/ползла́	по́лзать to crawl	
тащи́ть	таска́ть	to pull, drag (something)*

Except for е́здить and лете́ть , all the second-conjugation verbs have mobile stress. The alternations are given in brackets. Note бежа́ть, which is a mixture of the two conjugations.

Now, all those verbs were imperfective. There has to be a perfective, after all such verbs do cause changes: *Пошёл* дождь 'It rained/started to rain' Adding the prefix по- to the determinate verb, we get a perfective — this particularly applies to пое́хать and пойти́ (note what happens to идти́ when it has a prefix). They're often considered perfective-only, with the special sense 'to move *off*', but they also mean 'went', 'has gone'. There are volumes more to be said, but I'll hold back, for once.

We've seen from подписа́ть that verbal prefixes can create *new* verbs, which happen to be perfective: in, out, over, back, past, around, together, apart, up, down, up to, towards, away. Now look at a few examples, starting from the one-direction verbs — I split them into three groups, according to how the imperfective is created (work it out!):

perfective	imperfective	meaning
вы́везти	вывози́ть из + gen.	'to carry out'
перевести́	переводи́ть	'to convey, translate'
догна́ть	догоня́ть	'to catch up with, overtake'
сойти́сь	сходи́ться	'to come together'
прокати́ться	проката́ться	'to go for a drive'
прилете́ть	прилета́ть в/на + acc.	'to arrive by air at...'
унести́	уноси́ть	'to carry away'
разлете́ться	разлета́ться	'to fly apart/in different directions'
взойти́	всходи́ть на + acc.	'to walk up onto'
найти́	находи́ть	'to find (i.e. "come upon")'

perfective	imperfective	meaning
вбежа́ть	вбега́ть в + acc.	'to run in(to)'
переползти́	переполза́ть че́рез + acc.	'to crawl across'
вы́лезть	вылеза́ть из + gen.	'to crawl out (of)'
отплы́ть	отплыва́ть	'to depart by ship'
прое́хать	проезжа́ть ми́мо + gen.	'to drive past'
съе́хать	съезжа́ть с + gen.	'to drive down from'

And all these (and many more) are new, real aspect pairs in their own right. Once you know the basic verbs and prefixes/prepositions, you can guess the meanings of masses of useful verbs.

3. Moving with the genitive and dative, prepositionally speaking

There are two more cases, the genitive and the dative, the first roughly corresponding to English possession and 'of' and the second to 'to' and 'for' (the familiar sense of 'giving'). The genitive also provides the accusative of animate masculine nouns with a zero ending.

So, masculine nouns ending in a consonant have the ending -a or -я, depending on whether the final letter is, respectively, (i) a hard paired consonant, a husher, and ц, or (ii) a soft sign or -й. Most neuters have the same ending, -a replacing -o and -я replacing -e; those in -мя have -мени. Feminines, and masculine путь, in -ь replace the soft sign with -и. Last, feminines, and the very important masculines and epicenes, in -a and -я replace these endings with -ы and -и respectively (subject to the spelling rules: -a becomes -и after hushers and к, г, х).

The dative has -y, -ю for masculines in a consonant and for most neuters; путь has пути́ and вре́мя has вре́мени. Feminines in -ь are like путь; those in -a and -я both replace these endings with -e (except for -ия, which has -ии). So:

nominative	genitive	dative
ко́мната	ко́мнаты	ко́мнате
кни́га	кни́ги	кни́ге
душа́	души́	душе́
дя́дя	дя́ди	дя́де
фами́лия	фами́лии	фами́лии
уче́бник	уче́бника	уче́бнику
каранда́ш	карандаша́	карандашу́
слова́рь	словаря́	словарю́
Ива́н	Ива́на	Ива́ну
Евге́ний	Евге́ния	Евге́нию

nominative	genitive	dative
окно́	окна́	окну́
по́ле	по́ля	по́лю
зда́ние	зда́ния	зда́нию
ча́сть	ча́сти	ча́сти
мать	ма́тери	ма́тери
путь	пути́	пути́
вре́мя	вре́мени	вре́мени

The genitive or dative can stand on their own. Or some verbs require them, e.g. for the genitive: боя́ться, бою́сь, бои́шься 'to be afraid (of)', избега́ть, perf. избежа́ть 'to avoid'. Adjectives with the genitive include по́лный 'full (of)' and досто́йный 'worthy (of)', and the genitive is a way of doing 'than' after comparatives. Some verbs can take either the genitive or the accusative: the genitive tends to be more abstract, more general: хоте́ть 'to want', иска́ть, ищу́, и́щешь 'to look for', ждать, жду, ждёшь 'to wait for', проси́ть 'to request', e.g. Она́ иска́ла рабо́ты 'she was looking for work (any)' — Она́ иска́ла рабо́ту 'she was looking for work (a particular kind)'. The dative goes as you'd expect with many verbs of giving and communicating: saying, explaining, phoning, giving, reading, sending, writing. Where it might be unexpected is in the following verbs (note that помо́чь conjugates like мочь):

помога́ть, помо́чь 'to help'	по-сове́товать 'to advise'
по-меша́ть 'to disturb, hinder'	позволя́ть, позво́лить 'to permit, allow'
по-нра́виться 'to please'	зави́довать 'to envy'
по-ве́рить 'to believe, trust'	отвеча́ть, отве́тить 'to answer, reply'

and

за-смея́ться, -ею́сь, -еёшься
'to laugh at something' ('at somebody' = над + instr.)

улыба́ться, perf. улыбну́ться, улыбну́сь, улыбнёшься
'to smile' ('at' is as for смея́ться)

And учи́ть, учу́, у́чишь, perf. научи́ть 'to teach' (dative of the subject and accusative of the people taught): Она́ у́чит нас францу́зскому языку́ 'she's teaching us French'. If you make it reflexive, it becomes 'to study' and takes the dative, as you'd expect: Она́ у́чится му́зыке 'she's studying music'.

Нра́виться is a way of saying 'to like' — you just twist it round, like Spanish *gustar* 'to please', and make what you like the subject, e.g. А тебе́ понра́вилась пье́са? 'Did you like the play?'

Adjectives which take the dative include благода́рный 'grateful (to)' and ве́рный 'faithful (to)'.

4. And now for the prepositions

With the dative, first, к(о) 'towards', also used with people when 'to' means '[go] *to see* X'; in time expressions it means 'by', e.g. к четвергу́ 'by Thursday'. Secondly, благодаря́ 'thanks to'. And thirdly, the most ubiquitous, по 'along, according to'.

Prepositions most frequently take the genitive. For example:

без	'without'
вдоль	'along the side/length of'
во вре́мя	'during' (not with expressions involving numerals)
во́зле	'along the side of' (motion and stationary)
вокру́г	'around' (also an adverb)
впереди́	'in front of'
в тече́ние	'during'
для	'for; for the sake of'
из	'from, out of' (to be paired with в '(in)to', but see от)
кро́ме	'besides, apart from'
ме́жду	'between' (usually with the instrumental)
ми́мо	'past'
напро́тив	'across from, against, opposite'
о́коло	'close by, round about; approximately' (also an adverb)
от	'from, away from' (to be paired with к when used with persons and in an expression such as к ю́гу от 'to the south of', and with до when relating to places and referring to the distance between them)
позади́	'to the back of; at the back of'
про́тив	'across from, against, opposite'
с(о)	'from, down from/off; since' (often paired with до in referring to the opening hours of shops and with по + acc. if it's inclusive)
у	'at the house of, nearby, in the possession of' (extremely important)
до	'up to, as far as' (see от and с above) (the usual preposition for 'before')
по́сле	'after' (for 'immediately after' you can use по + prepositional)
среди́	'among, amid(st), in the middle of'

To cover spatial relationships we need to bring the instrumental and the accusative back in. Here goes:

пе́ред(о)	'in front of' ('immediately before' in time expressions)
за	'behind, beyond'
над(о)	'above'
под(о)	'under'

In the last three there's no motion involved. When there *is* motion, за and под are used with the accusative.

Над, when motion is involved, is replaced by че́рез + acc., which has senses of 'across, via, over'. Пе́ред + instr. may convey motion (впереди́ + gen. is more or less synonymous with пе́ред). By 'motion', by the way, is meant a change in relation to something else, since if you're *both* moving nothing changes. In other words, if your dog is walking behind you, за goes with the instrumental, but if it moves *into a position* behind you it goes with the accusative. Note that за + acc. has other uses, particularly to render 'for' in such constructions as плати́ть за 'to pay for', where there's a sense of 'in exchange for'.

Since 'before' and 'after' are important, it's useful to know за + acc. до + gen.: за ме́сяц до... 'a month before...' and че́рез + acc. по́сле + gen.: че́рез день по́сле... 'a day after...'. All this will fall into place as you meet more texts and see these constructions in use. Numerals hit you in Chapter 8. For practice you might try out the prepositions with some of the nouns you've met so far, say the lists in Chapter 3.

5. Bringing motion and prepositions together

You've seen that new verbs, perfectives, can be created using prefixes, and then that you can create imperfective partners for them by derivation, using suffixes. The verbs of motion really come into their own here (we saw some examples in Section 2), and can be constructed with prepositions. Here's a selection, with 'X' standing for the verb of motion:

в(о)-Х (въ- before e-) в + acc.	movement into
вы-Х из + gen.	movement out of
до-Х до + gen.	movement up to, as far as, 'reach'
за-Х за + instr. and/or в/на + acc. and/or к(о) + dat.	calling for something and/or at a place and/or on someone
от(о)-Х (отъ- before e-) от + gen.	movement slightly away from, or taking back, or departing
пере-Х + acc. or че́рез + acc.	movement across
при-Х (arrival: в/на + acc.; bringing)	arrival, bringing; = к + dat. if bringing someone to (see) someone

про-Х ми́мо + gen.	movement past something
раз-Х/рас-Х (разъ- before e-) -ся с + instr.	movement in different directions, separating from)
с(о)-Х (съ- before e-)	down from/off; with many-direction verbs creates perfective conveying a quick visit: 'drop in on/at/for, etc.' — see за-; here there will be some overlaps with imperfectives, e.g. слета́ть is a quick flying visit or an imperfective meaning flying down/off
с(о)-Х (съ- before e-) -ся с + instr.	movement together, joining with
у-Х (various preps)	movement away

When the prefix ends in a consonant, note the -o- which appears before -й- and in the past tense of verbs involving идти́: разойти́сь 'to separate', она́ разойдётся 'she'll separate', он разошёлся 'he separated', etc. In other words, given that the past tense masculine is influenced by the other past-tense forms, the -o- appears before *two* consonants.

Note that the prefix вы- is stressed when it creates a perfective and also when the verb is odd, say, it isn't paired for some reason, e.g. вы́глядеть, вы́гляжу, вы́глядишь + instr. 'to look X, have a X appearance', e.g. он вы́глядел гру́стным 'he looked sad'.

Exercises 1 and 2

1. Give the required form (provide both or all forms when the answer requires 'you' and when the verb could be masculine or feminine):

'we arrived' мы пришли́	'I arrived'	*я пришёл/я пришла́*
'I'll go out' я вы́йду	'we'll go out'	_____
'she'll come in' она́ войдёт	'they'll come in'	_____
'she went past' она́ прое́хала	'I went past'	_____
'you separated' вы разошли́сь	'I separated'	_____
'you'll go down' ты сойдёшь	'I'll go down'	_____
'we fly across' мы перелета́ем	'they fly across'	_____
'I'll take out' я вы́везу	'you'll take out'	_____
'he brought' он принёс	'you brought'	_____
'I'll go up' я взойду́	'he'll go up'	_____
'it flies down' он слета́ет	'I fly down'	_____
'they'll meet' они сойду́ться	'we'll meet'	_____

2. And now for some prepositions:

'plane' самолёт	'in в the plane'	в самолёте
'ship' пароход	'off с the ship'	_____
'building' здание	'out of из the building'	_____
'flat' квартира	'in front of перед the flat'	_____
'shelf' полка	'onto на the shelf'	_____
'table' стол	'under под the table'	_____
'shop' магазин	'next to рядом с the shop'	_____
'war' война	'before до the war'	_____
'lesson' урок	'after после the lesson'	_____
'girl' девушка	'at the house of у the girl'	_____

In рядом с, с takes the instrumental; it literally means something like 'in a row with', and рядом, from ряд 'row, series', is a very common adverb, meaning 'next door, nearby'.

6. Gilding the noun

For Isaak Babel' adjectives were something best left to *real* writers. Perhaps an exaggeration: an adjective like 'wooden' seems rather low-risk, even for the most hapless among us. Unless, though this is unlikely, he was thinking of all the forms you have to learn to say 'big' in Russian.

Indeed: six cases, three genders, and two numbers; that suggests thirty-six *big*s in Russian, before you even get to *bigger* and *biggest*. Don't worry; it's nowhere near as bad as that — you *do* have to make the agreements, but there's a lot of overlap and just one set of forms in the plural! And the comparative and superlative don't introduce anything new, though there *is* the *short* adjective, a treat in Chapter 11.

Let's take the singular of добрый 'good, kind', a very common type:

	masculine	neuter	feminine
nom.	добрый	доброе	добрая
acc.	добрый	доброе	добрую
gen.		доброго	доброй
dat.		доброму	доброй
instr.		добрым	доброй
prep.		добром	доброй

The stress doesn't move. Remember, by the way, animacy in masculine singulars, which means that the accusative singular of masculine animate nouns requires genitive agreement. If you *see your kind uncle*, you

ви́дишь *до́брого* дя́дю. And also remember that in the ending -ого /
-его the г is pronounced as if it were spelt в.

There are other adjective types, but the differences are largely
accounted for in terms of the spelling rules — see Chapter 2 and the
Reference Section.

There are, too, adjectives with the stress on the ending: here the -ы- and
-и- of the nominative and accusative singular masculine both appear as
-о́-; and unstressed -е- for -о- immediately after the last consonant
appears under stress as -о́-. Scrutinize and compare до́брый 'good' with
хоро́ший 'good' (neither stressed on the ending, but requiring different
spelling rules), then extend your gaze to худо́й 'thin, lean', большо́й 'big',
ти́хий 'quiet', and сухо́й 'dry' — identify the forms using the table above:

```
до́брый, до́брого, до́брому, до́брым, до́бром; до́брой; до́брое
худо́й, худо́го, худо́му, худы́м, худо́м; худо́й; худо́е

ти́хий, ти́хого, ти́хому, ти́хим, ти́хом; ти́хой; ти́хое
сухо́й, сухо́го, сухо́му, сухи́м, сухо́м; сухо́й; сухо́е

хоро́ший, хоро́шего, хоро́шему, хоро́шим, хоро́шем; хоро́шей; хоро́шее
большо́й, большо́го, большо́му, больши́м, большо́м; большо́й; большо́е
```

In other words, except in the instrumental singular masculine and neuter,
where the -ым/-им difference *remains*, adjectives in -ый, -к/г/х-ий, and
hushers + -ий all come together when end-stressed.

So now we can ask the crucial question, beloved of textbook and
exercise writers, which elicits adjectives (note the odd word order):

Како́й э́то мужчи́на?	'What sort of a man is this?'
Кака́я э́то же́нщина?	'What sort of a woman is this?'
Како́е э́то сло́во?	'What sort of a word is this?'

to which the answers might be:

Э́то до́брый мужчи́на	'This is a kind man.'
Э́то симпати́чная же́нщина	'This is a nice woman.'
Э́то ру́сское сло́во	'This is a Russian word.'

Play around with this using the adjectives below. Note how the adjective
како́й 'what (sort of) a' agrees with the noun, and э́то, which doesn't
change, comes in between. An alternative is to use the unchanging что э́то
за, a construction which goes, most often, with a nominative:

Что это за мужчина?	'What sort of a man is this?'
Что это за женщина?	'What sort of a woman is this?'
Что это за слово?	'What sort of a word is this?'

Here are a few adjectives, split into the declension types, plus a form which means 'it's...' and may serve as an adverb. You can get something close to the opposite of many an adjective by prefixing не-.

masculine	feminine	neuter	plural	'It's...'	meaning
новый	новая	новое	новые	—	new
вкусный	вкусная	вкусное	вкусные	вкусно	tasty
интересный	-ресная	-ресное	-ресные	-ресно	interesting
приятный	приятная	приятное	приятные	приятно	pleasant
чистый	чистая	чистое	чистые	чисто	clean
умный	умная	умное	умные	—	clever
красивый	красивая	красивое	красивые	красиво	beautiful
красный	красная	красное	красные	—	red
холодный	холодная	холодное	холодные	холодно	cold
чёрный	чёрная	чёрное	чёрные	—	black
белый	белая	белое	белые	—	white
жёлтый	жёлтая	жёлтое	жёлтые	—	yellow
зелёный	зелёная	зелёное	зелёныс	—	green
старый	старая	старое	старые	—	old
длинный	длинная	длинное	длинные	—	long (space)
трудный	трудная	трудное	трудные	трудно	difficult
тёплый	тёплая	тёплое	тёплые	тепло	warm
дешёвый	дешёвая	дешёвое	дешёвые	дёшево	cheap
прекрасный	-расная	-расное	-расные	-расно	really fine
удобный	удобная	удобное	удобные	удобно	comfortable
молодой	молодая	молодое	молодые	—	young
родной	родная	родное	родные	—	native
больной	больная	больное	больные	больно	ill, painful
худой	худая	худое	худые	—	thin
голубой	голубая	голубое	голубые	—	(light-)blue
маленький	-кая	-кое	-кие	—	small
английский	-ская	-ское	-ские	—	English
русский	русская	русское	русские	—	Russian
французский		-ская	-ское	-ские	— French
жаркий	жаркая	жаркое	жаркие	жарко	hot (weather)
короткий	короткая	короткое	короткие	—	short
тихий	тихая	тихое	тихие	тихо	calm, still
широкий	широкая	широкое	широкие	—	wide ...
узкий	узкая	узкое	узкие	—	narrow
высокий	высокая	высокое	высокие	—	high

masculine	feminine	neuter	plural	'It's...'	meaning
ни́зкий	ни́зкая	ни́зкое	ни́зкие	—	low
лёгкий	лёгкая	лёгкое	лёгкие	легко́	easy, light
до́лгий	до́лгая	до́лгое	до́лгие	до́лго	long (time)
дорого́й	дорога́я	дорого́е	дороги́е	до́рого	dear
плохо́й	плоха́я	плохо́е	плохи́е	пло́хо	bad
хоро́ший	хоро́шая	хоро́шее	хоро́шие	хорошо́	good, fine
горя́чий	горя́чая	горя́чее	горя́чие	—	hot (touch)
свё́жий	свё́жая	свё́жее	свё́жие	свежо́	cool
большо́й	больша́я	большо́е	больши́е	—	big
си́ний	си́няя	си́нее	си́ние	—	(dark-)blue
тре́тий	тре́тья	тре́тье	тре́тьи	—	third
-ли́цый	-ли́цая	-ли́цее	-ли́цые	—	-faced
-ше́ий	-шеяя	-ше́ее	-ше́ие	—	-necked

Exercises 3 and 4

3. Now insert some adjectives (refer back to Exercise 2):

большо́й	'in the big plane'	в большо́м самолёте
ру́сский	'off the Russian ship'	_____
гла́вный	'out of the main building'	_____
но́вый	'in front of the new flat'	_____
ве́рхний	'onto the top shelf'	_____
ма́ленький	'under the small table'	_____
кни́жный	'next to the bookshop'	_____
мирово́й	'before the world war'	_____
ва́жный	'after the important lesson'	_____
симпати́чный	'at the house of the nice girl'	_____
широ́кий	'with the wide window'	_____

4. Make up phrases from the following sequences:

большо́й, в, ко́мната   дорого́й, о́коло, рестора́н 'restaurant'
до, гла́вный, го́род   симпатичный, с, ма́льчик
краси́вый, над, ста́туя   вку́сный, по́сле, суп 'soup'
си́ний, за, маши́на   ни́зкий, че́рез, вход 'entrance'
тетра́дь, в, ру́сский   плохо́й, в, настрое́ние 'mood'

CHAPTER 8

1. First Orders, not to mention Last

For a basic command, e.g. 'Go!', 'Speak more slowly!', remove the last three letters from the second-person-singular form of the verb (if the verb's reflexive, don't include the particle in your count). If what's left ends in a vowel, add -й (that's (i) in the table below). Otherwise, and if the stress was on the ending in the first person singular, add -й (ii); and if the stress wasn't on the ending in the first person singular, add -ь unless the form ends in more than one consonant, in which case add -и (iii). There's just one exception, namely when the basic verb begins with the prefix вы- (stressed!): if the underived verb had the stress on the ending in the first person singular, the ending is -и (iv). To all these endings you just add -те to get the formal, polite singular or the plural form. So:

(i)	читáешь (читáю)	читá-	читáй(те)	read
	одевáешься (опдевáюсь)		одевá-	одевáйся
	get dressed			
			одевáйтесь	get dressed
(ii)	скáжешь (скажý)	скаж-	скажи́(те)	say
	говори́шь (говорю́)	говор-	говори́(те)	speak
(iii)	рéжешь (рéжу)	реж-	рéжь(те)	cut
	бýдешь (бýду)	буд-	бýдь(те)	be
	запóмнишь (запóмню)	запомн-	запóмни(те)	memorize
(iv)	вы́платишь (плачý)	выплат-	вы́плати(те)	pay off/out

There are exceptions, but very few! Thus, the verbs in -авáть, which lose -ва- in the non-past, keep it in the imperative: давáй 'let's be having you', узнавáй 'recognize, find out', не приставáй 'don't pester [me]' (by the way, you'll have noticed how Russian often leaves object pronouns out). And, though not really irregular, the group of useful verbs like пить 'to drink' have the non-past pattern пью, пьёшь,... пьют. Пь-? Well, the soft sign (and the hard one) were both once vowels, so here add -й: пьй! Oh well, still looks odd, but trust me and replace the soft sign with -е- . So we get пéй(те), and that's it. The others are лить 'to pour', шить 'to sew', бить 'to beat, break', вить 'to wind' — all the same.

How do you use them? Follow the rules for aspect — or better, go by the meaning. With a few verbs it can be politer to use the imperfective, but a lot depends on context — if a straight instruction is *expected* by the hearer, then a perfective won't offend (an imperfective might sound ironic). Use the imperfective if you're encouraging someone. You'd say, even repeat, бери(те)! 'take!' to someone, using the imperfective, if you wanted to encourage them to help themselves: 'go on, take it!' Возьми(те)! , the perfective, would be much more direct. Another thing is the negative imperative: a prohibition requires the imperfective and a warning a perfective. So if you can imagine 'watch out, mind' (that's смотри(те) in Russian) in front of a negative imperative, use the perfective: Смотри, не опоздай, он будет сердиться! 'Be careful, don't be late, he'll be angry'.

Now, what about 'let's...!', not to mention 'let me..!', 'let him, etc...!' The first one is the 'inclusive' imperative, so called because it includes *you* (that is, 'me' or 'us'). The others are not really commands, but rather wishes, 'optatives'. They use the non-past in the appropriate aspect preceded by пусть or пускай. Here's a nice example, from Venedikt Erofeev, fitting in nicely with the Soviet ethic of labour:

Они работают, ну и пусть работают, это очень мило с их стороны
'They're working, well let them work, that's very nice of them ["on their part"].'

Now, for 'let's...!', start with the first person plural of the perfective without мы: Напишем...! 'Let's write...!' That's *both* the ты *and* the вы form. There *is* a form in -те, but it can be rather colloquial and generally common only in particular verbs, e.g. Пойдёмте! 'Let's go!' Alternatively, put давай(те) in front of напишем (don't put the -те on напишем). If you want to have the imperfective, use давай(те) plus the *imperfective* infinitive: Давай(те) писать! 'Let's write!' By the way, for the negative, you don't have the aspect rule which applies to the exclusive imperative. But replace imperfective Давай(те) слушать радио! with Давай(те) не будем слушать радио, and if you want to say what you should do instead, insert лучше 'better': Давай(те) лучше играть в карты! 'Let's play cards instead!'

Exercise 1

Form imperatives from the following verbs, following the pattern as given (add a noun if suggested):

прочитать 'to read'	ты	*прочитай книгу!*
проходить 'to come "thru"/in'	вы	*проходите!*
выйти 'to go out'	ты	*выйди!*
сказать	вы	_____ (add 'me')
написать	ты	_____ (+ сочинение 'essay')
передать 'hand over'	ты	_____ (add 'to the boy the pencil')

познакóмиться	вы	_____	
постáвить 'put'	ты	_____	(+ тарéлка 'plate' onto table)
садúться 'sit down'	вы	_____	
откры́ть 'open'	ты	_____	(+ окнó)
закры́ть 'close'	вы	_____	(+ учéбник 'textbook')
пить	ты	_____	(+ вóдка/винó/пúво/водá 'vodka / wine / beer / water')
купúть 'buy'	вы	_____	(+ ромáн 'novel')
взять 'take'	ты	_____	(+ нож/вúлка/лóжка 'knife / fork / spoon')

2. A plurality of fun

It's time to get to know plurals.

Adjectives have no separate gender forms in the plural. This goes for nouns too, though history has left something of a mess as regards the nominative, accusative, and genitive. It's simplicity itself, however, for the dative, instrumental, and prepositional. Here's a table — for the citation forms -Ш(ь) indicates any husher and -С (of which there are two rows) indicates other consonants, and for the endings -ø indicates zero.

	nom./acc.	gen.	dat.	instr.	prep.
-С...	-ы/-и/-á/-я/...	-ов/-ев/...	-ам/-ям	-ами/-ями	-ах/-ях
...-С	...-ья/-ья/-е	...-ьев/-ей/-ø			
-Ш	-и	-ей	-ам	-ами	-ах
-й	-и	-ев	-ям	-ями	-ях
-Сь	-и	-ей	-ям/-ам	-ями/-ами	-ях/-ах
-а	-ы/-и	-ø	-ам	-ами	-ах
-я	-и	-ь (= zero)	-ям	-ями	-ях
-о	-а/-ья/-и	-ø/-ьев	-ам	-ами	-ах
-е	-я	-ей	-ям	-ями	-ях
-ие	-ия	-ий (= zero)	-иям	-иями	-иях
-мя	-мена	-мен (= zero)	-менам	-менами	-менах

Animacy, by the way, now applies to all the genders. So the genitive is used for animate masculines, feminines, and even neuters.

For the nominative, the choice between -ы and -и is to do with the spelling rules. The stressed endings -á/-я are found with quite a few frequent nouns and with names of professions: гóрод 'town' — городá, глаз 'eye' — глазá, áдрес 'address' — адресá, нóмер 'number, hotel room' — номерá, профéссор 'professor' — профессорá. Note the endings -ья and -ья: there aren't many such nouns, but you just have to learn them, or at least to recognize them, and note that with one rare exception the unstressed one goes with genitive plural -ьев and the stressed one with genitive plural -ей: брат 'brother' — брáтья, брáтьев;

сын 'son' — сыновья́, сынове́й; друг 'friend' — друзья́, друзе́й (only друг has that consonant change). The ending -e applies to a certain number of nouns of groups or nationalities, e.g. англича́нин, usually in -ин, and -ин is removed first: англича́не 'Englishmen, English people'.

Looking at the neuters in -o, plurals in -ья and -и are to be found in only a few nouns (as usual, they're quite frequent), e.g. крыло́ 'wing' — кры́лья, gen. кры́льев; перо́ 'feather' — пе́рья, gen. пе́рьев; плечо́ 'shoulder' — пле́чи, gen. плеч.

Focussing on the genitive in masculines, one has a zero ending in a few nouns, which have to be learnt (some of them are to do with terms for soldiers and nationalities, and pairs and measures, where quantities are routine, so one does without an ending — numerals involve the genitive!). The ending -ей (very often stressed) is that found after hushers and soft consonants. After -ц one has -о́в if stressed and -ев if unstressed: оте́ц 'father' — отцы́, отцо́в; па́лец 'finger' — па́льцы, па́льцев. And for -й one has -ев, when stressed -ёв: геро́й 'hero' — геро́ев, слой 'layer, stratum' — слоёв. Otherwise one has -ов, stressed or unstressed: стол 'table' — столо́в, огоро́д 'kitchen garden' — огоро́дов.

Before we continue, let's have a few examples (cast into an exercise). Don't bother about the stresses.

Exercise 2

The following don't cover *all* possibilities for the nominative and genitive plural, but you should be able to derive the dative, etc. from them.

студе́нт 'student'	студе́нты	студе́нтов
рестора́н 'restaurant'	рестора́ны	рестора́нов
стол 'table'	_____	_____
дива́н 'sofa'	_____	_____
о́фис 'office'	_____	_____
каранда́ш 'pencil'	карандаши́	карандаше́й
нож 'knife'	_____	_____
ключ 'key'	_____	_____
врач 'doctor'	_____	_____
слова́рь 'dictionary'	словари́	словаре́й
портфе́ль 'briefcase'	_____	_____
путь 'way'	_____	_____
пло́щадь 'square'	_____	_____
ночь 'night'	_____	_____
вещь 'thing'	_____	_____
музе́й 'museum'	музе́и	музе́ев
геро́й 'hero'	_____	_____

англича́нин 'Englishman'	англича́не	англича́н
гражданин 'citizen'	_____	_____
крестья́нин 'peasant'	_____	_____

а́дрес 'address'	адреса́	адресо́в
но́мер 'hotel room'	_____	_____
край 'edge'	_____	_____
по́езд 'train'	_____	_____
учи́тель 'teacher'	_____	_____
ве́чер 'evening'	_____	_____
дом 'house'	_____	_____

| брат 'brother' | бра́тья | бра́тьев |
| стул 'chair' | _____ | _____ |

друг 'friend'	друзья́	друзе́й
муж 'husband'	_____	_____
сын 'son' (insert -ов-)	_____	_____

сло́во 'word'	слова́	слов
лицо́ 'face'	_____	_____
ме́сто 'place'	_____	_____

де́рево 'tree'	дере́вья	дере́вьев
перо́ 'feather'	_____	_____
крыло́ 'wing'	_____	_____

| мо́ре 'sea' | моря́ | море́й |
| по́ле 'field' | _____ | _____ |

| зда́ние 'building' | зда́ния | зда́ний |
| мне́ние 'opinion' | _____ | _____ |

вре́мя 'time'	времена́	времён
и́мя 'first name'	_____	_____
пле́мя 'tribe'	_____	_____
зна́мя 'banner' (note: знамёна)	_____	_____

голова́ 'head'	го́ловы	голо́в
ко́мната 'room'	_____	_____
гора́ 'mountain'	_____	_____
жена́ 'wife' (note: е becomes ё)	_____	_____
страна́ 'country'	_____	_____
рука́ 'hand, arm'	_____	_____
нога́ 'foot, leg'	_____	_____

| мать 'mother' | ма́тери | матере́й |
| дочь 'daughter' | _____ | _____ |

3. Vowels that don't know whether they're coming or going

In the previous section you'll have noticed that in the genitive plural there are quite a few possibilities for *zero* endings, particularly among feminine and neuter nouns. What could be simpler than a zero ending — just nothing, no ending to learn! However, there's a catch: if the zero ending is preceded by two consonants (which may be separated by a soft sign), a vowel is often inserted between them. Thus, комнатка 'little room' provides комнатк which becomes комнаток, and земля 'earth' provides земль which becomes земель. Learn them as you come across them.

We've also had палец 'finger' and its genitive пальца . This is an instance of a zero ending too, but it doesn't seem quite as tricky because we tend to learn the nominative singular first! If -е- drops from -ле-, the result will be -ль-. Otherwise (almost without exception), it's absolutely nothing.

The soft sign hints to you that something used to be there. And indeed there was, as this pattern was started off by a soft sign or a hard sign (they were both once vowels) between the consonants. They either disappeared (typically if a full vowel followed in the next syllable), or became -е- and -о- respectively. Think of день 'day' — дня (there was once a soft sign), лён 'flax' — льна (a soft sign again; does it make you think of *linen*?), and сон 'sleep, dream' — сна (a hard sign). This also gave the pattern for inserted vowels where there had never been a vowel before. This could happen in nouns, but it could happen in verbs too. Thus, we know гнать 'to chase'; if we want to chase something in different directions, we use разогнать (*о* is inserted before two consonants), but its non-past will be разгоню, etc. and its imperfective разгонять.

Let's now have a few examples, and work them into an exercise.

Exercise 3

кусóк 'piece, bit'	кускá	кускú	кускóв
молотóк 'hammer'	_____	_____	_____
огонёк 'little fire'	_____	_____	_____
(insert ь here)			
кружóк 'little circle'	_____	_____	_____
афгáнец 'Afghan'	афгáнца	афгáнцы	афгáнцев
канáдец 'Canadian'	_____	_____	_____
конéц (note the stress)	_____	_____	_____
индúец 'Indian'	индúйца	_____	_____
малúец 'Mali person'	_____	_____	_____
австрúец 'Austrian'	_____	_____	_____

ча́шка 'cup'   ча́шек   руба́шки 'shirt'   руба́шек
де́вушка 'girl'   _____   де́вочка 'girl'   _____
привы́чка 'habit'   _____   то́чка 'dot'   _____

note the next two, which exemplify the 'rule' for consonant + -ня:

ба́сня 'fable'   ба́сен   ба́шня 'tower'   _____
пе́сня 'song'   _____   пека́рня 'bakery' _____

but:

ба́рышня 'young lady' ба́рышень   дере́вня 'village' _____

and, just for illustration, because it's all alone:

ку́хня 'kitchen'   ку́хонь

You'll note that when к, г, х are around, -o- tends to be favoured.

окно́ 'window'   о́кон   ви́лка 'fork'   _____
бе́лка 'squirrel'   _____   буты́лка 'bottle'   _____
оши́бка 'mistake'   _____   прогу́лка 'walk'   _____
скри́пка 'violin'   _____   поку́пка 'purchase' _____

but not if preceded by a husher, when you have to have -e-: ру́чка — ру́чек, но́жка — но́жек.

and some you have to be careful of:

сестра́ 'sister'   сестёр   кре́сло 'armchair' кре́сел
весло́ 'oar'   вёсел   ведро́ 'bucket'   вёдер

4. The plural just won't leave one alone: adjectives...

Well, the adjective, wherever the stress, collapses into a mere four forms:

nom.	-ые	до́брые	ру́сские	больши́е	зде́шние	тре́тьи
acc.	-ые	до́брые	ру́сские	больши́е	зде́шние	тре́тьи
gen.	-ых	до́брых	ру́сских	больши́х	зде́шних	тре́тьих
dat.	-ым	до́брым	ру́сским	больши́м	зде́шним	тре́тьим
instr.	-ыми	до́брыми	ру́сскими	больши́ми	зде́шними	тре́тьими
prep.	-ых	до́брых	ру́сских	больши́х	зде́шних	тре́тьих

Note here that -ы- becomes -и- after the velars and hushers (and in the rare длинноше́ий), and that the special ('possessive') adjectives and тре́тий have -ьи, -ьи, -ьих, -ьим, -ьими, -ьих. As usual, animates use the genitive. See the Reference Section.

5. Les pronoms-adjectifs possessifs et les pronoms-adjectifs démonstratifs, en passant par les pronoms personnels

Well, why not another language for a line or two! All this English gets boring.

If anything is going to be irregular in a language, the personal pronouns are likely to be up there among the contenders. Russian is no exception, though, as usual, it's not as bad as it could be. Basically, Russian has words for 'I' and 'we' and 'you (familiar singular)' and 'you (polite singular, all plural)' And there are words for 'he/it', 'she/it', 'it/it' (sex/gender respectively!), and a single plural 'they'.

	I	*you*	*we*	*you*	*he/it*	*it/it*	*she/it*	*they*
nom.	я	ты	мы	вы	он	оно́	она́	они́
acc.	меня́	тебя́	нас	вас	его́		её	их
gen.	меня́	тебя́	нас	вас	его́		её (ей)	их
dat.	мне	тебе́	нам	вам	ему́		ей	им
instr.	мной	тобо́й	на́ми	ва́ми	им		е́ю (ей)	и́ми
prep.	мне	тебе́	нас	вас	нём		ней	них

Added to these is a special reflexive form, себя́ '-self', without a nominative (any idea why?) and changing just like тебя́. From the first four you can at least see that there are only four *different* forms; just note that the singular and plural patterns don't coincide — well, they aren't really singular and plural, are they? For the third person, setting aside the nominative, you should be experiencing a sense of *déjà vu* — the endings of adjectives. Do pronounce *déjà vu* correctly, by the way; so many English speakers pronounce it as if it was *déjà vous* — the Russians get it right: дежа́ вю (Russians use ю for French *u*).

Just one *very* important note: the AGDIP case-forms of the third-person pronouns acquire н- at the beginning whenever they are governed by a preposition — you can see this already in the prepositional, of course! There are a very few prepositions which don't cause this. This is the *n* which was at the end of в and с, mentioned earlier, and which transferred to the pronoun and then spread to practically all prepositions.

Now let's have the possessives and demonstratives, starting with four which *never* change: его́ 'his/its', её 'her(s)/its', его́ 'its', их 'their(s)'. They never change because they're already in the genitive, just like English *his*, *her*, *its*, *their*, so compare у него́ at his place' with у его́ дру́га 'at his friend's place'. The other possessives are as follows, and they're *all* used much less than in English — I mix them here.

	masc. my/-ne	neut. my/-ne	fem. your(s)	pl. refl.	masc. our(s)	neut. our(s)	fem. your(s)	pl. your(s)
N	мой	моё	твоя́	свой	наш	на́ше	ва́ша	ва́ши
A	мой	моё	твою́	свой	наш	на́ше	ва́шу	ва́ши
G	мое́го		твое́й	свои́х	на́шего		ва́шей	ва́ших
D	моему́		твое́й	свои́м	на́шему		ва́шей	ва́шим
I	мои́м		твое́й	свои́ми	на́шему		ва́шей	ва́шими
P	моём		твое́й	свои́х	на́шем		ва́шей	ва́ших

Remember that the genitive is used for the accusative singular masculine and for the plural when they qualify an animate noun.

A key pattern here is Чей э́то дом? 'Whose house is this?' Just make the questioned noun agree with the appropriate form of чей, чья, чьё, чьи and put э́то after it if it's a 'Whose... is this?' type of question.

	masc.	neut.	fem.	pl.
nom.	чей	чьё	чья	чьи
acc.	чей	чьё	чью	чьи
gen.	чьего́		чьей	чьих
dat.	чьему́		чьей	чьим
instr.	чьим		чьей	чьи́ми
prep.	чьём		чьей	чьих

As for demonstratives, Russian has two, the one formed from the other: тот 'that', typically used to contrast with э́тот 'this, that'.

	'this'				'that'			
	masc.	neut.	fem.	pl.	masc.	neut.	fem.	pl.
nom.	э́тот	э́то	э́та	э́ти	тот	то	та	те
acc.	э́тот	э́то	э́ту	э́ти	тот	то	ту	те
gen.	э́того		э́той	э́тих	того́		той	тех
dat.	э́тому		э́той	э́тим	тому́		той	тем
instr.	э́тим		э́той	э́тими	тем		той	те́ми
prep.	э́том		э́той	э́тих	том		той	тех

Exercise 4

Slot the appropriate forms of the demonstratives and possessives into the following answers (in brackets I give the masculine singular nominative as default form):

1. В како́м до́ме он живёт?   В _____ (тот)
2. Како́му челове́ку он даёт кни́гу?   _____ (тот)
3. Каку́ю учи́тельницу ты бо́льше лю́бишь?   _____ (э́тот)
4. От како́й во́дки он опьяне́л?   _____ (э́тот)

5. Какие любят погорячее?   _____ (тот)

Больше любить is the most common way of saying 'to prefer' (lit. 'to like more'); you'll also come across предпочитáть, which you might find a mouthful. Опьянéть means 'to get drunk (perf.)' — there are many, many expressions to do with drinking in Russian. Its imperfective is пьянéть, пьянéю, пьянéешь — verbs like this, formed from adjectives (пьяный 'drunk'), are common and productive. As second-conjugation verbs, i.e. пьянить, they have the sense 'to make someone drunk', etc. The last question is derived from Нéкоторые любят погорячее 'Some like it hot'.

6. В чьей квартире она сейчас?   В _____ (мой)
7. С чьей кошкой собака поссорилась?   С _____ (егó)
8. Чья дочка приéдет к нам завтра?   _____ (твой)
9. От чьегó решéния они зависят?   От _____ (ваш)
10. В чей офис она поступила работать? В _____ (их)

The verb поссóриться 'to fall out, row' is the perfective of ссóриться. Its opposite is помириться, помирюсь, помиришься (perf.; usually plural) 'to make up'. Зависеть от + gen. (imperf. only) means 'to depend on'. Поступить, imperf. поступáть, means 'to take up' of a job, etc. It's very useful in a set and productive construction which flouts the animacy rule: поступить в студéнты/политики 'to become a student/politician'; note the set phrase выйти в люди 'to get on in the world'. Simplifying, it's the old accusative, now the nominative.

6. Adding things up, comparing, contrasting

How does Russian do English 'and', 'or', and 'but'? The simplest answer is и, или, and но respectively. Dealing with the last can be awkward, as there is the very common word a as well. A brings in the sense of a denial: Он ученик, a [она не ученица,] она учительница 'He's a pupil, but [she's not a pupil,] she's a teacher', or Он не инженéр, a мéнеджер 'He's not an engineer, but a manager'. It's also very common at the beginning of a sentence, as if signalling something new (so possibly implicitly denying what's gone on before) — a bit like 'And what about...?'. Нó can often suggest 'in spite of X, Y', e.g. 'He's reading with great concentration, but isn't working'. Дá can also mean both 'and' and 'but'. And there are particles, e.g. же, which must come second and suggests a contrast. A useful alternative, roughly 'however', is the slightly bookish однáко. If и doesn't make sense as 'and' in a sentence, it's likely to mean 'also, too': он был и в Москвé 'he was in Moscow too'. For 'both... and...', use и..., и...

or как..., так и.... For 'or' you also come across либо. 'Either... or...' is
или..., или or либо..., либо...

7. Out for the count

Russian numerals are hard. Here are the first few:

	0	ноль (нуль in scientific contexts)		
1	один, одна, одно, одни		*6*	шесть
2	два, две		*7*	семь
3	три		*8*	восемь
4	четыре		*9*	девять
5	пять		*10*	десять

The first, ноль, is a masculine noun. If constructed with a noun, the noun
will go into the genitive, singular or plural as appropriate: ноль градусов
'zero degrees'. Один agrees in case, number, and gender with the noun it
counts — and it loses its -и- when declined. It changes like этот, but is
stressed on the very end except for instrumental plural одними, where it's
on the end*ing*.

The next three can be taken together, but do note that два is used with
masculine and neuter nouns, and две with feminines (similar is оба, обе
'both'). With these three, when the case required by the sentence is the
nominative or accusative, the noun counted goes into the genitive singular
and the adjective (as a general rule) into the genitive plural: два брата
'two brothers', три сестры 'three sisters', четыре высоких окна 'four
high windows' — you'll note exceptions in the texts, e.g. Gogol's два
русские мужика in Chapter 7). Any other case, they just agree with the
noun counted, which goes into that required case. So, for 'in the two big
houses' start with в, then в домах, insert the adjective, thus в больших
домах, then the prepositional of два, thus в двух больших домах. This
is more or less true for every numeral between 'one' and 999,999 — for
Russian numerals you need vitamin tablets. The case forms are:

nom./acc.	два две	три	четыре
gen.	двух	трёх	четырёх
dat.	двум	трём	четырём
instr.	двумя	тремя	четырьмя
prep.	двух	трёх	чстырёх

Animacy applies to these numerals as well as to один, when they're used
on their own and for один (but not два, три, четыре) in compounds, e.g.
'22'. It also applies to оба/обе , which respectively decline обо-, обе-
plus -их, -им, -ими, -их in the GDIP.

The good news about 5-10 is that they decline just like feminines ending in a soft sign (keep them in the singular!), that they have the stress fixed on the ending (except as in пя́тью пять 'five times five'), and that when required to be in the nominative or accusative they take the genitive plural and nothing else (if you put something in front of the numeral it goes into the nominative or accusative plural, and even genitive if animacy is relevant, though the numeral itself will remain in the accusative): пять ма́льчиков 'five boys', с пятью ма́льчиками 'with five boys', я зна́ю э́тих пять ма́льчиков 'I know these five boys'.

'11-19', the tens, and the hundreds all behave like 5-10, but any compounds, e.g. 21, 143 obey the last component as regards following nouns and adjectives, except that animacy only affects those ending in '1' — the bigger the number, the less animacy seems salient, if you think about it. The compounds, by the way, are formed by simple concatenation (no *and*s): два́дцать семь де́вушек '27 girls', в двадцати́ семи́ дома́х 'in 27 houses', я зна́ю два́дцать одного́ ма́льчика 'I know 21 boys'. '11-19' are feminines in a soft sign, with a fixed stress this time.

оди́ннадцать, двена́дцать, трина́дцать, четы́рнадцать, пятна́дцать, шестна́дцать, семна́дцать, восемна́дцать, девятна́дцать

Of the tens, два́дцать 'twenty' and три́дцать 'thirty' decline like feminines in a soft sign, with the stress fixed on the ending. Со́рок 'forty', девяно́сто 'ninety', and also сто 'hundred', have the GDIP сорока́, девяно́ста, and ста. The others, namely пятьдеся́т 'fifty', шестьдеся́т 'sixty', се́мьдесят 'seventy', and во́семьдесят 'eighty' (note the spellings) decline like feminines in a soft sign, but do it twice over and have the stress on the ending of the first bit. So: пяти́десяти (GDP), пятью́десятью (instr.; in the spoken language пяти́десятью).

The hundreds other than сто also doubly decline, with the stress on the second component throughout 500-900 and overall in the GDIP:

две́сти, три́ста, четы́реста, пятьсо́т, шестьсо́т, семьсо́т, восемьсо́т, девятьсо́т

nom./acc.	две́сти	три́ста
	четы́реста	пятьсо́т
gen.	двухсо́т	трёхсо́т
	четырёхсо́т	шестисо́т
dat.	двумста́м	трёмста́м
	четырёмста́м	семиста́м
instr.	двумяста́ми	тремяста́ми
	четырьмяста́ми	восемьюста́ми
prep.	двухста́х	трёхста́х
	четырёхста́х	девятиста́х

Plodding on, тысяча 'thousand' is a normal feminine noun. If you like, on its own and in a multiple it can *always* be followed by the genitive plural of what it counts, whatever the case it goes into: в тысяче домов 'in a thousand houses'. But in the GDIP it can also have what it counts in the same case, which might fit with a more numeral-like instrumental, тысячью. The lover of tidiness might like с тысячью домами as against с тысячей домов 'with a thousand houses'.

Could English *thousand* be related to тысяча? It is. The -сяч- bit is related to сто which is related to Latin *centum* which is related to *hundred*, and the ты-manifests itself in a verb you don't find much in Russian now, namely тыть 'to become fat', so тысяча is a 'fat hundred'. For some Slavs a 'week' is a 'fat day', e.g. Ukrainian тиждень.

Really coming down to earth, a 'million' is миллион, and it's a boring old masculine noun, always constructed with the genitive plural.

'Once, one time', by the way, is раз — you can use it also when counting instead of один; 'once' in the sense 'one day, in the past' is однажды ('once upon a time' is жил-был: Жила была старая ведьма 'Once upon a time there was an old witch'). For 'twice', etc. you have дважды, трижды, четырежды, but it's fine to use два/три/четыре раза, then пять раз (note the zero ending), etc. — in this same vein you can have один раз 'once'. And be careful over не раз 'many a time' and ни разу 'not a single time' (if a verb goes with ни разу, make it negative: я ни разу не был у него 'I've not been a single time at his place'). And, for people, on the whole use человек as the genitive plural of человек: сто человек 'a hundred people'.

Recall that the compounds are formed by simply putting one numeral after the other (in decreasing order). Every component is declined, as a rule, but where there are more than two there's apparently a tendency to decline just the first and last. Quite honestly, having mastered the declensions and rules you might feel rather miffed about that. I confess I find it easier to decline them all. I'd get confused otherwise.

Exercise 5

(a) Try to write out (and even read out loud!) the following numbers:

3, 7, 16, 21 (a choice here), 38, 40, 55, 64, 79, 82 (and here), 97, 101, 243, 385, 442, 519, 666, 789, 2345.

(b) And now try case forms other than the nominative:

1. Бли́зко от 'near' тех (3) домо́в.
2. (21) (ко́шка).
3. В (5) (магази́н).
4. Со (сто) (друг).
5. Те (9) упражне́ний.
6. К (ты́сяче) (червь).

7. Я отвеча́ю (тот) (23) (симпати́чый) (злоде́й)
8. Она́ уви́дела (тот) (31) (де́вушка)
9. В ко́мнате бы́ло (6) (челове́к)
10. (7) (де́ти) разгова́ривало с (7) (стари́к)

It's tricky. Упра́жне́ние is 'exercise'; note the zero-ending, there's just the spelling to get your mind around. Червь means 'worm' and is masculine. Ч often goes back to a *k* sound, so could it be related to *crimson* and, stretching credibility further, indeed *vermilion*, and indeed *worm*? Do you think worms could give you a red dye? Злоде́й is 'villain (lit. "evil-doer")', and стари́к is 'old man'. I have no doubt whatsoever that you can work out the genitive plural of де́ти 'children' — just in case, see the end of this paragraph. Note, by the way, how the subject numeral phrases go with singular and, in the past, neuter verbs. They can go with plurals, especially '2-4', but if in doubt,... Оди́н, when it's on its own, i.e. not in '21', etc., takes singular and, in the past tense, gender agreement. (дете́й)

And don't forget Jack Weinberg's ageist Не верь никому́ бо́льше тридцати́ — can you work it out? Ве́рить 'to believe' takes the dative for *whom* you believe and 'than' after comparatives (here бо́льше 'more') can be the genitive (the word лет, genitive plural of год 'year', is understood — look it up); check out Chapter 19 for никому́ and negatives.

6. Practice with plurals

Here's a slightly adapted passage from Il'f and Petrov's *Двена́дцать сту́льев The Twelve Chairs* (1928) — see Chapter 15. It's really good for plurals. How about it, just try to translate it for yourself! Or find a translation (you'll have to find it in the translation — I'm not giving any hints other than that it's the beginning of a chapter) and compare the two, making *exhaustive* use of a dictionary and writing it all up in your vocabulary book — don't forget all the grammatical information too. Of course, there are forms here you haven't come across, notably participles — check out Chapters 13 and 17.

Стати́стика зна́ет всё. То́чно учтено́ коли́чество па́хотной земли́ в СССР.

Изве́стно, ско́лько и како́й пи́щи съеда́ет в год сре́дний граждани́н респу́блики. Изве́стно, ско́лько э́тот сре́дний граждани́н выпива́ет в сре́днем во́дки с приме́рным указа́нием потребляемой закуски. Известно, сколько в стране охотников, балерин, собак всех пород, велосипедов, памятников, девушек, маяков и швейных машинок.

Как много жизни, полной пыла, страстей, и мысли, глядит на нас со статистических таблиц!

Кто он, розовощёкий индивид, сидящий с салфёткой на груди за столиком и с аппетитом уничтожающий дымящуюся снедь? Вокруг него лежат стада миниатюрных быков. В специальном статистическом бассейне плещутся бесчисленные осетры. На плечах, руках и голове индивида сидят куры. В облаках летают гуси, утки и индейки. Под столом сидят два кролика. На горизонте возвышаются пирамиды из печёного хлеба. Небольшая крепость из варенья смывается молочной рекой. Огурец, величиною в пизанскую башню, стоит на горизонте. За крепостными валами из соли и перца маршируют вина, водки и наливки. В арьергарде жалкой кучкой плетутся безалкогольные напитки — нарзаны, лимонады.

Кто же этот розовощёкий индивид — обжора, пьянчуга и сластун?.. Это — средний гражданин, съедающий в среднем за свою жизнь всю изображённую на таблице снедь. Это — нормальный потребитель каллорий и витаминов — тихий, сорокалетний холостяк, служащий в госмагазине галантерёи.

Just four notes:

(i) for учтено look up учесть (related to учтивый 'polite, considerate'),;

(ii) плещутся is from плескаться (an alternation I didn't burden you with in Chapter 5)

(iii) каллорий nowadays has one л;

(iv) госмагазине is a compound noun, with гос a truncation of the adjective государственный 'State'. If we were to spell it out in full here, it would be государственном.

CHAPTER 9

1. Yet more verb patterns

Just to stress that I'm not deceiving you in saying how regular the Russian verb is, the next set of patterns, apart from the past-tense forms, again misses bits out — a useful exercise. An asterisk marks the perfectives and a dagger those which are one-off. For the past-tense forms, recall that '-á' means that the feminine form is ending-stressed, while '÷' or 'л÷' means that all the endings are stressed. Look at them and make connections.

пить	откры́ть*	петь	бри́ть†	умере́ть*	лечь*†	боле́ть
drink	open	sing	shave (tr.)	die	lie down	be ill
пью	откро́ю	пою́	бре́ю	умру́	ля́гу	боле́ю
пьёшь	откро́ешь	поёшь	бре́ешь	умрёшь	ля́жешь	боле́ешь
пил(á)	откры́л	пел	брил	у́мер(лá)	лёг(л÷)	боле́л

сесть*†	пла́кать	дрема́ть	стать*	оде́ть*	врать	поня́ть*
sit down	weep	drowse	become	dress (tr.)	fib	understand
ся́дете	пла́чете	дре́млете	ста́нете	оде́нете	врёте	поймёте
ся́дут	пла́чут	дре́млют	ста́нут	оде́нут	врут	пойму́т
сел	пла́кал	дрема́л	стал	оде́л	врал(á)	по́нял(á)

снять*	лгать	плева́ть	рискну́ть*	тре́бовать	со́хнуть	вы́нуть*
take off	tell a lie	spit	risk	demand	dry (itr.)	take out
сниму́	лгу	плюю́	рискну́	тре́бую	со́хну	вы́ну
сни́мем	лжём	плюём	рискнём	тре́буем	со́хнем	вы́нем
снял(á)	лгал(á)	плева́л	рискну́л	тре́бовал	сох(л-)	вы́нул

звать	рвать	печь	плести́	греть	класть	созрева́ть
call	tear	bake	braid	heat	put	ripen
зовёшь	рвёшь	печёшь	плетёшь	гре́ешь	кладёшь	созрева́ешь
зову́т	рвут	пеку́т	плету́	гре́ют	кладу́т	созрева́ют
звал(á)	рвал(á)	пёк(л÷)	плёл(÷)	грел	клал	созрева́л

спать†	боле́ть	вари́ть	молча́ть	посети́ть*	отве́тить*	корми́ть
sleep	ache	cook	be silent	visit	reply	feed
сплю	--	варю́	молчу́	посещу́	отве́чу	кормлю́
спят	боля́т	ва́рят	молча́т	посетя́т	отве́тят	ко́рмят
спал(á)	боле́л	вари́л	молча́л	посети́л	отве́тил	корми́л

Открьіть has a sense of 'uncovering' and belongs to quite a rich family: If you put the cover *over* something, you 'shut' it, so закрьіть . The imperfectives are in -крывáть. Note умерéть; its imperfective is умирáть which, as with most derived imperfectives, conjugates without any surprises. Do you think it might be connected to things *moribund*? 'Death' is смерть (fem.) — German *der Schmerz*? Note the verbs in -чь, which have a -г- or a -к- surfacing in the non-past and past. The non-past stress tends to be fixed on the ending, but мочь and лечь are exceptions. Note болéть, with its different conjugation when meaning 'to ache' — third-person forms only. Note (за)плáкать 'to weep', with its first-person singular identical, barring the stress, to that of (за)платúть 'to pay'. There ought to be a connection! Note одéть; its imperfective is одевáть : the imperfective suffix is -ва-, so it doesn't belong to the very productive group of verbs with -ова-/-ева-, e.g. трéбовать and плевáть . Note снять, понять, вьінуть : they all belong to the important 'take' family; their imperfectives are снимáть, понимáть, вынимáть. And record the changes in the first person singular of some of the second-conjugation verbs (the last box): that between посетúть and отвéтить comes out too in their imperfectives: посещáть, отвечáть.

Do remember that all this is repetition and exemplification — there *are* a few more patterns, but still requiring nothing beyond the need to learn the infinitive plus, say, the 'I' form and one other of the non-past.

2. Getting impersonal, and what happens when your postillion has been struck by lightning

Russian verbs are often linked to something in the nominative case as subject — and so they should be, you'll say. But Russian also makes great use of verbs without a nominative subject: 'impersonal' constructions. Russian goes far beyond English equivalents such as 'it's getting dark, it's cold, it's raining', though it has some of those as well, e.g.

смеркáется	'dusk is falling'	lit. 'it's dusking'
вечерéет	'evening is falling'	lit. 'it's eveninging'

Many Russian impersonals exploit the *meanings* of cases. For example, in English you will say 'I open the door', 'the door opens', and 'the key opens the door'. Fine in Russian too, but it's only in the first that 'I' as a subject is 'normal': active, doing it. In the second, well, doors don't open without some sort of help, it's really the door that is opened, so you make дверь the accusative with a form of the verb for 'one..., people...', viz. the third-person plural without онú: дверь открывáют (clearer with a feminine in -a: кнúгу открывáют 'the book is opened'). What about the key? It doesn't open the door, the door gets opened with it, it's the instrument. So, using the instrumental, Ключóм открывáют дверь. Other examples:

Лес рýбят, щéпки летя́т'[If] the forest is felled, splinters fly' (said by Stalin?);	
Шкóлу ремонти́руют	'The school is being repaired';
У нáс не кýрят	'No smoking here';
Уйди́, говоря́т тебе!	'Go away, I'm telling you!'

Note that this third person plural without они́ is very generalized or indefinite; someone using it might well have a single person at the back of their mind. Similar is the use of the second-person singular (usually without ты), a bit like English 'you' as in 'You turn right, go straight on, then you're there'. So:

На войнé встречáешь рáзных людéй
'In war you meet different sorts of people';
Без трудá не вы́нешь и ры́бку из прудá'
'Without hard work you won't get even one fish out of a pond (prov.)'
За двумя́ зáйцами погóнишься, ни одногó не поймáешь
'[If] you chase after two hares, you won't even catch one (prov.)'

The writer Venedikt Erofeev had a reasonable variation on the last:

И éсли уж гня́ться, то не мéньше, как за двумя́ зáйцами
'And if you're going to chase, then not after less than two hares'

How about 'the room is cold'? Odd? In Russian it's better to say 'in the room it's cold': В кóмнате хóлодно. If you had кóмната холóдная, it could be saying something about the qualities of the room. This hits you in 'I'm cold', where if you just feel cold it's Мне хóлодно. Frigidity would be suggested by Я холóдный/холóдная.

The wonders of case take off with 'the bullet killed the soldier'. You can do it literally, as bullets are extremely dangerous things. But better Russian would go 'the-soldier it-killed by-the-bullet': Солдáта уби́ло пýлей. Likewise 'the wind tore the boy's hat off': Вéтром сорвáло шля́пу мáльчика 'By-the-wind it-tore-off the-hat of-the-boy'. By the way, see if you can find some of these words in the dictionary, i.e. work out their citation form.

A very common construction is where you make a verb reflexive and construct it with a dative, giving a sense of 'feeling like': емý не спи́тся 'he doesn't feel like sleeping'; вам не рабóтается 'you don't feel like working', and мне не хóчется 'I don't feel like...' (the feeling can be quite strong: Мне э́того так не хотéлось 'I so didn't want this').

CHAPTER 9

Not to mention a few nouns used as impersonals: лень 'laziness', пора́ 'time'. Both feminine, but their 'past' tense gives the game away: мне лень бы́ло рабо́тать 'I felt too lazy to work', им пора́ бы́ло уходи́ть 'it was time for them to leave'. Another example is ей жаль до́чку 'she's sorry for her daughter' (with a genitive object it would mean 'begrudge': ему́ жаль бы́ло истра́ченных де́нег 'he begrudged the money he'd spent (lit. "the spent money")').

Not everything you expect is impersonal: 'it's raining' is идёт дождь, where the masculine noun дождь 'rain' is the subject, as is clear from пошёл дождь 'it started raining', isn't it? If it rains all the time, by the way, you still use идти́. Don't be tempted by ходи́ть — the rain comes in a pretty straight line, only one direction, and one-way, however often!

Quite a few impersonal expressions use adjectives with the ending -o: тепло́ 'it's warm', жа́рко 'it's hot', за́тхло and ду́шно 'it's stuffy', хорошо́ 'it's good', прохла́дно 'it's cool', темно́ 'it's dark', светло́ 'it's light'. Similar-looking forms function as adverbs: интере́сно 'interestingly' or 'it's interesting'. Very useful ones constructed with a dative subject include: легко́ 'easy', тру́дно 'hard', жа́лко 'feel sorry for, begrudge' (just like жаль), ску́чно 'boring', интере́сно 'interesting', гру́стно 'sad', ве́село 'happy', бо́льно 'painful', and оби́дно 'offensive (as impers. = "hurt, offended")' all with a sense of 'feel/find it X'. Plus those for how hot, warm, or cold you feel: Кому́ хо́лодно? 'Who's cold?'

Russian goes much further with impersonal expressions, using them extremely frequently to convey 'can, may, ought, must', with the subject in the dative and, optionally, an infinitive: на́до and ну́жно 'it is necessary to, must, have to', необходи́мо 'it's indispensable to' (look at this one: it's literally 'it is not-walk-round-able'), мо́жно 'it is possible to', нельзя́ 'it is not allowed to (+ imperf.)' and 'it is impossible to (+ perf.)'. To form the past tense add бы́ло, and for the future add бу́дет.

Ну́жно has another existence as a neuter; the other forms are ну́жен, нужна́, нужны́ — can you guess which is which? In Russian you say 'a book is necessary to me': Мне нужна́ кни́га. Note the agreement. And, just to confirm all this, a sentence from Venedikt Erofeev's notebooks:

Евро́пе ну́жен бык, быку́ нужна́ Евро́па
'Europa needs a bull, the bull needs Europa'

Similar is до́лжен, должна́, должно́, должны́ 'must, obliged' (it can also have the probability overtones of 'must', as in the nice little expression должно́ быть 'very likely'), though there's no reversal as in ну́жен. So 'I must (= "I have a duty to") work' is Я должна́ рабо́тать, using a female subject. In the past and future put the forms of the verb быть *after* it: Я должна́ была́ / бу́ду рабо́тать 'I had to / will have to work'.

91

Here are a few more examples. Amazing how useful most of them are — and play around, changing the 'subject'.

Accusative subjects:

> Ма́шу тошни́т от э́того 'Masha feels sick as a result of this';
> Ива́на тя́нет домо́й/на пи́во 'Ivan feels homesick/is longing for a beer';
> Меня́ зноби́т 'I feel shivery, shudder';
> Её лихора́дит 'She feels feverish';
> Его́ бро́сило/ки́нуло в пот/жар/дрожь 'He burst into a sweat / fever / trembling';
> Её всю дёргало 'She was twitching all over';
> Нас коро́бит от его́ слов 'His words jar on us';
> Его́ крючило от бо́ли 'He was writhing in pain';
> Его́ мути́т 'He feels sick';
> Его́ внеза́пно осени́ло 'It suddenly dawned on him' (can be personal: Его́ осени́ла мысль 'The thought struck him');
> Меня́ передёрнуло от отвраще́ния/бо́ли 'I was convulsed with disgust/pain';
> Её рвёт 'She throws up';
> Его́ трясёт от стра́ха 'He's shaking with dread'.

Genitive subjects

> Воды́ приба́вилось 'There was an increase in water';
> Де́нег (не) хвата́ет 'There is(n't) enough money'.

and very often with negatives:

> Катастро́фы не произошло́ 'There was no catastrophe (lit. "it didn't happen of a catastrophe")' (if not negative, we have: произошла́ катастро́фа 'a catastrophe occurred' — note the agreement).

and compare (some Russians dispute this):

> Он не́ был до́ма = 'he wasn't/hadn't been home', stating a fact, *or* about to say where he was/had been;
> Его́ не́ было до́ма = 'he wasn't/hadn't been at home'.

Dative subjects:

> Что вам не сиди́тся? 'How come you can't sit still?';
> Нет, пей, пока́ пьётся 'No, drink while you feel like it' (subject omitted here);
> Мне нездоро́вится 'I feel unwell';
> Нам ве́рится с трудо́м 'We have difficulty believing'.

Им удалóсь 'They were successful, they managed to...' (удавáться, perf. удáться);
Ей придётся 'She'll have to/be forced/fated to...' (приходи́ться, perf. прийти́сь);
Нам надоéло игрáть в шáхматы 'We're fed up playing chess' (надоéсть, imperf. надоедáть — the perfective past is usual in this construction; it can also be personal, meaning 'to tire, pester' plus dat. of 'whom' and instr. of 'how, with what').

including the reflexives, which are often imperfective

Ему дрéмлется/кáшляется/икáется/чихáется 'He feels like dozing, coughing, hiccupping, sneezing' (these are not usually negative);

but one can get perfectives, e.g.

Емý чихнýлось 'He felt a need to sneeze'
Ей зевнýлось 'She felt a need to yawn'
Мне хорошó пописáлось 'I feel I got a good bit of writing done'.

and

Мне не по себé 'I'm not myself/out of sorts';
Им не до смéху 'They're not in a laughing mood';
Ей не до пéсен 'She's in no mood for songs';
Что емý до...? 'What does he care about...?'
Мне повезлó 'I had a stroke of luck' (using везти́ 'to convey' impersonally);
Ей крышка 'She's had it';
Не фарти́т нам 'We're out of luck' (very colloquial);
Мне ви́дно/слы́шно (+ acc. if a direct object) 'I can see/hear...';
Вчерá всем достáлось от Андрéя 'Yesterday everyone got told off by Andrei';
Капýт старикý 'The old man's had it';
Рáдоваться рáно 'It's [a bit] early to rejoice';
Мне éсть когдá прийти́ к вáм 'I have the time to come to see you';
Мне нéкогда прийти́ к вáм 'I haven't the time to come to see you' (Chapter 19);
Тури́стам было где отдохнуть 'The tourists had somewhere to take a rest';
Ей двáдцать лет 'She's twenty years old'.

Prepositional-phrase subjects (do note some of the cases involved):

На нéбе пáсмурно 'The sky is cloudy' (lit. 'in the sky it's cloudy');
У меня в гóрле перши́т 'I've got a tickle in my throat';
У неё заложи́ло нос 'She's got a stuffed-up nose';
У негó лóмит спи́ну 'His back aches';
У них боя́т зýбы 'They have toothache';
У меня дух захвáтывает 'I can't get my breath';

У меня в глазáх потемнéло 'Everything's gone dark before my eyes';
У меня кóлет в бокý 'I've a stitch';
У меня под лóжечкой сосёт 'I can feel cramps in the pit of my stomach';
У меня в носý щекóчет 'I've an itchy nose';
У негó в сердце колет 'He has a stitch'.
С отцóм невáжно 'Our father's not well';
С цемéнтом тýго 'There's a shortage of cement' (тýго = 'it's tight');
В больнице было тихо 'The hospital was calm';
За окнóм льёт, как из ведрá 'Outside it's raining cats and dogs';
Из дýша кáпает 'There's a leak in the shower';
В избé пáхло лýком 'The izba smelt of onions';
В избé вонЯло гнилóй капýстой 'The izba stank of rotten cabbage';
В избé несёт лýком 'The izba smells of onions';
Там потянýло сыростью 'There came a blast of dampness there'.

If you know them, you'll never be at a loss! And there are many more.

3. Impersonal even for possession

If any verb was going to be personal it would be 'to have'. But in Russian it's normally expressed by what's at first sight an impersonal construction, the verb быть accompanied by the preposition у + genitive. The only exceptions concern set phrases and where what is possessed is 'abstract', where we may have имéть , non-past имéю, имéешь : Нарушéния *имéют мéсто* в цéнтре гóрода 'There are disturbances in the centre of town', я имéю честь... 'I have the honour (to)...'. Otherwise, 'to have' is:

у меня	есть/бýдет/был	нóж	'I have/will have/had a knife'
у тебя	есть/бýдет/былá	тетрáдь	'you ... an exercise book'
у негó	есть/бýдет/было	полотéнце	'he ... a towel'
у неё	есть/бýдут/были	друзья	'she ... friends'
у Ивáна	есть/бýдет/былá	тарéлка	'Ivan ... a plate'
у Елéны	есть/бýдет/было	рáдио	'Elena ... a radio'
у нас	есть/бýдет/был	карандáш	'we ... a pencil'
у вас	есть/бýдут/были	пластинки	'you ... records'
у них	есть/бýдет/был	дóм	'they ... a house'
у дéвушек	есть/бýдет/было	бюрó	'the girls ... an office'

Note that 'to be' in this construction is usually actually expressed in the present tense. The literal meaning is 'In X's possession there is... Y' (you may prefer to see есть, etc. as meaning 'is' rather than 'there is' here and what is possessed, in the *nominative*, as the subject, giving you a personal expression — this comes out in the future and especially the past). Есть may be omitted, but normally only when the sense of possession is reduced, say when the nominative is qualified by an adjective, e.g. у меня́ больша́я колле́кция гравю́р — хо́чешь посмотре́ть? 'I've a big collection of etchings — do you want to see them?' But I'm advised to recommend you *do* express есть. Now compare the negative forms:

у меня́	нет/не бу́дет/не бы́ло	ножа́
у тебя́	нет/не бу́дет/не бы́ло	тетра́ди
у него́	нет/не бу́дет/не бы́ло	полоте́нца
у неё	нет/не бу́дет/не бы́ло	друзе́й
у Ива́на	нет/не бу́дет/не бы́ло	таре́лки
у Еле́ны	нет/не бу́дет/не бы́ло	ра́дио
у нас	нет/не бу́дет/не бы́ло	карандаша́
у вас	нет/не бу́дет/не бы́ло	пласти́нок
у них	нет/не бу́дет/не бы́ло	до́ма
у де́вушек	нет/не бу́дет/не бы́ло	бюро́

Here it *does* seem impersonal (and *so easy*): the verb is singular and, in the past, neuter. What is not possessed must be in the genitive (ра́дио and бюро́ don't decline): Без ка́йфа нет ла́йфа 'Life's a drag without fun' (lit. 'without fun there isn't life' — youth slang). This is important. Negatives and genitives go together in Russian — after negative verbs what would otherwise be accusative tends to be genitive.

Нет, не бу́дет, and не́ бы́ло are not restricted to 'to have' — they also express *absence*, and *must* be constructed with the genitive of what's absent: «Ма́ма до́ма?» — «Нет. Ма́мы сего́дня нет.» — «Когда́ она́ бу́дет?» — «Не зна́ю. Её не бу́дет ещё не́сколько дней. Да и на про́шлой неде́ле её не́ бы́ло» 'Is your mum at home?' — 'No, mum's not [here] today' — 'When will she be around?' — 'I don't know. She won't be around for several days more. And last week too she wasn't around'.

Exercise 1

How about revising the adjective?

	masc.	neut.	fem.	fem.	masc	neut.
nom.		ру́сское		зде́шняя		
acc.			хоро́шую			
gen.	до́брого					
dat.				зде́шней		
instr.					тре́тьим	
prep.						большо́м

	masc.	neut.	fem.	fem.	masc	neut.
nom.	добрые					
gen.			рýсских			
dat.				большúм		
instr.					здéшними	
prep.						трéтьих

And let's exercise (or is it 'exorcise'?) the verbs from Chapter 6:

брать	взять	мочь	хотéть	начáть	сказáть	слышать
to take	to take	can	to want	to start	to say	to hear
	возьмý				скажý	
берёшь			хóчешь			
		мóжет				
					начнёте	
			хотят			слышат

бежáть	дать	есть	послáть	смотрéть		слýшать
	торговáть					
to run	to give	to eat	to send	to watch	to listen (to)	to trade
бегý						
			пошлёшь			
					слýшает	
бежúм						
						торгýете
				смóтрят		

And can you work out what these verbs mean?

выeverзти	вывозúть из + gen.	_____
перевестú	переводúть	_____
догнáть	догонять	_____
сойтúсь	сходúться	_____
прилетéть	прилетáть в/на + acc.	_____
унестú	уносúть	_____
разлетéться	разлетáться	_____
взойтú	всходúть на + acc.	_____
найтú	находúть	_____
вбежáть	вбегáть в + acc.	_____
проéхать	проезжáть мúмо + gen.	_____
отплыть	отплывáть	_____
съéхать	съезжáть с + gen.	_____

CHAPTER 10

After Ivan the Terrible came the Смутное время, Борис Годунов, and the beginning of the Романов dynasty. The seventeenth century was a century of consolidation, of reorganization. This was confirmed by 1649, with the new code of laws, the Уложение. As usual, and for more than another two hundred years, the peasants (remember most of them were *slaves*) were left out of account. Under the first three Romanovs, Михаил, Алексей, and Фёдор, there were numerous peasant risings.

So consolidation neglected the people, but the strengthening of the state set down reasonably firm foundations (lots of skeletons in them) for the future. Contacts with the West had increased dramatically, giving people a taste for something different. This took a giant leap forward with Пётр I, Пётр Великий, Peter I, the Great (1682-1725): the reduction of the Church to a government 'Ministry', the Holy Synod, the reform of the calendar and the alphabet, the push to the Baltic, and the building of St Petersburg. But progress was built on tyranny. After a strong leader, the familiar story. The period up to the accession of Екатерина II, Catherine the Great (1762-1796), might be seen as decay, but it might equally be seen as a period of settling down. Everything Western became highly fashionable in higher circles. Moreover, it was, with the polymath peasant Lomonosov and his founding of Moscow University, a period of real importance in the shaping of the Russian language. And Catherine came, stained with the blood of her husband emperor. She had something of the benevolent despot — on the whole more of the despot. But she was successful in her foreign policy and expansion of Russia, and laid more political and cultural foundations.

By now Russia is fully on the European scene, something confirmed by its involvement in the Napoleonic Wars and rôle in Napoleon's defeat and the creation of a new Europe. Александр I, Aleksandr I (1801-1825), with his retiring, withdrawn attitude, aroused hopes of liberalism and reform, but he died suddenly and enigmatically, and his apparent otherworldliness may have drawn Russia back from Europe. It was a time of questionings by Russians of their identity and of whether the road ahead lay with or without the West: a division into славянофилы 'Slavophiles' and западники 'Westernizers', which was never quite as simple, or as much of a division, as that. The real division? As ever, from the people. The hiatus between the death of Aleksandr and accession of

Николáй I, Nikolai I (1825-1855) was marked by the failure of the Декабрúстское восстáние Decembrist Uprising. This, along with the unpreparedness of Nikolai (he hadn't been first in line), meant caution, in other words firmness and oppression. The contemporary buzzwords were самодержáвие, правослáвие, нарóдность autocracy, orthodoxy, 'nationalism'. By the revolution in Paris of 1848 this oppressive autocrat, absolute leader of a stifling state, its 'best' characterized in literature by what Turgenev would call the лúшний человéк 'the superfluous man', would have become the жандáрм Еврóпы 'the gendarme of Europe'. And yet great literature was in the making, a triumph of language and mind in a society enriched over the course of the preceding century by influences from abroad, particularly the West.

Among the Slavophiles, names to conjure with include Николáй Карамзúн (perhaps a surprise, given his rôle in the development of the language as reflected in the salons of Russian high society), the brothers Ивáн and Пётр Кирéевский, Алексéй Хомякóв, and the brothers Константúн and Ивáн Аксáков. Ivan Aksakov outlived the others by many years and ended up as a Slavonic nationalist reactionary, perhaps the only outcome for the Slavophiles' idealization of the past, belief in the central position of Orthodoxy, and rejection of the West as a model. For many Russians, the Aksakovs make one think more of their father, Сергéй (1791-1859) and his depictions of Russian provincial life. And among the Westernizers: Пётр Чаадáев, keen to consolidate Russia's emergence from cultural isolation, Виссариóн Белúнский, the radical literary critic devoted to individual freedom and the importance of knowledge and education, and Алексáндр Гéрцен, in the West away from Russia from 1847 to his death in 1870, a liberal keen that Russia learn from the French Revolution and contemporary German thinkers, hoping for a truly democratic state but aware of the natural barriers to such an ideal — his publication Кóлокол The Bell, based in London, provided his main platform, though no one should neglect his memoirs, not least for their excellent Russian: Былóе и дýмы My Past and Thoughts (1855-1869).

Now for two contemporary writers. First, Гончарóв, renowned for his great novel Облóмов Oblomov (1857-1858). He wrote other works, and some of them are still very readable, but one worries about a man whose three main works begin with the letters об: Обыкновéнная истóрия An Ordinary Story, Облóмов, and Обрыв The Precipice. I'll take the very beginning of the novel, setting the scene in the apartment of the tragic and lovable figure, Oblomov — quite honestly, it was hard to keep the extract short, so compelling is the scene-setting:

В Горо́ховой у́лице, в одно́м из больши́х домо́в, народонаселе́ния кото́рого ста́ло бы на це́лый уе́здный го́род, лежа́л у́тром в посте́ли, на свое́й кварти́ре, Илья́ Ильи́ч Обло́мов.

Э́то был челове́к лет тридцати́ о́т роду, сре́днего ро́ста, прия́тной нару́жности, с тёмно-се́рыми глаза́ми, но с отсу́тствием вся́кой определённой иде́и, вся́кой сосредото́ченности в черта́х лица́. Мысль гуля́ла во́льной пти́цей по лицу́, порха́ла в глаза́х, сади́лась на полуотворённые гу́бы, пря́талась в скла́дках лба, пото́м совсе́м пропада́ла, и тогда́ во всём лице́ те́плился ро́вный свет беспе́чности. С лица́ беспе́чность переходи́ла в по́зы всего́ те́ла, да́же в скла́дки шлафро́ка.

Иногда́ взгляд его́ помрача́лся выраже́нием бу́дто уста́лости и́ли ску́ки; но ни уста́лость, ни ску́ка не могли́ ни на мину́ту согна́ть с лица́ мя́гкость, кото́рая была́ госпо́дствующим и основны́м выраже́нием, не лица́ то́лько, а всей души́; а душа́ так откры́то и я́сно свети́лась в глаза́х, в улы́бке, в ка́ждом движе́нии головы́, руки́. И пове́рхностно наблюда́тельный, холо́дный челове́к, взгляну́в мимохо́дом на Обло́мова, сказа́л бы: «Добря́к до́лжен быть, простота́!» Челове́к поглу́бже и посимпати́чнее, до́лго вгля́дываясь в лицо́ его́, отошёл бы в прия́тном разду́мье, с улы́бкой.

[...]

Как шёл дома́шний костю́м Обло́мова к поко́йным черта́м лица́ его́ и к изне́женному те́лу! На нём был хала́т из перси́дской мате́рии, настоя́щий восто́чный хала́т, без мале́йшего намёка на Евро́пу, без кисте́й, без ба́рхата, без та́лии, весьма́ помести́тельный, так что и Обло́мов мог два́жды заверну́ться в него́. Рукава́, по неизме́нной азиа́тской мо́де, шли от па́льцев к плечу́ всё ши́ре и ши́ре. Хотя́ хала́т э́тот и утра́тил свою́ первонача́льную све́жесть и места́ми замени́л свой первобы́тный, есте́ственный лоск други́м, благоприобретённым, но всё ещё сохраня́л я́ркость восто́чной кра́ски и про́чность тка́ни.

Хала́т име́л в глаза́х Обло́мова тьму неоценённых досто́инств: он мя́гок, ги́бок; те́ло не чу́вствует его́ на себе́; он, как послу́шный раб, покоря́ется самомале́йшему движе́нию те́ла.

Обло́мов всегда́ ходи́л до́ма без га́лстука и без жиле́та, потому́ что люби́л просто́р и приво́лье. Ту́фли на нём бы́ли дли́нные, мя́гкие и широ́кие; когда́ он, не гля́дя, опуска́л но́ги с посте́ли на́ пол, то непреме́нно попада́л в них сра́зу.

In Gorokhovaia Street, in one of the-large houses, [of] the-population of-which would be-enough [бы with the past tense gives the conditional] for a-whole uezd city [chief town of an uezd district], in-the-morning lay in bed, in his apartment, Il'ia Il'ich Oblomov.

This was a-person of about thirty years from birth [reversing 'years' and 'thirty' gives approximation], of-medium height, of-a-pleasant appearance, with dark-grey eyes, but with an-absence of any/every definite idea, any/every concentration in the-features of-[his]-face. A-thought promenaded like-a-free bird over [his]-face, fluttered in [his]-eyes, perched ['sat down'] on [his]-half-opened lips, hid in the-folds of-[his]-forehead, then completely disappeared, and then in all [his]-face glimmered the-even light of-unconcern. From [his]-face unconcern moved-over into the-poses of-[his]-whole body, even into the- folds of-[his]-'sleeping-coat'.

Sometimes his glance became-clouded with-an-expression as-it-were of-fatigue or boredom; but neither fatigue nor boredom could for [not] even a-minute chase off [his]-face the-softness which was the-ruling and basic expression, not of-[his]-face only, but of-[his]-whole soul; and [his]-soul so openly and clearly shone in [his]-eyes, in [his]-smile, in every movement of-[his]-head, arm. And a superficially observant, cold person, having-glanced [a gerund — Chapter 16) in-passing, would say: 'A-good-natured fellow he-must be, simplicity!' A-person [who was] more-profound, more-likeable, long looking-into [a gerund] into his-face, would go-off in pleasant rêverie, with a-smile.

[...]

How went the-domestic costume of-Oblomov to the-placid features of-[his]-face and to [his]-pampered body! On him was a-*khalat* ['dressing gown', Oblomov's trademark!] out-of Persian material, a-genuine eastern *khalat*, without the-slightest hint of-Europe, without tassels, without velvet, without a-waist, exceedingly capacious, so that even Oblomov could twice wrap-himself-up in it. The-sleeves, according-to the-unchanging Asiatic fashion, went from the-fingers to the-shoulder ever wider and wider. Although this *khalat* even had-lost its original freshness and in-places replaced its primordial, natural sheen with another, well-acquired, [but] all the same it-retained the-brightness of-[its]-eastern colouring/dyeing and the-firmness of-[its]-cloth.

The-*khalat* had in the-eyes of-Oblomov a-mass [lit. 'darkness'] of-unappreciated qualities: it [was] soft, supple [two short adjectives — Chapter 11]; [his]-body does not feel it on itself; it, like an-obedient slave, submits to-the-very-slightest movement.

Oblomov always walked-about at-home without a-tie and without a-waistcoat, because he-loved space and freedom. The-slippers on him were long, soft, and broad; when he, without-looking [another gerund], lowered [his]-feet from the-bed onto the-floor, then unfailingly [he]-went into them at-once [попадáть, perf. попáсть is a very useful verb for 'getting somewhere'].

And now a poem by Тютчев (1803-1873), often overlooked and certainly rather laid-back regarding his creation, and yet the creator of some of the best Russian love poetry (often seen through the eyes of the woman) and of one of Russian poetry's most memorable lines — see if you can guess it, in *Silentium!* (don't pay too much attention to the stresses here!).

Молчи, скрывайся и тай	Be-silent, hide and conceal
И чу́вства и мечты́ свои́ —	both your feelings and dreams —
Пуска́й в душе́вной глубине́	let in the-soul's depths
Встаю́т и захо́дят оне́	rise and set [them = they (arch.)]
Безмо́лвно, как звезды́ в ночи́, —	speechlessly, like stars in the-night, —
Любу́йся и́ми — и молчи́.	admire them — and be-silent.
Как се́рдцу вы́сказать себя́?	How for-the-heart to-express itself?
Друго́му как поня́ть тебя́?	for-another how to-understand you?
Поймёт ли он, чем ты живёшь?	will he understand, by-what you live?
Мысль изречённая есть ложь.	an-expressed-thought is a-lie.
Взрыва́я, возмути́шь ключи́, —	stirring-up, [you]-'ll-cloud the-springs,
Пита́йся и́ми — и молчи́.	be-nourished by-them — and be-silent.
Лишь жить в себе́ само́м уме́й —	Only know-how to-live within yourself
Есть це́лый мир в душе́ твое́й	there-is a-whole world in your soul
Таи́нственно-волше́бных дум;	of-mysterious-magical thoughts;
Их оглуши́т нару́жный шум,	them will-deafen the-outside noise,
Дневны́е разгоня́т лучи́, —	the-day's rays will-scatter [them], —
Внима́й их пе́нью — и молчи́!	heed their singing — and be-silent!

Tiutchev's language can be somewhat archaic. Note the gerunds in the fifth
line, and the short adjectives in the sixth and eighth — see how short
горька́ goes with как (if it were long, you would have кака́я го́рькая);
and note the use of dative cases. The form стра́жду, from страда́ть 'to
suffer', is obsolete; nowadays the verb is like чита́ть.

Exercises

Here we can take tables from Chapters 8 and 9, with gaps for you to fill in and the
odd variation. Try not to peek!

1. Personal pronouns:

	I	you	we	you	he/it	it/it	she/it	they
nom.							она́	
acc.	меня́							их
gen.					его́			
dat.		тебе́						
instr.			на́ми				им	
prep.				вас				

2. Possessives:

	masc. my/-ne	neut. your(s)	fem. our(s)	pl. refl.	masc. your(s)	neut. our(s)	fem. your(s)	pl. my/-ne
nom.			на́ша					
acc.	мой						твою́	
gen.		твоего́						мои́х
dat.				свои́м				
instr.						на́шему		
prep.					ва́шем			

3. Whose?:

	masc.	neut.	fem.	pl.
nom.	чей		чья	
acc.		чьё		
gen.		чьего́		
dat.				
instr.				чьи́ми
prep.				

4. Demonstratives:

	'this'				'that'			
	masc.	neut.	fem.	pl.	masc.	neut.	fem.	pl.
nom.						то	та	
acc.	этот							
gen.			этой					
dat.								тем
instr.			этими					
prep.								

5. '2, 3, and 4':

	m./n.	fem.	—	—
nom./acc.				
gen.		двух		
dat.		трём		
instr.			четырьмя́	
prep.				

6. Have a go at 'to have' (don't forget the noun endings):

y	нóж-	'I will have a knife'
y	тетрáд-	'you have an exercise book'
y	полотéнц-	'he had a towel'
y	друг	'she will have friends'
y	тарéлк-	'Ivan had a plate'
y	рáд-	'Elena has a radio'
y	карандáш-	'we will have a pencil'
y	пласти́нк-	'you had records'
y	дóм-	'they will have a house'
y	бюр-	'the girls have an office'

7. And now make them negative:

y	нóж-	'I won't have a knife'
y	тетрáд-	'you haven't an exercise book'
y	полотéнц-	'he hadn't a towel'
y	друг	'she won't have friends'
y	тарéлк-	'Ivan hadn't a plate'
y	рáд-	'Elena hasn't a radio'
y	карандáш-	'we won't have a pencil'
y	пласти́нк-	'you hadn't records'
y	дóм-	'they won't have a house'

Wordplay

Putting and saying

Let's look briefly at two families of words in Russian.

First, in English we may have the catch-all word *put*, but in Russian the tendency is to be more precise: you can put something lying down, standing up, sitting, or hanging, and all this is extraordinarily symmetrical, as you'll see, and even links in with *being* in one of those positions and *getting into* one of those positions!

Note how the *be* verbs are second-conjugation and how three of the four *getting-into* verbs form unusual aspect pairs. Bear in mind that they're often used with prepositions. Here, use в and на with the accusative where there's movement (the first and third columns) and the prepositional where there's none (the second). You *will* find the prepositional with the third column at least; it seems to give a nuance of your having been there a while or, perhaps, just that the prepositional phrase is connected less closely with the verb. So (the first line of each section is for the imperfective, the second for the perfective):

	put ('cause to be')	*be*	*move ('cause self to be')*
'lie'	класть, кладу́, кладёшь; кла́л	лежа́ть, лежу́, лежи́шь	ложи́ться, ложу́сь, ложи́шься
perf.	положи́ть, положу́, поло́жишь	—	лечь, ля́гу, ля́жешь; лёг(л-́)
'sit'	сажа́ть or сади́ть	сиде́ть, сижу́, сиди́шь	сади́ться, сажу́сь, сади́шься
perf.	посади́ть, посажу́, поса́дишь	—	сесть, ся́ду, ся́дешь; сёл
'stand'	ста́вить, ста́влю, ста́вишь	стоя́ть, стою́, стои́шь	станови́ться,-овлю́сь, -о́вишься
perf.	поста́вить	—	стать, ста́ну, ста́нешь; стал
'hang'	ве́шать	висе́ть, вишу́, виси́шь	ве́шаться
perf.	пове́сить, пове́шу, пове́сишь	—	пове́ситься

There's another verb for 'put': деть, де́ну, де́нешь, a perfective verb pairing with дева́ть, though the pair is somewhat odd (like most!). It has a sense of 'mislay', and when reflexive can mean 'to disappear' — intentional mislaying! If you really want to emphasize 'mislay', then задева́ть will do — guess what aspect! I hope you were wrong: it's perfective. Don't despair! There's a perfectly normal pair: заде́ть, задева́ть, and that has the sense of just touching, grazing someone or something, and, figuratively, offending someone. It can be impersonal: Его́ заде́ло за живо́е! 'He was cut to the quick!' Did I tell you that живо́й 'living' and *quick* are historically identical? One judges, after all, between the quick and the dead.

More important is that you use this verb for dressing, putting on, and taking off: одева́ть, оде́ть + acc. 'to dress someone' (use в + acc. for 'in something'), одева́ться, оде́ться 'to get dressed', надева́ть, наде́ть + acc. (+ на + acc.) 'to put something on' (add 'on your head' if need be), and раздева́ть, разде́ть + acc. 'to undress (someone)', раздева́ться, разде́ться 'to get undressed' — or just to take your coat off. So don't feel embarrassed (or get the wrong idea) if your host tells you: Разде́нься! / Разде́ньтесь! Do you see a link with the word for 'clothes': оде́жда? (You might be able to take away some of the ambiguity by using the imperative of снять 'to take off': Сними́те оде́жду/пальто́! 'Take off your clothes/overcoat!'

And while we're here: носи́ть is 'to wear', but in a habitual sense. If you want just to refer to what you're wearing at the moment, then you can use он/она́ оде́т/оде́та в + acc. '(s)he's dressed in...', or use a

preposition: я в + prep. or на мнé + nom.: он одét в прекрáсную
шýбу — он в прекрáсной шýбе — на нём прекрáсная шýба 'He's
wearing a beautiful fur coat'. Interestingly, one tends not to use одét with
я!

Now how about 'saying'? We'll leave говорйть alone here and take its
perfective, сказáть, скажý, скáжешь. Full marks if you think c- is a
prefix, in spite of the fact that you can use сказ- as a unit to create new
verbs, e.g. рассказáть, imperf. расскáзывать 'to tell, narrate'. So:

доказáть	to prove (+ acc.)
заказáть	to book, reserve, order (+ acc.)
наказáть	to punish (+ acc.)
оказáть	to render, offer (услýгу 'a service')
оказáться	to prove to be, turn out to be (+ instr.)
показáть	to show (+ acc.), point out (+ на + acc.)
приказáть	to command, order (+ dat. + inf.)
отказáть	to refuse (someone something = + dat. + в + prep.)
отказáться	to refuse (± inf.)
указáть	to point out (+ на + acc.), indicate (+ acc.)

All the imperfectives are on the pattern докáзывать and, as usual, entirely
regular. Just use the dative for X-ing something *to*.

Did you notice *-dic-* in *indicate*? That's related to 'saying': Latin *dico* 'I
say'. Think of French, Spanish, Italian. And there's a technical word in
English, from Ancient Greek, *deictic*, often used to talk about pronouns
that *point*, like *this* and *that*. The Greek original means 'to show'. Speaking,
showing, indicating, digits, it all comes together. And the *index finger*? —
указáтельный пáлец.

CHAPTER 11

1. The century marches on

Nikolai I began to see the need for modernization, and with it the abolition of serfdom отмéна крепостнóго прáва. The Crimean War Крьíмская войнá had laid bare the inefficiency of the system. The problem would be the difficulty of change and how to do it without undermining autocracy. Aleksandr II (1855-1881) took this on, whether from liberal conviction or from a concern to maintain power, or both. Whatever the case may be, great effort went into carrying out the reform, completed on 19th February, 1861. An immense operation, unavoidably imperfect and creating shock waves throughout the system, there was dissatisfaction both on the part of the peasants and on that of the landowners. This was a short period of liberalism, of reform, and yet not enough: the backwardness of rural life and slowness with which the reforms had any impact, the inability of the bureaucracy to keep up with headlong industrial development, the authorities' resistance to constitutional rule, the absence of a sizable middle class. Rank and old-fashioned prestige still held sway, but were more and more out of touch.

Unrest resided with the intelligentsia — an unusual one, an intelligentsia not based in a bourgeoisie. Russia was still catching up: it was now Russia's Age of Enlightenment, though эпóха Просвещéния *does* refer to the eighteenth century. Scrutiny of the agitators among the intelligentsia, the нарóдники Populists and нигилúсты Nihilists, reveals them to be somewhat ridiculous; but can anyone withstand close examination? 'We all fear the deep-directed gaze' Все мы боймся глубокоустремлённого взóра, in Gogol's words.

But they engaged in outrages, with assassinations of important figures and attempts on the tsar's life. And, in the end, his assassination in 1881 by members of the Нарóдная вóля 'People's Will' group, the very day when an increasingly reactionary but still pragmatic tsar had agreed to go ahead with a programme of progressive reform proposed by Михаúл Лóрис-Мéликов Loris-Melikov, meant political reaction: Aleksandr III (1881-1894) and, finally, the fatally weak Nikolai II (1894-1917). Russia was hurtling along in Gogol's troika, going no one knew where, along the дорóга, all-important to a Russian, over the empty steppe to the occasional halt in an idyllic village. Self-deception in Gogol's divine comedy, but apposite and reflected in *fin-de-siècle* literature.

Alongside all this, some of the best of world literature, which you simply *have* to read in Russian. Start with Turgenev, Ива́н Серге́евич Турге́нев (1818-1883): *Пе́рвая любо́вь First Love* (1860), *А́ся Asia* (1858; not the continent!), the play *Ме́сяц в дере́вне A Month in the Country* (1855) anticipating Chekhov, and, though, there's much else, his great novels, a chronicle of the age: *Ру́дин Rudin* (1856), *Дворя́нское гнездо́ A Nest of Gentlefolk* (1859), *Накану́не On the Eve* (1860), and the one which had most impact, due to its ambiguous presentation of the nihilist База́ров Bazarov, *Отцы́ и де́ти Fathers and Children* (1862).

So many other authors claim our attention: the great dramatist Алекса́ндр Никола́евич Остро́вский Ostrovskii (1823-1886) — his magnum opus *Гроза́ The Thunderstorm* is doubtless best-known as Janáček's *Kát'a Kabanová*; then Алексе́й Феофила́ктович Пи́семский, Pisemskii (1821-1881) and his novel *Ты́сяча душ A Thousand Souls* (1858), the poets Афана́сий Афана́сьевич Фет Fet (1820-1892) and Никола́й Алексе́евич Некра́сов Nekrasov (1821-1878). And a writer whose language, through its very inventiveness and his depiction of provincial, merchant, and peasant life, is difficult, but who musn't be neglected: Никола́й Семёнович Леско́в Leskov (1831-1895), one of whose novellas was taken as subject matter for what is Shostakovich's most arousing opera: *Леди Макбе́т Мце́нского уе́зда Lady Macbeth of Mtsensk* (1865).

We're leaving two writers out for the moment. For now an extract from Turgenev's *Пе́рвая любо́вь*, autobiographical and written when he was at the height of his powers.

На сле́дующее у́тро, когда́ я сошёл к ча́ю, ма́тушка побрани́ла меня́ — ме́ньше, одна́ко, чем я ожида́л — она́ заста́вила меня́ рассказа́ть, как я провёл накану́не ве́чер. Я отвеча́л ей в немно́гих слова́х, выпуска́я мно́гие подро́бности и стара́ясь прида́ть всему́ вид са́мый неви́нный.

— Всё-таки они́ лю́ди, не *comme il faut*, — заме́тила ма́тушка, — и тебе́ не́чего к ним таска́ться, вме́сто того́ чтоб гото́виться к экза́мену да занима́ться.

Так как я знал, что забо́ты ма́тушки о мои́х заня́тиях ограни́чатся э́тими немно́гими слова́ми, то я и не почёл ну́жным возража́ть ей; но по́сле ча́ю оте́ц взял меня́ под руку и, отпра́вившись вме́сте со мно́ю в сад, заста́вил рассказа́ть всё, что я ви́дел у Засе́киных.

Стра́нное влия́ние име́л на меня́ оте́ц — и стра́нные бы́ли на́ши отноше́ния. Он почти́ не занима́лся мои́м воспита́нием, но никогда́ не оскорбля́л меня́; он уважа́л мою́ свобо́ду — он да́же был, е́сли мо́жно так вы́разиться, ве́жлив со мно́ю ... то́лько он не допуска́л меня́ до себя́. Я люби́л его́, я любова́лся им, он каза́лся мне образцо́м мужчи́ны — и, Бо́же мой, как бы я стра́стно к нему́ привяза́лся, е́сли б я постоя́нно не чу́вствовал его́ отклоня́ющей руки́! Зато́, когда́ он хоте́л, он уме́л почти́ мгнове́нно, одни́м сло́вом, одни́м движе́нием возбуди́ть во мне́ неограни́ченное дове́рие к себе́. Душа́ моя́ раскрыва́лась — я болта́л с ним, как с разу́мным дру́гом, как с снисходи́тельным наста́вником ... пото́м он так же внеза́пно покида́л меня́ — и рука́ его́ опя́ть отклоня́ла меня́ — ла́сково и мя́гко, но отклоня́ла.

On the-following morning, when I had-gone-down to tea, mamma scolded me — less, however, than I had-expected — she made me [to]-tell how I had-spent the evening before [on the eve the evening]. I answered her in a-few words, leaving-out many details and trying to-attribute to-everything the-most innocent air.

'None-the-less they [are] people, not *comme il faut*,' remarked mamma, 'and there-is-no-reason for-you to-drag-yourself-off to them, instead of-the-fact that to-prepare-yourself for the-exam and to-study.'

As I knew that mamma's anxieties about my studies will-be-limited [indirect speech, Chapter 18] by-these few words, then I didn't even consider [it] necessary to-object to-her; but after tea father took me by the-arm and, having-set-off together with me into the-garden, made [me] to-recount everything that I had-seen at the-Zasekins.

Father had a-strange influence on me — and our relations were strange. He almost did not occupy-himself with-my upbringing, but [he] never offended me; he respected my freedom — he was even, if it-is-possible to-express-oneself so, polite with me ... only he did not admit me to him. I loved him, I admired him, he seemed to-me a-model of-a-man — and, my God, how passionately I would have become-attached to him, if [only] I did not constantly feel his holding-[me]-at-bay hand. And-yet, when he wanted, he knew-how, almost in-an-instant, with-one word, with-one movement to-arouse in me boundless confidence in him. My soul opened — I chatted with him as with a-sensible friend, as with a-condescending mentor ... then he just as suddenly abandoned me — and his hand again held-at-bay me — kindly and softly, but held-[me]-at-bay.

Some sort of commentary would certainly help with many of the texts I've been giving you, but I've decided the approach I've adopted is the ме́ньшее из двух зол 'lesser of two evils'. Many of the forms you meet are dealt with in this book, but only a thorough grammatical presentation would come anywhere near to clarifying the multitude of possibilities; I'll just slip things in here and there, and remember, learning a language is a journey without an end.

Among the verbal forms, you will come across those ending in -я or -a, and -в or -(в)шись — these are gerunds, literally meaning 'doing' and 'having done', or when negative 'without doing' and 'without having done', and are tackled in Chapter 16. You will have noticed a number of adjectives too, related to verbs, some in -щий(ся) and -(в)ший(ся) — these are the active participles, and others in -нный or -тый — these are the past passive participles; the meanings are respectively and roughly 'who/which is doing' and 'who/which was doing/has done' for the actives, and 'who/which has been done' for the passive — all but the last are reckoned to be bookish. There's more information in Chapters 13 and 17. Do dip in here and there — Chapter 12 will be helpful too.

2. The long and the short of it

Apart from the odd one or two, the adjectives we've met so far have been 'long'! They're the form you must use when the idea is 'who/which is X', i.e., a 'white house' is a 'house which is white' (this is called 'attributive') and 'the boy, tired and expectant' is 'the boy, who was tired and expectant' (this is called 'in apposition').

In the past there were also short adjectives, and they could be used in the same constructions. No longer. You can't use them in either of the constructions just mentioned, so that leaves 'the boy is tired'. This is called a predicative construction. Here there's no immediately obvious interpretation 'who is tired', and this is when the short adjective is a possibility. However, only in a number of admittedly useful adjectives is there a preference for, indeed an obligation to use, the short form — and remember, even then *only* when it's predicative. Note too that in this construction the only case available is what looks like the nominative.

There are fossilized forms of other cases than the nominative, e.g. снóва 'again, (anew)', от мáла до велúка 'everyone (from small to large)'. Most interesting, perhaps, and most alive, is the expression друг дрýга 'each other'. This has nothing to do with 'friends', but is the short form of другóй 'other'. It makes sense for the first to remain invariable, in the 'nominative' (it refers back to a part of the subject), and the second to be in whatever case is appropriate to the verb: мы вúдим друг дрýга 'we see each other', онú разговáривают друг с дрýгом 'they chat with each other'. So you have all the cases — but only the singular, and the masculine covers everything: in the preceding sentence it could be Tania and Masha chatting, or Vania and Igor, or a mixture. Any preposition comes in between the two, though you may see it before them both: прóтив друг дрýга 'against each other'.

Let's look at some adjectives which are quite often found short. Note that overall they're all qualitative adjectives, like 'big, small, beautiful, ready, interesting'. Sometimes they can have slightly different meanings when they're short from when they're long. Thus the short forms of хоро́ший 'good' and дурно́й 'bad', хоро́ш/хороша́ (собо́й) and дурён/дурна́ (собо́й) often mean 'handsome' and 'ugly' respectively (note how they tend to have the собо́й expansion). Others, from большо́й — ма́ленький 'big — small', высо́кий — ни́зкий 'high — low', широкий — у́зкий 'wide — narrow', дли́нный — коро́ткий 'long — short', and ста́рый — молодо́й 'old — young' are respectively вели́к — мал, высо́к — ни́зок, широ́к — у́зок, дли́нен — ко́роток, стар — мо́лод, can have the specialized sense '*too* X' and as such, once again, are often *expanded*, with a dative or для 'for' + genitive, e.g. 'too big *for me*'. And one might note живо́й 'lively' as against жив 'alive' (does one say 'an alive woman' in English? Makes you think), пра́вый 'right = just' as against пра́в 'right = correct', and злой 'evil, wicked' as against зол 'angry'.

So, an adjective, I am assured, *has* to be short when predicative *and* expanded, by an infinitive, a case form of a noun, or a preposition plus a noun. Long adjectives can be expanded too. Here's an example from a poem of 1917 by О́сип Мандельшта́м Mandel'shtam, a great believer in the essential power of Russian as a non-written language:

Одиссе́й возврати́лся, простра́нством и вре́менем по́лный.
'Odysseus returned, full of space and time.'

Particularly common examples are to be found in the following list (I leave out the common construction where an instrumental follows an adjective in the sense 'because of, through, as a result of, for', e.g. кни́жка интере́сна свое́й развя́зкой 'the book is interesting for its dénouement', она́ слаба́ здоро́вьем her health is weak (lit. "she is weak through her health")'). Some long forms are approximate, and placed in brackets.

Long	Short	Meaning	+ inf	+ case/+ prep
бе́дный	бе́ден, бедна́, бе́дно, бе́дны	'poor in'	—	+ instr.
благода́рный	благода́рен, -да́рна, -о, -ы	'grateful to/for'	—	+ dat. 'to', за + acc. 'for'
бли́зкий	бли́зок, -зка́, -зко, бли́зки	'close to, intimate with'	—	с + instr.
бога́тый	бога́т, бога́та, -о, -ы	'rich in'	—	+ instr.
больно́й	бо́лен, -льна́, -льно́, -льны́	'ill, sick with'	—	+ instr.
винова́тый	винова́т, -а, -о, -ы	'guilty of something, *vis-à-vis* someone'	—	в + prep. 'of', пе́ред + instr.

110

Long	Short	Meaning	+ Inf	+ case/+ prep
гото́вый	гото́в, -а, -о, -ы	'ready (for)'	✔	к + dat., на + acc.
(до́лжный 'due, proper')	до́лжен, -жна́, -жно́, -жны́	'owe to someone something', 'must, have a duty to'	— ✔	+ dat. + acc. —
досто́йный	досто́ин, досто́йна, -о, -ы	'worthy of'	—	+ gen.
за́нятый or arguably занято́й	за́нят, занята́, за́нято, за́няты	'busy'	—	'with' = + instr.
злой	зол, зла, зло, злы	'angry at/with'	—	на + acc.
знако́мый	знако́м, -а, -о, -ы	'acquainted with'	—	с + instr.
—	наме́рен, -а, -о, -ы	'intend'	✔	—
подо́бный	подо́бен, -бна, -бно, -бны	'like, similar to'	—	+ dat.
похо́жий	похо́ж, -а, -е, -и	'like, similar to'	—	на + acc.
по́лный	по́лон, полна́, по́лно, полны́	'full of'	—	+ gen. or + instr.
пре́данный	пре́дан, -а, -о, -ы	'devoted to'	—	+ dat.
равноду́шный	равноду́шен, -шна, -шно, -шны	'indifferent to'		к + dat.
ра́вный	ра́вен, -вна́, -вно́, -вны́	'equal to'	—	+ dat.
—	рад, ра́да, ра́до, ра́ды	'glad to/of'	✔	+ dat.
свобо́дный	свобо́ден, -дна, -дно, -дны	'free (to do something)'	✔	—
серди́тый	серди́т, -а, -о, -ы	'angry at/with, on account of'	—	на + acc. 'at someone', из-за + gen. 'because of something'
си́льный	си́лен/силён, сильна́, -о, -ы	'strong, "good" at (e.g. something academic)'	—	в + prep.

Long	Short	Meaning	+ inf	+ case/+ prep
слабый	слаб, слаба, слабо, слабы	'weak in/at (e.g. something academic)'	—	по + dat.
согласный	согласен, -сна, -сно, -сны	'agree with/to'	✔	с + instr. 'with', на + acc. 'to'
способный	способен, -бна, -бно, -бны	'good at/capable of'	✔	к + dat. 'at', на + acc. 'of'
уверенный	уверен, -а, -о, -ы	'sure of'	—	в + prep.

The variations for готов and способен are, respectively, 'ready because the work has been done', 'ready to accept the consequences', and 'capable because intelligent enough', 'capable of anything': Иван готов к этому заданию — Иван готов на всё 'Ivan is ready for this task — Ivan is ready for anything', Аня способна к языкам — Аня способна на всё 'Ania is good at languages — Ania is capable of anything'. They mean 'ready' and 'capable' when expanded by an infinitive. Do remember that short adjectives don't *have* to be expanded: Я готов 'I'm ready'.

Other adjectives which very often occur short include:

виден (-дна)	visible
женат (fixed stress)	married
здоров (fixed stress)	healthy, well
неправ (-а)	wrong
слышен (-шна)	audible
спокоен (-ойн-; fixed stress)	calm
счастлив (from счастливый)	happy
чреват (fixed stress) + instr.	fraught with

Most of these are straightforward. Worth bearing in mind among the others are виден and слышен. The subject can be what you can see or hear, but alternatively you can use the 'neuter' form with the accusative of what you can see: thus either Видна дача or Видно дачу 'I can see the dacha'. And if it's negative: Не видно дачи 'I can't see the dacha' — the negation triggers the genitive case. If the 'logical' subject, i.e. 'I, you, etc.', were made explicit, it would be conveyed in the dative case, e.g. Ивану не видно дачи 'Ivan can't see the dacha'. Just a few examples:

Мне нужна грамматика этого языка	'I need a grammar of this language'
Там видна лодка/Там видно лодку	'The boat can be seen there'

Тут слышна вода́/Тут слышно во́ду	'Water can be heard here'
Он здоро́в те́лом и душо́й	'He is healthy in body and soul'

Of course, lots more adjectives have this option, so we need some hints. Start with больно́й 'sick'. Both она́ больна́я and она́ больна́ mean 'she's sick', but there's a difference, resp. 'she's chronically sick' and 'she's sick (today)'. The long adjective implies something relative, potentially characteristic of a person: 'she's a sick person/one'. The short form can be provisional; as such, it's more absolute, and that lends it to use in exclamations and generalizations: 'she's sick'! What is perhaps most useful is to know is that, where there's a choice, you can practically always get away with the long form.

What of when you have 'was/will be/would be interesting', in other words, something other than the present tense of быть? Well, setting aside those adjectives that favour the short form, now you could have a three- (not two-) way choice: short form, long form nominative, long form instrumental. The simple answer is: long form instrumental. The long form nominative is quite common these days, but, overall, expect everything and if in doubt go for the long form instrumental.

Just one little thing: when you're using вы, and an adjective is involved, a short form must be in the *plural*, whether it's one person or more. If a long form is involved, choose the appropriate form: singular masculine, singular feminine, plural. This might make you think of the past tense. Thus 'you're strong' (overlooking nuances):

вы сильны́ =	вы сильный *or* вы сильная *or* вы сильные	

Exercise 1

1. Here I use adjectives which tend to occur in the short form when the circumstances are right. Choose the correct form:

1. Она́ была́ (за́нятый) весь день — 'She was busy all day.'
2. Она́, (по́лный) энтузиа́зма, рабо́тала — 'She, full of enthusiasm, worked.'
3. У (больно́й) же́нщины... — 'The sick woman has...'
4. Они́ все (согла́сен) на э́то — 'They all agree to this.'
5. Мы (скло́нный) оста́ться до́ма — 'We're inclined to stay at home.'
6. Мне (ну́жный) больша́я су́мка — 'I need a big bag.'
7. Вдали́ (ви́ден) о́зеро — 'In the distance one can see a lake.'
8. Мужчи́на (досто́йный) уваже́ния — 'The man is worthy of respect.'

3. Short adjectives in the flesh

Short adjectives deserve a short text. Here's an extract from Goncharov's piece of travel writing *Фрегáт «Паллáда»* *The Voyage of the Frigate Pallada* (1858). It's quite straightforward — enjoy reading it and use your dictionary to translate it (the more you suffer with a dictionary now, the less you will later). As usual, there's a lot more to it than short adjectives.

Вы мóжете упрекнýть меня, что, говоря обо всём, что я вúдел в Áнглии, я ничегó не сказáл о жéнщинах. Но говорúть о нúх повéрхностно — не хóчется, а наблюстú их глýбже и прúстальнее — нé было врéмени.

Я не успéл познакóмиться с семéйными домáми и потомý видáл жéнщин в церквáх, в магазúнах, в лóжах, в экипáжах, в вагóнах, на ýлицах. От этого могý сказáть тóлько — и то для тогó, чтоб избежáть предполагáемого упрёка, — что онú прекрáсны, стрóйны, с удивúтельным цвéтом лицá, несмотря на то, что едя́т мнóго мя́са, пря́ностей и пьют крéпкие вúна. Едвá ли в другóм нарóде рáзлито стóлько красоты́ в мáссе, как в Áнглии. Не судúте о красотé англичáн и англичáнок по этим ры́жим господáм и госпожáм, котóрые дезертúруют из Áнглии под úменем шкúперов, учителéй и гувернáнток, осóбенно гувернáнток: это обóрвыши; красúвой жéнщине нéзачем бежáть из Áнглии: красотá — капитáл. Англичáнки бóльшею чáстью высокú рóстом, стрóйны, но немнóго горды́ и спокóйны, — по словáм мнóгих, дáже холодны́. Цвет глаз и волóс до бесконéчности разнообрáзен: есть совершéнные брюнéтки, то есть с чёрными, как смоль, волосáми и глазáми, и в то же врéмя с необыкновéнною белизнóй и я́рким румя́нцем; потóм слéдуют каштáновые вóлосы, и всё-таки бéлое лицó, и, наконéц, те нéжные лúца — фарфóровой белизны́, с тóнкою прозрáчною кóжею, с лёгким рóзовым румя́нцем, окаймлённые льня́ными кýдрями, нéжные и хрýпкие создáния с лебедúною шéей. Нáдо сказáть, что и мужчúны достóйны этих лéди по красотé.

4. More numerals: is there no end, is there an infinity of them?

Well, we can add the following: двóе, трóе, чéтверо (you can go higher, but just seeing пят-, etc. might be enough!). They are often referred to as the 'collective' numerals and do have their own declensions (gen. двоúх, троúх, четверы́х and so on, like an adjective), but the normal cardinals are often used for the GDIP now. The somewhat dated declension fits in with the declension of óба, óбе 'both, the one and the other'. It also, as we learned, takes the genitive singular, while двóе, etc., take the genitive plural, and agree in the GDIP. And when can these collectives be used? First, with groups of males (двóе мужчи́н 'two men'), with children (трóе дете́й 'three children'), and with the young of animals (че́тверо медвежáт 'four bear cubs' — the young of animals often end in -ёнок or -онок in the singular, here медвежóнок, all of this replaced by -ята or -ата in the plural). Also with nouns indicating groups of people, e.g. лю́ди 'people', or an adjective being used as a noun (че́тверо люде́й 'four people', трóе бéдных 'three poor souls'), with personal pronouns (нас бы́ло трóе 'there were three of us'), with names referring to pairs (трóе рук 'three (pairs of) hands'), and with nouns found only in the plural (двóе су́ток 'two days'). The collectives are more likely in certain of these, but obligatory only with the nouns found only in the plural; here, in compound numerals (where they aren't used), you insert a qualifier such as шту́ка, пáра, e.g. двáдцать две пáры нóжниц 'twenty-two pairs of scissors' (нóжницы 'scissors'), or a permissible word with a similar meaning, e.g. день 'day' for су́тки 'day (period of 24 hours)'.

And how about 'how many?' and the like? Well, several words arise here; they all look like neuter singulars and are followed by the genitive (singular or plural, as appropriate), but in the GDIP have adjectival plural endings. And animacy should be borne in mind. It's possible to argue that the NA and GDIP are separate words, but that's a nicety. The words in question are: мнóго 'much, many', немнóго 'a little, a few' (the diminutive немнóжко is used just in that form), мáло 'little, few' (doesn't decline, but very useful, e.g. мáло где 'hardly anywhere', мáло кто 'few people'), достáточно 'enough' (decline it by turning it into an adjective agreeing with коли́чество 'quantity'), скóлько 'how much/many', нéсколько 'several', and стóлько 'so much, so many'. Here goes:

nom./acc.	скóлько	мнóго
gen.	скóльких	мнóгих
dat.	скóльким	мнóгим
instr.	скóлькими	мнóгими
prep.	скóльких	мнóгих

One finds (не)мнóгие too, perhaps equivalent to English '(not) many a...', used both agreeing with nouns and on its own. Even the singular occurs: мнóгое 'many a thing', во мнóгом 'in many respects'. And one also has нéкоторые 'certain, a few', close to, but more definite than, нéсколько.

Do recall that the important word челове́к 'man, person' (refers to both sexes — that's why I keep translating it as 'person') normally has as plural лю́ди, люде́й, люде́й, лю́дям, людьми́, лю́дях (note the odd instrumental, found in дéти - детьми́ 'children' too). After numerals which require a genitive plural, and after ско́лько and не́сколько, one has челове́к instead, unless the idea of 'people' is less crucial (i.e. if there's an adjective there as well, in which case люде́й can be used). There's one other noun with an odd genitive plural where numerals and similar terms are concerned, namely год (no, not Him, that's бог) 'year', with лет, lit. 'summers': пять лет 'five years' — you'll use this after all those numerals and other 'quantifiers'.

Exercise 2

Here are a few plural-only nouns, with their all-important genitives — without a singular you don't seem to have a gender, and gender can be helpful in working out the genitive.

брю́ки, брюк	'trousers'	де́ньги, де́нег	'money'
ша́хматы, ша́хмат	'chess'	трусы́, трусо́в	'underpants'
но́жницы, но́жниц	'scissors'	пла́вки, пла́вок	'swimming trunks'
сли́вки, сли́вок	'cream'	часы́, часо́в	'clock, watch'
очки́, очко́в	'spectacles'	кани́кулы, кани́кул	holidays'
вы́боры, вы́боров	'elections'	по́хороны, похоро́н	'funeral'
хло́поты, хлопо́т	'fuss, bother'	шо́рты, шорт	'shorts'
черни́ла, черни́л	'ink'	воро́та, воро́т	'gate, goal'
дрова́, дров	'firewood'	ро́ды, ро́дов	'childbirth'

Now slot in the correct form of the word in brackets (I use (не)мно́го as citation form for simplicity — some people might disagree):

1. Их бы́ло (два ог дво́е?).
2. Ско́лько у вас (брю́ки)?
3. У нас бы́ло сто́лько (хло́поты) с ним.
4. В (немно́го) города́х.
5. Из (ско́лько) музе́ев.
6. С кра́сными (черни́ла).
7. Во вре́мя (вы́боры).
8. В (сли́вки) пла́вала му́ха.
9. С (дрова́) сошла́ Ната́ша.
10. (Оди́н) пла́вки.
11. Тро́е (очки́).
12. Он вошёл без (трусы́).

Wordplay

It's all in the family: remembering

The basic word for 'to forget' is perfective забы́ть, which conjugates just like быть : забу́ду, etc., and забы́л (the stress stays fixed). The imperfective is забыва́ть, conjugated just like чита́ть.

How about remembering? The basic word is по́мнить, non-past по́мню, по́мнишь,... по́мнят. Nothing spectacular. Bearing in mind that по- is usually a prefix, we can imagine -мн- is basic, and that might well re**mind** us that **mind** contains both *m* and *n*. They're originally the same!

But why, if по́мнить is made up of a prefix on a simple verb, isn't it perfective? Well, that's history. At least it arguably doesn't have a perfective, which does hint at something special: it can just mean 'to have/keep something in mind', though I do find it fitting my idea of 'remember'. There is a perfective, вспо́мнить, and you can say that *that* has an imperfective вспомина́ть, and that that's the real pair. Note the -и-surfacing between the м and н; that tells you there was something like an *i* there all the time (remember *mind*) — it was a soft sign, which historically is a short *i*; the *i* we actually see in Russian was often a long *i*, so you can see that some aspect pairs are connected by having a short or a long vowel, which has become respectively nothing or a vowel: soft sign (or zero) — и, hard sign (= zero) — ы (do you recall назва́ть and называ́ть in Chapter 6?). There are lots of related verbs, e.g.

напо́мнить, imperf. напомина́ть	to remind someone (dat.) of something (acc. or о + prep.)
припо́мнить, imperf. припомина́ть	to recollect, recall (used with a dative of a person and an accusative of whatever it is, this can be used to promise revenge: я тебе́ э́то припо́мню! 'I'll get you for this!')
упомяну́ть (упомяну́, упомя́нешь,... упомя́нут), imperf. упомина́ть	to mention (+ acc. or о + prep.) (note the weird perfective)
запо́мнить, imperf. запомина́ть	to memorize

CHAPTER 12

1. Достоéвский Dostoevsky

Фёдор Михáйлович Достоéвский (1821-1881) — he may not have quite the same place in Russians' hearts as Pushkin, but if there was one reason for anyone in the world to read Russian literature, this writer would be it. Some of his works are a mess, but a most compelling mess, and at his best, as in *Брáтья Карамáзовы The Brothers Karamazov* (1879-1880; don't pronounce the *z* as *ts*!) he is up there with the very greatest writers and, given that he really touches the spirit of us all, can't but be there in much of the best of twentieth-century literature — do remember, the *best*, there isn't ever that much of it. And please don't imagine there's such a thing as 'progress' in literature — it was all there already in Aeschylus. Though one can appreciate what Dostoevsky meant when he said that we have all emerged 'from under Gogol's greatcoat'.

Dostoevsky was not so concerned with society, however firmly set many of his works might be in specific places and times — you can follow the steps of Раскóльников, protagonist of *Преступлéние и наказáние Crime and Punishment* (1866), around St Petersburg, or in the context of specific social problems: alcohol, prostitution. His focus might be the dilemma of man's social and psychological selves; but it's more than that, there are so many selves, so many voices, and ultimately his arena is the mind. Start, as he did, with *Бéдные лю́ди Poor Folk* (1846), arguably a 'humanization' of Gogol's *Шинéль The Greatcoat*, and of the period before his four great novels read at least *Запи́ски из подпóлья Notes from the Underground* (1864), which broaches so many of the issues central to Dostoevsky's work, implicitly targetting the worst, and most 'rationalist', Russian novel, Chernyshevskii's *Чтó дéлать? What is to be done?* (1863). If you manage to read *Запи́ски* and never ask yourself thereafter, as you approach someone head-on in the street, 'Will he move first?', then I recommend you stick with Chernyshevskii. And, though I won't name more than one of them, don't neglect Dostoevsky's less well-known works — several of them are the best of reads and fit in with particular themes in nineteenth-century Russian literature, e.g. *Селó Степáнчиково и егó обитáтели The Village of Stepanchikovo and its Inhabitants* (1859), a tale of the decay of a family, the pinnacle of which is Салтыкóв-Щедри́н Saltykov-Shchedrin's *Господá Головлёвы The Golovlëv Family* (1875-1880). And there is so much else.

Of his greatest novels I haven't mentioned *Идиóт The Idiot* (1868) and
Бéсы The Devils (1871-1872). The first is Dostoevsky's doomed portrayal
of the perfect man, transfixed by chaos. And for once we have an
exploration of the depths of the soul in two extraordinary female characters
— it's not just men. But for an extract let's come to his greatest work,
Брáтья Карамáзовы, a 'simple tale of parricide'. But the fact is that
everyone is guilty, and that what happens is permanently there in society
— or is it the human condition? The family, society, has burst asunder —
for Dostoevsky what is needed to bind everything together is faith, for him
that of Orthodox Christianity. I begin the extract at the very end of the
story told by the rationalist, intellectual brother Ivan, *Велúкий
инквизúтор The Grand Inquisitor*, to the brother embodying faith,
Alësha. As Alësha sees only too well, Ivan's portrayal of an earthly
paradise, a régime run by a benevolent despot, is undermined by Ivan's
language itself. The culmination, as often in *Брáтья Карамáзовы*, is in a
confrontation, here between the Inquisitor and his silent prisoner, who,
instead of condemning him, kisses him on the lips. We don't meet the
brother embodying emotion, Dmitrii, but he's mentioned; nor the
illegitimate brother, and parricide, Smerdiakov. The passage makes us
think about the name *Карамáзов*. You won't find it in an ordinary
dictionary; but it means 'swarthy; of dark complexion'. What you *will* find
is *черномáзый*, with the same meaning, which looks more like it. *Kara* is
Turkish for 'black'; *маз* is probably related to *мáзать*, an Indo-European
word in Russian meaning 'to smear' and doubtless related to *мáсло* 'butter'.
Perhaps we have here something of the breadth of the Russian nature,
giving it richness, chaos, and boundless freedom.

Плéнник ухóдит.
— А старúк?
— Поцелýй горúт на егó сéрдце, но старúк остаётся в
прéжней идéе.
— И ты вмéсте с ним, и ты? — гóрестно восклúкнул Алёша.
Ивáн засмеялся.
— Да ведь это же вздор, Алёша, ведь это тóлько бестолкóвая
поэма бестолкóвого студéнта, котóрый никогдá двух стихóв не
написáл. К чему ты в такóй серьёз берёшь? Уж не дýмаешь ли
ты, что я прямо поéду тепéрь тудá, к иезуúтам, чтобы стать в
сóнме людéй, поправляющих егó пóдвиг? О гóсподи, какóе мне
дéло! Я ведь тебé сказáл: мнé бы тóлько до тридцатú лет
дотянýть, а там — кýбок óб пол!
— А клéйкие листóчки, а дорогúе могúлы, а голубóе нéбо, а
любúмая жéнщина! Кáк же жúть-то бýдешь? — гóрестно
восклицáл Алёша. — С такúм áдом в грудú и в головé это

возмо́жно? Нет, и́менно ты е́дешь, что́бы к ним примкну́ть... а е́сли нет, то убьёшь себя́ сам, а не вы́держишь!

— Есть така́я си́ла, что всё вы́держит! — с холо́дною уже́ усме́шкой проговори́л Ива́н.

— Кака́я си́ла?

— Карама́зовская... си́ла ни́зости карама́зовской.

— Это потону́ть в развра́те, задави́ть ду́шу в растле́нии, да, да?

— Пожа́луй, и э́то... то́лько до тридцати́ лет, мо́жет быть, и избе́гну, а там...

— Ка́к же избе́гнешь? Чем избе́гнешь? Это невозмо́жно с твои́ми мы́слями.

— Опя́ть-таки по-карама́зовски.

— Это чтобы «всё позво́лено»? Всё позво́лено, та́к ли, та́к ли?

Ива́н нахму́рился и вдруг ка́к-то стра́нно побледне́л.

— А, э́то ты подхвати́л вчера́шнее словцо́, кото́рым так оби́делся Миу́сов... и что так наи́вно вы́скочил и переговори́л брат Дми́трий? — кри́во усмехну́лся он. — Да, пожа́луй: «всё позво́лено», е́сли уж сло́во произнесено́. Не отрека́юсь. Да и реда́кция Ми́тенькина не дурна́.

Алёша мо́лча гляде́л на него́.

— Я, брат, уезжа́я, ду́мал, что име́ю на всём све́те хоть тебя́, — с неожи́данным чу́вством проговори́л вдруг Ива́н, — а тепе́рь ви́жу, что и в твоём се́рдце мне нет ме́ста, мой ми́лый отше́льник. От фо́рмулы «всё позво́лено» я не отреку́сь, ну и что́ же, за э́то ты от меня́ отречёшься, да, да?

Алёша встал, подошёл к нему́ и мо́лча ти́хо поцелова́л его́ в гу́бы.

—Литерату́рное воровство́! — вскрича́л Ива́н, переходя́ вдруг в како́й-то восто́рг, — э́то ты укра́л из мое́й поэ́мы! Спаси́бо, одна́ко. Встава́й, Алёша, идём, пора́ и мне и тебе́.

Они́ вы́шли, но останови́лись у крыльца́ тракти́ра.

— Вот что́, Алёша, — проговори́л Ива́н твёрдым го́лосом, — е́сли в са́мом де́ле хва́тит меня́ на кле́йкие листо́чки, то люби́ть их бу́ду, лишь тебя́ вспомина́я.

The-prisoner departs.
'And the-old-man?'
'The-kiss burns on his heart, but the-old-man remains in the-former idea.'
'And you together with him, you?' Alësha exclaimed sorrowfully. Ivan laughed.
'But, you-know, this [is] nonsense, Alësha, you-know this [is] only the-senseless poem of-a-senseless student, who never wrote two lines of-poetry. For what [purpose] do you take [it] so seriously? Do you not think that I now will-go

straight there, to the-Jesuits, in-order to-take-my-place in the-congregation of-people correcting his achievement? O O-Lord, what matter [is it] to me! You-know I have-told you: for-me would-be only to-drag-out [my life] till thirty years, and there — [to smash] the-cup against the-floor!'

'But the-sticky little-leaves, and the-dear graves, and the-blue sky, and the-beloved woman! How will-you live?' sorrowfully exclaimed Alësha. 'With such-a hell in [your] breast and in [your] heart [is] this possible? No, you're going precisely in-order to-join [to] them... and if not, then [you] yourself will-kill yourself, and [you] won't endure [it].'

'There-is such-a force, which will-endure everything!' uttered Ivan now with a-cold grin.

'What force?'

'The-Karamazov [force]... the-force of-Karamazov baseness.'

'That-is to-drown in debauchery, to-stifle [your] soul in corruption, yes, yes?'

'Perhaps, and that... only to thirty years, perhaps I'll escape, and then...'

'How will-[you]-escape? By-what-means will-[you]-escape? That's impossible with your thoughts.'

'Again in-the-Karamazov-way.'

'[Is] that that 'Everything is-permitted'? Everything is-permitted, like that, like that?' Ivan scowled and suddenly somehow strangely went-pale.

'Ah, [that's] you've picked-up yesterday's little-phrase, at which Mïusov so was-offended... and that brother Dmitrii so naively jumped-out-at and said-again?' he wryly grinned. 'Yes, perhaps: 'Everything is-permitted', if the-phrase [lit. word] already has-been-pronounced. I don't take-it-back. And Mitia's version isn't bad either.'

Alësha silently looked at him.

'I, brother, going-away, thought that [I] have [indirect speech — see Chapter 18] in the-whole world at-least you,' Ivan uttered with unexpected feeling. 'But now [I] see that also in your heart there-isn't a-place for-me, my dear anchorite. I shall not take-back the-formula "Everything is-permitted"; so then, for this you will-repudiate me, yes, yes?'

Alësha stood-up, went-up to him and silently, softly kissed him into the-lips.

'Literary theft!' Ivan shouted, suddenly moving-over into some-sort-of rapture. 'You stole that from my poem! But thank-you. Do-get-up, Alësha, let's-go, it's-time for-you and for-me.'

They went-out, but stopped by the-porch of-the-inn.

'Look here, Alësha,' uttered Ivan in-a-firm voice. 'If really there's-enough [time] for-me for the-sticky little-leaves, then I-shall love them, only remembering you.'

Now, that's difficult, and I've stuck to a desire to give you a translation-gloss. I couldn't pretend to do a good translation. Note the use of little particles here and there. Very often they come second in a clause, or are attached to a word, and have a sense of 'but, however', or may be emphatic. Very like Ancient Greek. And there's the rather freer one, ведь, which means 'after all; you know'. It's difficult sometimes to translate non-past forms of the verbs 'according to the rules', i.e. present for the imperfective and future for the perfective — this isn't the first time it's happened, and it just indicates how there is more to it than our English tenses, useful though they are as an approximation. And no word-list: that's what the rough translation is for. Be serious and use a dictionary.

2. If only there were no subjunctive!

The Russian conditional is the past tense accompanied by the particle бы, and this combination is used in some of the circumstances where French or Spanish would have a subjunctive.

So the Russian conditional looks like this: я хотéл(а) бы 'I would like...', мы вы́брали бы... 'we would choose...' The safe place to put the бы (which is never stressed and may sometimes be found as б) is straight after the verb. But you can put it wherever you like (but not first, and not far from the beginning of the sentence), provided you realize that what comes in front of it is emphasized: Пошлá бы я домóй! 'Oh that I'd like to go/have gone home', Онá взялá бы мою́ жизнь 'she would have taken my life' — Онá бы взялá мою́ жизнь 'it is she who would have taken my life' — Мою́ бы жизнь онá взялá 'it's *my* life she would have taken' (and so on!). It can also soften a suggestion, introduce a tentative note: я сказáла бы, что ты непрáв 'I'd say you were wrong', or make an appearance in '-ever' ('concessive') sentences: Гдé бы онá ни жилá, онá постоя́нно звони́т мне 'Wherever she lives, she's constantly phoning me' (note ни here — see Chapters 16 and 19). A good way of saying you'd better be off is simply something like Ну, я пошёл! — it sounds like you're wishing you'd already gone. And why not! So Пошли́! or Поéхали! can mean 'Let's go!'

It can also be used with nouns, adverbs, impersonals like ну́жно, and infinitives, providing a sort of impersonal conditional: Конéц бы нáшим забóтам! 'Would there be an end to our cares!', Хорошó бы побывáть в Крыму́! 'How good it would be to spend time in the Crimea!, Ну́жно бы сбéгать за хлéбом! 'I should pop out for some bread!' (or just Сбéгать бы за хлéбом!, which might mean 'I wish I could pop out for some bread!'), and Пойти́ бы домóй! 'Oh to go home!' *or* 'I wish I could go home!' If you express a 'subject' with an infinitive, use the dative.

Though the flexibility of Russian is awesome, that sense of freedom is also wonderful — you begin to wonder whether Dostoevsky's feeling of how important, and how terrible, and how terribly important, man's freedom just was had something to do with the language! You can be adventurous, mess around. But you've *got* to learn the forms — there's a discipline fundamental to all freedoms.

First of all, let's get the conditional as a pretend subjunctive out of the way. Well, if you want/require/command/tell someone to do something or if it's necessary that someone do (look, English has one too!) something, you use it. And how? Well, you use что to join two clauses in он говори́т, что они́ прие́хали 'he says that they've arrived', and you use что́бы to join two clauses in those sentences requiring the subjunctive (because the subjects are different, otherwise you'd just use the infinitive). Whatever the time referred to, the verb goes into the past-tense form, because бы is there in the clause:

она́ хо́чет / жела́ет / выража́ет жела́ние / предлага́ет / сове́тует / про́сит / тре́бует / прика́зывает, что́бы вы *пришли́* на ве́чер
'she wants / desires / expresses a desire / suggests / advises / requests / demands / orders you to come to the party'.

Contrast these with:

она́ хо́чет / жела́ет / выража́ет жела́ние / предлага́ет / сове́тует / про́сит / тре́бует / прика́зывает *прийти́* на ве́чер
'she wants / desires / expresses a desire / proposes / advises / requests / demands / orders to come to the party'

Some of these might need some massaging in English. And some verbs allow you to do it по-англи́йски 'in the English way':

она́ предлага́ет вам / сове́тует вам / про́сит вас / прика́зывает вам *прийти́* на ве́чер
'she proposes to you/advises you/asks you/orders you *to come* to the party'.

And you can use the subjunctive after ну́жно 'it is necessary', на́до 'it is necessary, must', обяза́тельно 'it is necessary', and жела́тельно 'it is desirable'. Also, if you have a feeling that there's a sense of 'in order that, so that' in the sentence, you can use что́бы; thus 'I take care that / struggle so that they might be left in peace' я забо́чусь / борю́сь, что́бы их оста́вили в поко́е (from забо́титься, боро́ться). And then there are verbs or expressions of communication, e.g. сказа́ть 'to tell', написа́ть 'to write', ва́жно 'it's important', заинтересо́ван 'interested' (see the example for the nuance here) — you can imagine these in sentences where one states both a fact and a desire, a stipulation:

> Мне сказа́ли, что́бы я согласи́лся.
> 'They told me to agree.'
>
> Мы заинтересо́ваны в том, что́бы вы там бы́ли.
> 'It's of interest to us that you should be there.'

123

If you used что, here's what they would mean (note what happens to the second):

Мне сказáли, что я согласúлся.	'They told me that I had agreed.'
Интерéсно, что вы там бы́ли.	'It's interesting that you were there.'
Интерéсно, что вы там бу́дете.	'It's interesting that you will be there.'

And if there any suggestions of uncertainty, of doubt, something which can go along with generalizations, you are likely to use чтобы — you have to use your intuition here:

Чтóбы онá согласúлась? Не ду́маю.	'I can't imagine she's agreed.'
Ей нрáвится, чтобы там бы́ло тúхо.	'She likes it being calm there.'

Я рéдко слы́шал, чтобы так хорошó пéли.
'I've rarely heard such good singing.'

And, last, the verb боя́ться 'to fear' — note the negative:

Онá бойтся, чтобы он/как бы он не пришёл.	'she's afraid he might come.'
Онá бойтся, что он придёт.	'she's afraid he'll come.'
Онá бойтся, что он не придёт.	she's afraid he won't come.'

3. If only...

And now let's look at 'if', or conditional, sentences, by which I mean sentences with the pattern 'If I..., [then] I/you, etc...' The two bits have the splendid names *protasis* (the 'antecedent') and *apodosis* (the 'consequent'). Now, if in the English apodosis one has 'would', then in Russian one has the conditional in *both* halves. These tend to be rather unreal conditions, of the sort 'If I were to do this, he would do that'. If, however, in the English apodosis one has the future tense (or something which might have a vague future implication, e.g. the imperative), then in Russian one has the future in both halves (but *keep* an imperative). These tend to be more real conditions: 'If he comes, I'll give him a piece of my mind' — 'Give him a piece of your mind, if he comes'. And if neither of these situations arises, one has the same in Russian as in English.

The Russian word for 'if' is éсли , and it may be balanced in the apodosis by то — Russian likes balancing its clauses. In unreal conditions the бы usually comes immediately after éсли. So:

> Éсли бы вы пришли завтра, мы посмотрели бы передачу.
> 'If you came tomorrow, we'd watch the programme.'
>
> Éсли бы он пришёл вовремя, мы бы успели в театр.
> 'If he arrived in time, we would manage to get to the theatre.'
>
> Éсли вы придёте завтра, мы посмотрим передачу.
> 'If you come tomorrow, we'll watch the programme.'
>
> Éсли я приходила рано, то они всегда ужинали со мной.
> 'If I came early, they would always have supper with me.'
>
> Оттащи его в сторону, если ты сможешь. (В. Ерофеев)
> 'Drag him off to the side, if you can.'
>
> Бери, не пожалеете. '[If you] take it, you won't be sorry.'

And then there's the 'if' which is synonymous with 'whether' — see Chapter 18.

Exercise 1

Slot the appropriate forms into the following sentences:

1. Она хочет (, / чтобы / я / вернуться 'to come back') домой) — 'She wants me to come back home.'
2. Веня, (пойти / бы / ты / поиграть в теннис) — 'Venia [Венедикт], you ought to go and play a bit of tennis.'
3. Мы советуем (вы / взяться за работу) — 'We advise you to get down to work.'
4. Они предлагают (, / чтобы / мы / купить дневник) — 'They suggested we bought a diary.'
5. Ей хочется (, / чтобы / Ваня / попросить / у неё руки) — 'She feels a desire for Vania to ask for her hand.'

Now a bit harder:

6. I'm afraid he might be against the proposal (быть против (+ gen.) 'to be against', предложение 'proposal'; быть за (+ acc.) 'to be for').
7. I want them to give me their books.
8. I do this, so that they can help me.
9. I insist you see that film. (посмотреть фильм)
10. Oh, I'd love to have a little sleep! (Just think of the possibilities: something to eat, to have a drink, read *Das Kapital*.)

LEARN RUSSIAN

4. A bit of something in the cherry orchard

Occasionally, in the genitive and prepositional of masculine nouns ending in a hard or soft consonant, you'll find the endings -у, -ю instead of the expected -а/-я and -е respectively. These are usually rather small nouns, one or at most two syllables in the nominative.

Regarding the genitive, these endings are nowadays found in nouns denoting things you can't usually count without adapting the meaning, i.e. you can't say 'two breads' unless you mean two 'sorts' of bread. These are words you can put 'some' or 'any' in front of, e.g. 'some bread', 'some tea', etc. Of course, such nouns aren't only masculine ones ending in a consonant — what of вода 'water'! Well, you can use the genitive of any 'non-count', 'mass' noun to convey 'some', 'a bit of': он попил воды 'he had a little drink of water'. It's just that in a few masculine consonant-final nouns you have this special ending. Examples of words which have this are табак 'tobacco' (табаку), мёд 'honey' (мёду), народ 'people' (народу), сахар 'sugar' (сахару), сок 'juice' (соку), чай 'tea' (чаю, often in the diminutive: чайку from чаёк; also кофейку from the diminutive of the indeclinable masculine кофе 'coffee'), шум 'noise' (шуму). You find them after appropriate verbs, e.g. дать 'to give' and взять 'to take', after words like много 'much', немного 'a little', and нет 'there isn't any...', and after nouns such as фунт 'a pound', кило 'a kilo', чашка 'a cup', стакан 'a glass', банка 'a jar', and кусок 'a piece'. This is restricted to quantity, i.e. not after a word such as цена 'price' or when the non-count noun is qualified by an adjective, e.g. крепкого чая 'some strong tea'. *Do* use them, but bear in mind they tend in modern Russian to be restricted to set phrases, e.g. Мне *до зарезу* нужны деньги 'I *really* need the money', Мы говорили *с глазу на глаз* 'We were having a tête-à-tête', она *сбила меня с толку* 'She muddled me', Нет о нём *ни слуху ни духу* 'Not a word's been heard from him'.

And what about the prepositional! Well, just as that special genitive is sometimes called the 'partitive', so this special prepositional is sometimes called the 'locative', and it's so called because it can only be used when there is a reference to location, almost always place, but in a few instances time. The difference here is that you *have* to use it. The ending is always stressed and only to be found after в and на. Here are a few:

ад 'hell'	в аду 'in hell'
бок 'side (of the body)'	на боку 'on his side'
бред 'delirium'	в бреду 'in delirium'
век 'century; age'	на нашем веку 'in our lifetime'
верх 'top'	на верху 'on the top (of)'
год 'year'	в прошлом году 'last year'
край 'edge'	на краю 'on the edge'

126

круг 'circle'	в кругу́ друзе́й 'amongst friends'
лёд 'ice'	на льду́ 'on the ice'
лес 'forest'	в лесу́ 'in the forest'
мост 'bridge'	на мосту́ 'on the bridge'
рай 'paradise'	в раю́ 'in paradise'
ряд 'row'	в э́том ряду́ 'in this row'
сад 'garden'	в саду́ 'in the garden'
снег 'snow'	в снегу́ 'in the snow'
цвет 'blossom'	в цвету́ 'in blossom'
шкаф 'cupboard'	в шкафу́ 'in the cupboard'
бе́рег 'bank, shore'	на берегу́ 'on the shore'

Generally these locatives have concrete senses — where they don't, they tend to be set phrases, e.g. име́ть в виду́ 'to have in mind, think', or figurative, e.g. он зна́ет толк в ле́се 'He knows a lot about forestry', в «Вишнёвом са́де» Че́хова 'In Chekhov's *The Cherry Orchard*'.

5. Getting back at yourselves and each other

Over the last few chapters we've encountered the personal pronoun себя́, the reciprocal pronoun друг дру́га, and the odd verb with the particle -ся or -сь attached to the endings. It's the last which characterizes what are usually considered the reflexive verbs of Russian. The particle is what's left of an unstressed form or forms of the pronoun себя́, and себя́ is sometimes actually used, e.g. он лиша́ет себя́ возмо́жности игра́ть гла́вную роль в пье́се 'he deprives himself of the opportunity to play the main part in the play' (лиша́ться + gen. means 'to lose, be deprived of'), or unavoidable when a preposition is involved, e.g. он смо́трит на себя́ в зе́ркало 'he looks at himself in the mirror'.

In its form -ся the particle is added to tense and imperative forms ending in a consonant and to all participial forms (see Chapter 13); in its form -сь the particle is added to all tense and imperative forms ending in a vowel — remember that й is a consonant.

The verbs thus obtained express varying degrees of reflexivity, from мы́ться, мо́юсь, мо́ешься,... 'to wash *oneself*' to здоро́ваться, здоро́ваюсь, здоро́ваешься,... 'to greet *each other*' to находи́ться 'to be situated, find itself', боя́ться + gen. 'to be afraid (of)', смея́ться 'to laugh', улыба́ться 'to smile', открыва́ться 'to open (intr.)', закрыва́ться 'to shut (intr.)', начина́ться 'to begin (intr.)', and конча́ться 'to end (intr.)', where there seems to be little reflexivity. A passive might be лиша́ться 'to lose, be deprived of (+ gen.)', mentioned above. Imperfective reflexive verbs are also an important way of conveying the imperfective passive: Сло́во пи́шется с большо́й бу́квы 'The word is written with a capital letter', Пото́м пи́шется письмо́ и отправля́ется клие́нту 'Then the letter is written and sent to the client'. For the perfective passive see Chapter 17.

6. Unreservedly adverbially

Many adverbs can be formed from adjectives (and also from participles), and their form coincides with the neuter form of the short adjective: хорошо́ 'well', пло́хо 'badly', ло́вко 'deftly', кра́йне 'extremely' (from кра́йний), и́скренно/и́скренне 'sincerely' (from и́скренний), взволно́ванно 'excitedly', одобря́юще 'approvingly', ра́но 'early' (from ра́нний), по́здно (from по́здний).

Different, but very important, are adverbs formed from adjectives in -ский and -цкий ; these have the endings -ски and -цки, thus траги́чески 'tragically', логи́чески 'logically', дура́цки 'foolishly'. They are particularly common preceded by по-, to be found in menus: по-ки́евски 'à la Kiev' (or just 'Kiev'), or to refer to speaking a language: они́ бесе́довали по-англи́йски 'they were chatting in English'. One resists lists, but why not work out for yourselves what languages or cuisines, or just à las, the following refer to:

по-венге́рски	по-по́льски	по-испа́нски	по-болга́рски
по-францу́зски	по-неме́цки	по-голла́ндски	по-шве́дски
по-норве́жски	по-фи́нски	по-украи́нски	по-че́шски

7. Filling the gaps: a few more 'pronouns'

	весь 'all (the)'				сам 'self'			
	masc.	*neut.*	*fem.*	*pl.*	*masc.*	*neut.*	*fem.*	*pl.*
nom.	весь	всё	вся	все	сам	само́	сама́	са́ми
acc.	весь	всё	всю	все	сам	само́	саму́	са́ми
gen.	всего́		всей	всех	самого́		само́й	сами́х
dat.	всему́		всей	всем	самому́		само́й	сами́м
instr.	всем		всей	все́ми	сами́м		само́й	сами́ми
prep.	всём		всей	всех	само́м		само́й	сами́х

Весь agrees with the noun it qualifies and usually means 'all *the*, the whole'. Indefinite, though it doesn't have to be, is це́лый 'entire, whole'. 'Each, every' is ка́ждый. And there is вся́кий , which is slightly less definite, namely 'any sort of, every manner of'. Useful expressions are во вся́ком слу́чае 'in any case, at any rate' and на вся́кий слу́чай 'just in case'. More indefinite is любо́й 'any': любо́й цено́й 'at any price' (more in Chapter 17). Regarding весь, note the difference between всё and все, resp. 'everything' and 'everyone'. Всё is *one* word where the two dots are

128

often actually written, though they don't need to be. It also means 'all the time', 'still' (often as всё ещё); and note всего 'in all, altogether'.

Сам is an emphatic pronoun. It has a neuter form, e.g. as in само собой разумеется 'it goes without saying', but most often qualifies animates, *following* personal pronouns and *preceding* nouns (this isn't a rule!), e.g. она сама 'she herself', сам учитель 'the teacher himself'. There is, by the way, a wonderful alternative accusative singular feminine, самоё (doesn't it look a bit like её?), something just to keep in the back of your mind. Similar is the adjective самый, which might more often be used with inanimates, which it precedes: самый факт 'the very fact' (this type is actually rather rare and best learnt with particular nouns). If you put it in front of an adjective, it provides the superlative (see Chapter 18), so if you want to avoid that you must use сам.

You may be tempted to think it means 'same'. Well, that *can* come into it — тот же самый: В ту же самую минуту 'At that same moment'. Compare В ту самую минуту 'At that very moment'. Simplest is to have тот же, without самый, for 'same'. An alternative is to use один, as in Она живёт в одном доме со мной 'She lives in the same house as I'. You can do this with тот же too: Она живёт в том же доме, что я.

CHAPTER 13

1. Толстóй Tolstoy

After Dostoevsky, Tolstoy. Different as he may be, Лев Николáевич Толстóй (1828-1910; apparently Tolstoy preferred Лёв) is no less great than Dostoevsky. That Russia should have produced two such writers in the mid to late nineteenth century, and with one, Chekhov, still to come, is astonishing, and no doubt connected with the carving out, within a stifling and restless national atmosphere, of a sense of self, of identity, through fiction. Whatever one thinks of the structure of Войнá и мир War and Peace (1865-1869) — just how many novels are there in there? — it's the work of a master craftsman, a work of universal appeal shaped by Tolstoy's wide reading in the classics of literature and philosophy. Like so much of his work, it is a revelation of his self, the aristocrat, the proud and passionate individual. Many a Russian is critical of his Russian — it wasn't quite a foreign language for him, steeped though he may have been in French; perhaps that helps it read so comparatively easily.

So many other works repay reading: from the early years at least Дéтство, Óтрочество, Ю́ность Childhood, Boyhood, Youth (1852-1857), Семéйное счáстье Family Happiness (1859), not least for its study of a woman's psychology, and Казáки The Cossacks (1863) (the usual stress is казакú). And from the late seventies: Úсповедь My Confession (early 1880s), where his mid-life crisis is related, Смерть Ивáна Ильичá The Death of Ivan Il'ich (1886), a wonderful study of society hypocrisy and death, Крéйцерова сонáта The Kreutzer Sonata (1890), an extraordinarily open study of the psychology of sexuality, his powerful, dark tragedy Власть тьмы The Power of Darkness (1888), and Воскресéние Resurrection (1899).

And we've left out Áнна Карéнина Anna Karenina (1875-1877), among the best nineteenth-century studies of passion. A product of a more troubled period in his life: misogyny, existential doubt. Speculation as to why Anna's life works out that way will never cease — I certainly get irritated with her (and with her lover Vronskii), but basically it is the stuff of life and shows how involved Tolstoy gets us. And the other story, that of Levin and his spiritual quest, was in the ascendant in Tolstoy. What it boils down to, within a framework of inimitable craftsmanship and observation, is stated plainly in the first sentence.

CHAPTER 13

Все счастли́вые се́мьи похо́жи друг на дру́га, ка́ждая несчастли́вая семья́ несчастли́ва по-сво́ему. Всё смеша́лось в до́ме Обло́нских. Жена́ узна́ла, что муж был в связи́ с бы́вшею в их до́ме францу́женкою-гуверна́нткой, и объяви́ла му́жу, что не мо́жет жить с ни́м в одно́м до́ме. Положе́ние э́то продолжа́лось уже́ тре́тий день и мучи́тельно чу́вствовалось и сами́ми супру́гами, и все́ми чле́нами семьи́, и домоча́дцами. Все чле́ны семьи́ и домоча́дцы чу́вствовали, что нет смы́сла в их сожи́тельстве и что на ка́ждом постоя́лом дворе́ случа́йно соше́дшиеся лю́ди бо́лее свя́заны ме́жду собо́й, чем они́, чле́ны семьи́ Обло́нских. Жена́ не выходи́ла из свои́х ко́мнат, му́жа тре́тий день не́ было до́ма. Де́ти бе́гали по всему́ до́му, как поте́рянные: англича́нка поссо́рилась с эконо́мкой и написа́ла запи́ску прия́тельнице, прося́ прииска́ть ей но́вое ме́сто; по́вар ушёл ещё вчера́ со двора́, во вре́мя обе́да; чёрная куха́рка и ку́чер проси́ли расчёта.

На тре́тий день по́сле ссо́ры князь Степа́н Арка́дьич Обло́нский — Сти́ва, как его́ зва́ли в све́те, — в обы́чный час, то есть в во́семь часо́в утра́, проснýлся не в спа́льне жены́, а в своём кабине́те, на сафья́нном дива́не. Он поверну́л своё по́лное, вы́холенное те́ло на пружи́нах дива́на, ка́к бы жела́я опя́ть засну́ть надо́лго, с друго́й стороны́ кре́пко обня́л поду́шку и прижа́лся к ней щеко́й; но вдруг вскочи́л, сел на дива́н и откры́л глаза́.

All happy families [are] similar to each other, every unhappy family [is] unhappy in-its-own-way. Everything was-mixed-up in-the-house of-the-Oblonskiis. The-wife had-found-out that the-husband was [had been?] in a-relationship with-the-former [who-had-been] in their house Frenchwoman-governess, and had-declared to-the-husband that [she] cannot live with him in one house. This situation was-continuing already the-third day and was-felt painfully by-the-spouses themselves and by-all the-members of-the-family, and by-the-house-servants. All-the members of-the-family and house-servants felt that there-is-no sense in their living-together and that at any staging inn by-chance come-together people are more connected between themselves than they, the-members-of-the-family of-the-Oblonskiis. The-wife didn't come-out of her rooms, the-husband already a-third day wasn't at-home. The-children were-running-about the-whole house, like lost people: the-Englishwoman had-fallen-out with the-housekeeper and written a-note to-a-woman-friend, asking to-find for-her a-new position; the-cook had-left as-recently-as yesterday from the-'household' during lunch; the-unskilled-[lit. 'black']-cook and the-coachman had-asked-for the-account ['given in their notice'].

On-the-third day after the-falling-out Prince Stepan Arkad'ich Oblonskii — Stiva, as him [people] called in society [lit. 'the world'], — at-the-usual hour, that is at eight o'clock in-the-morning, awoke not in the-bedroom of-[his]-wife, but in his study, on the-morocco-leather couch. He turned his stout, pampered body on the-springs of-the-couch, as it-were wishing again to-fall-asleep for-a-long-time, on the-other side firmly embraced the-pillow and pressed-himself to-it with-[his]-cheek; but suddenly jumped-up, sat on the couch and opened [his]-eyes.

2. The howmanieth chapter?

Numerals again: it'll be enough in this book to call a halt with the 'ordinals': first, second, third, millionth. These are nothing but good news, as they're adjectives in form. And they behave just like English ones, in that '123rd' in Russian is exactly that: 'one hundred + twenty + *third*' (no *and*): сто двáдцать трéтий. The only thing that changes is the ordinal.

Here's a list, and you'll get plenty of practice when telling the time and saying in which year things happened! So:

1st	пéрвый	50th	пятидесятый
2nd	вторóй	60th	шестидесятый
3rd	трéтий	70th	семидесятый
4th	четвёртый	80th	восьмидесятый
5th	пятый	90th	девянóстый
6th	шестóй	100th	сóтый
7th	седьмóй	200th	двухсóтый
8th	восьмóй	300th	трёхсóтый
9th	девятый	400th	четырёхсóтый
10th	десятый	500th	пятисóтый
11th	одиннадцатый	600th	шестисóтый
12th	двенáдцатый	700th	семисóтый
13th	тринáдцатый	800th	восьмисóтый
20th	двадцáтый	900th	девятисóтый
21st...	двáдцать пéрвый...	1000th	тысячный
40th	сороковóй	1000000th	миллиóнный

One might add послéдний 'last (of all)' and предпослéдний 'last-but-one' (compare прóшлый 'last (before now)' and its counterpart позапрóшлый).

Ordinals suggest a text, so here's Даниил Хармс Kharms's *Случай Incidence*, *Вывáливающиеся стару́хи The Plummeting Old Women*, to choose the -*ing* word in Neil Cornwell's translation:

Однá стару́ха от чрезмéрного любопы́тства вы́валилась из окнá, упáла и разби́лась.

Из окнá вы́сунулась другáя стару́ха и стáла смотрéть вниз на разби́вшуюся, но от чрезмéрного любопы́тства тóже вы́валилась из окнá, упáла и разби́лась.

Потóм, из окнá вы́валилась трéтья стару́ха, потóм четвёртая, потóм пя́тая.

132

Когда́ вы́валилась шеста́я стару́ха, мне надое́ло смотре́ть на них, и я пошёл на Ма́льцевский ры́нок, где, говоря́т, одному́ слепо́му подари́ли вя́заную шаль.

Here's a list of words for once.

стару́ха, -и	old woman
чрезме́рный	excessive
любопы́тство, -а	curiosity
вы́валиться, imperf. выва́ливаться	to tumble out
упа́сть, упаду́, упадёшь, imperf. па́дать	to fall
разби́ться, разобью́сь, разобьёшься, imperf. разбива́ться	to crash, break up
то́же	also
друго́й	other, second
стать, ста́ну, ста́нешь, imperf. станови́ться	to become, begin (+ imperf. inf.)
вниз (without motion = внизу́)	down[wards], downstairs (adv., motion)
пото́м	after that, then
надое́сть, imperf. надоеда́ть + dat.	to be fed up (usually past perf., and note the construction)
ры́нок, ры́нка	market ('in, at' = на)
слепо́й	blind, blind person
подари́ть, imperf. дари́ть, дарю́, да́ришь	to give
вя́заный	knitted
шаль, -и (fem.)	shawl

The opposites of вниз, внизу́ are наве́рх, наверху́. Разби́вшуюся is a past active participle, which you're at last about to be told about!

Exercise 1

Write out the following ordinals:

(a) На 123 страни́це ('page')
(b) 4 ма́рта (gen.sing.neut. 'on the 4/iii')
(c) В 6 часу́ (prep. of час 'hour'; = '5-6')
(d) 163 авто́бус (No.163 bus)
(e) 12 за́поведь ('commandment', fem.)
(f) В 1999 году́ (prep. of год 'year')
(g) 22 попы́тка ('attempt')
(h) По́сле 9 рома́на
(i) 2 том ('volume')
(j) При 1 возмо́жности

Choose the endings from: -ого, -ом, -ая, -ая, -ого, -ом, -ом, -ой, -ый, -ой.

3. The walking along the street man smiled at the sitting in the café woman

Well, this works in bookish Russian, but in English the nearest you come is in putting 'walking along the street' and 'sitting in the café' straight after 'man' and 'woman' respectively. More common, in both languages, is to use a 'who/which', i.e. relative, clause, which we'll soon find out about. But Russian has participles for this sort of thing too and, just as in Ancient Greek, they're incredibly useful and something you can do with learning about pretty early on (and this whole book is 'early days'). You'll be told they're bookish; well, yes, but lots of us talk like books, and what about writing?

There are four participles in Russian, two active (present and past) and two passive (present and past). I'll do the passives in Chapter 17; one of them is both the most widely-used and the trickiest to form (isn't it always like that!) — Chapter 17 seems a bit late for something so important, but this book is a whole, not something progressive.

The present active is formed from imperfective verbs, and you just replace the -т at the end of the 'they' form with -щий (-щийся if the verb is reflexive — and *always* -ся). As for the stress, first-conjugation verbs tend to have that of the 'they' form: идýт, so идýщий; плáчут, so плáчущий, and пишут, so пишущий. Second-conjugation verbs have it there too *if* it is also there in the masculine form of the past tense; if not, it goes where it is in the past, e.g. кýрят, but курил 'smoked', so курящий; мéдлят and мéдлил (from мéдлить 'to linger ("over" = c + instr.)'), so мéдлящий. There are only a few exceptions, e.g. first-conjugation мочь 'to be able' — мóгут, but могýщий, and second-conjugation дышáть 'to breathe' — дышáл, but дышащий, любить 'to love' — любил, but любящий, and служить 'to serve' — служил, but слýжащий.

The past active, which can be formed from both aspects, is straightforward too. Take the past masculine. If it ends in -л (as it does usually), replace the -л with -вший (-вшийся if reflexive — and *always* -ся). If it doesn't end in -л, simply add -ший or -шийся. The stress is generally on the same vowel as in the past masculine, but a more effective rule can be to take the stress of the infinitive (unless it's -ти):

> (про)читáть 'to read' — (про)читáл, so (про)читáвший
> (по)стрóить 'to build' — (по)стрóил, so (по)стрóивший
> (по)нести 'to carry' — (по)нёс, so (по)нёсший
> (о)слéпнуть 'to become blind' — (о)слéп, so (о)слéпший
>
> начáть 'to begin' — нáчал, but начáвший
> умерéть 'to die' — ýмер, but умéрший

The only exceptions to bear in mind relate to the verbs with an underlying д or т. Some of these are regular: класть 'to put' — клал, non-past кладу — клавший, сесть 'to sit down' — сел, non-past сяду — севший. But on the whole the -д- or -т- reappears and, if there was a -ё- in the past masculine, it is replaced by -e-. Thus:

> вести 'to lead' — вёл, веду — ведший
> идти 'to go' — шёл, иду — шедший

All this is very well, and it will solve most of your problems when trying to get the gist of something in Russian, especially as in English we just say or write 'walking', etc. On the whole, the perfective past will be straightforward; it will mean 'who has done/finished/changed'. But choosing between the other two is tricky, and if in doubt you should go for the present active. Basically, if the two processes (of the main verb and of the participle) more or less overlap, you may use the present active; but if the main verb is past, you have the option of using either the present or the past active — imperfective often conveys synchronicity and overrules tense. You might find it easier just to use the participle corresponding to what you would expect if the verb were expressed in a tensed form.

As an adjective the participle agrees in case, number, and gender with the noun to which it refers and, unless it comes in front of that noun, it will be preceded by a comma. Here are a few examples:

> На углу стоял мальчик, читающий/читавший газету.
> 'At the corner there stood a boy reading a newspaper.'
>
> Она налила ему ещё стакан из большого, весело кипящего самовара.
> 'She poured him another glass from the big, gaily boiling samovar.'
>
> Я не знаю мужчин, идущих нам навстречу.
> 'I don't know the men coming towards/to meet us.'

Quite often participles turn into adjectives proper: будущий 'future', блестящий 'brilliant', выдающийся 'outstanding', бывший 'former'.

Well, they're good and useful forms to know, you really need to know them if you're ever going to get past a sentence or two of written Russian, and you *will* hear people use them in speech.

Exercises 2 and 3

2. Form present and past active participles from the following verbs:

1. пить 'drink'	8. брать 'take'	15. ýжинать 'dine'
2. обéдать 'lunch'	9. зáвтракать 'breakfast'	16. начинáть 'begin'
3. отходить 'depart'	10. отправлЯться 'set off'	17. оставáться 'remain'
4. дéлать 'do'	11. чýвствовать 'feel'	18. болéть 'ache'
5. болéть 'be ill'	12. умывáться 'wash oneself'	19. жить 'live'
6. говорить 'say'	13. учить(ся) 'learn'	20. читáть 'read'
7. смотрéть 'watch'	14. знать 'know'	21. игрáть 'play'

3 And form past active participles from these:

1. дать 'give'	5. убрáть 'tidy up'	9. пообéдать 'lunch'
2. купить 'buy'	6. отдохнýть 'take a rest'	10. начáть 'begin'
3. отойти 'depart'	7. напрáвиться к 'make for'	11. остáться 'remain'
4. подождáть 'wait'	8. раздéться 'undress'	12. заработáть 'earn'

No key — you should be able to do it. Third person plural, masculine past — read the preceding section! It's *all* regular. Be confident!

4. It's all relative

In Chapter 4 I introduced кто and что and said they could cover for 'who' and 'which' in relative clauses, but especially after forms of тот and весь. Normally, however, the relative pronoun is something quite different: котóрый, a straightforward adjective. All you have to do to use it, because Russian insists on expressing it, is precede it (or a preposition governing it) by a comma, and make it agree in number and gender with the noun it refers to and take on the case appropriate to the relative clause. If that sounds complicated, take a look at these examples:

> Мы вышли в сад, котóрый спускáлся к рекé.
> 'We came out into the garden, which went down to the river.'
>
> Вчерá к нам пришли друзьЯ, котóрых мы давнó не видели.
> 'Yesterday some friends came to visit us whom we'd not seen for a long time.'
>
> Они наконéц нашли книгу, о котóрой мáма им говорила.
> 'They've finally found the book about which mum had been telling them.'

In the first we have masculine singular because it refers to сад and nominative because it's the subject of спускáлся. In the second we have plural because it refers to друзьЯ and genitive because it's the animate object of a verb (and the verb is negative, which would normally require the genitive for the accusative too). And in the third we have feminine singular because it refers to книгу and prepositional because it's governed by the preposition o.

Кото́рый, by the way, can be used as an interrogative, though it tends to be replaced nowadays by како́й. Formerly, кото́рый would refer to 'which (one)?' in a series, while како́й would ask 'what sort?' You still find кото́рый in, for example, Кото́рый час? 'What time is it?' and В кото́ром часу́? 'At what time?'

Exercise 4

Create single sentences with relative clauses from the following pairs of sentences:

1. Ви́ктор вхо́дит в магази́н. Магази́н стои́т на углу́.
2. Ната́ша купи́ла кни́гу по филосо́фии. В кни́ге мно́го интере́сного.
3. На́ши де́ти нашли́ ко́шку. Ко́шку они́ о́чень лю́бят.
4. К нам в го́сти приду́т Пу́шкины. Мы их давно́ не ви́дели.
5. На столе́ лежи́т каранда́ш. Карандашо́м я рису́ю портре́т отца́.
6. Он познако́мил меня́ с Ма́рксом. Я Ма́ркса охо́тно чита́ю.
7. Она́ обрати́ла внима́ние на же́нщину. Же́нщина гро́мко разгова́ривала.
8. Я поздра́вил дру́га с днём рожде́ния. Дру́гу бу́дет 16 лет за́втра.
9. Я пригласи́л их на ве́чер. Ве́чер бу́дет в суббо́ту.

Choose from: кото́рого, кото́рый, кото́рому/кото́рой, кото́рый, в кото́рой, кото́рых, кото́рую, кото́рым, кото́рой.

идти́/пойти́ в го́сти к + dat. 'to go and visit' у́гол, угла́ 'corner'
быть в гостя́х у + gen. 'to be visiting' на-рисова́ть 'to draw'
охо́тно 'willingly, with pleasure' день рожде́ния 'birthday'
приглаша́ть/пригласи́ть 'to invite' в суббо́ту 'on Saturday'

обраща́ть/обрати́ть внима́ние на + acc. 'to pay attention to'
поздравля́ть/поздра́вить 'to congratulate' (+ acc.; note с + instr. for 'on')

CHAPTER 14

1. Чéхов Chekhov

Антóн Пáвлович Чéхов (1860-1904) makes the story of Russian literature in the nineteenth and early twentieth centuries almost too much for the imagination to cope with. Don't be misled by the 'atmosphere' of his plays and stories: Chekhov was quite a lad, really one of us all (I'm referring to both men *and* women), politically incorrect, sexist, ageist,... you name it, and all you'd want someone to be as well. And, more than anything, a free artist (as he indeed referred to himself). *And* a genius. The stories and the plays involve us and leave it to us, though despair breaks through in a claustrophobic masterpiece such as *Палáта №6 Ward No.6* (1892), seen by many as a portrayal of Russia itself. From his early stories read at least *Смерть чинóвника Death of a Civil Servant* (1883) and *Тóлстый и тóнкий Fat and Thin* (1883), a couple of pages each and 99% readable in an hour by *you*, *now*, with a dictionary. Later and more serious stories to read must include the poetic masterpiece *Степь The Steppe* (1888), the melancholy *Скýчная истóрия A Boring Story* (1889), suggesting the emptiness of a life without real feeling, human companionship, and some sort of faith, and *Дáма с собáчкой The Lady with the Dog* (1899), one of the most tantalizing of Chekhov's stories, probably autobiographical, transferred perfectly to the screen in Heifetz's film. The stories are less well-known than the plays, which in performance cannot but reach out simultaneously to so many more people. At least four of them should be read and read: *Чáйка The Seagull* (1896), *Дя́дя Вáня Uncle Vania* (1896-1897), *Три сестры́ Three Sisters* (1901), and *Вишнёвый сад The Cherry Orchard* (1904). If you like Mrs Gaskell,... Anyway, here I've chosen a passage from the end of *Дáма с собáчкой*, where Гýров Gurov is on his way to see Áнна Сергéевна Anna Sergeevna, first accompanying his daughter to school.

С ним шла егó дочь, котóрую хотéлось емý проводи́ть в гимнáзию, э́то бы́ло по дорóге. Вали́л крýпный мóкрый снег.
— Тепéрь три грáдуса теплá, а мéжду тем идёт снег, — говори́л Гýров дóчери. — Но ведь э́то тóлько на повéрхности земли́, в вéрхних же слоя́х атмосфéры совсéм другáя температýра.

— Па́па, а почему́ зимо́й не быва́ет гро́ма?

Он объясни́л и э́то. Он говори́л и ду́мал о то́м, что вот он идёт на свида́ние, и ни одна́ жива́я душа́ не зна́ет об э́том и, вероя́тно, никогда́ не бу́дет знать. У него́ бы́ли две жи́зни: одна́ я́вная, кото́рую ви́дели и зна́ли все, кому́ э́то ну́жно бы́ло, по́лная усло́вной пра́вды и усло́вного обма́на, похо́жая соверше́нно на жизнь его́ знако́мых и друзе́й, и друга́я — протека́вшая та́йно. И по кому́-то стра́нному стече́нию обстоя́тельств, быть мо́жет случа́йному, всё, что бы́ло для него́ ва́жно, интере́сно, необходи́мо, в чём он был и́скренен и не обма́нывал себя́, что составля́ло зерно́ его́ жи́зни, происходи́ло та́йно от други́х, всё же, что бы́ло его́ ло́жью, его́ оболо́чкой, в кото́рую он пря́тался, что́бы скрыть пра́вду, как, наприме́р, его́ слу́жба в ба́нке, спо́ры в клу́бе, его́ «ни́зшая ра́са», хожде́ние с жено́й на юбиле́й, — всё э́то бы́ло я́вно. И по себе́ он суди́л о други́х, не ве́рил тому́, что ви́дел, и всегда́ предполага́л, что у ка́ждого челове́ка под покро́вом та́йны, как под покро́вом но́чи, прохо́дит его́ настоя́щая, са́мая интере́сная жизнь. Ка́ждое ли́чное существова́ние де́ржится на та́йне, и, быть мо́жет, отча́сти поэ́тому культу́рный челове́к так не́рвно хлопо́чет о том, что́бы уважа́лась ли́чная та́йна.

Проводи́в дочь в гимна́зию, Гу́ров отпра́вился в «Славя́нский база́р». Он снял свою́ шу́бу внизу́, подня́лся наве́рх и ти́хо постуча́л в дверь. А́нна Серге́евна, оде́тая в его́ люби́мое се́рое пла́тье, утомлённая доро́гой и ожида́нием, гляде́ла на него́ и не улыба́лась, и едва́ он вошёл, как она́ уже́ припа́ла к его́ груди́. То́чно они́ не ви́делись го́да два, поцелу́й их был до́лгий, дли́тельный.

— Ну, как живёшь там? — спроси́л он. — Что но́вого?

— Погоди́, сейча́с скажу́... Не могу́.

Она́ не могла́ говори́ть, так как пла́кала. Отверну́лась от него́ и прижа́ла плато́к к глаза́м.

«Ну, пуска́й попла́чет, а я пока́ посижу́», — поду́мал он и сел в кре́сло.

Пото́м он позвони́л и сказа́л, что́бы ему́ принесли́ ча́ю; и пото́м, когда́ пил чай, она́ всё стоя́ла, отверну́вшись к окну́... Она́ пла́кала от волне́ния, от ско́рбного созна́ния, что их жизнь так печа́льно сложи́лась; они́ ви́дятся то́лько та́йно, скрыва́ются от люде́й, как во́ры! Ра́зве их жизнь не разби́та?

— Ну, переста́нь! — сказа́л он.

With him went his daughter whom he wanted to-accompany to school, it was on the-way. Large damp snow was-falling.

'Now three degrees of-warmth, and yet it's snowing,' Gurov said to-the-daughter. 'But, you-know, this [is] only on the-surface of-the-earth, and in the-upper layers of-the-atmosphere there's a completely different temperature.'

'Papa, but why in-winter isn't there thunder?'

He explained this too. He spoke and thought about the-fact that here he's going to a rendez-vous and not one living soul knows about this and, probably, never will know. He had two lives: one open, which saw and knew everyone [= subject], to-whom this was necessary, full of-conventional truth and conventional deception, completely similar to the-life of his acquaintances and friends, and another — secretly flowing-past. And through some strange confluence of-circumstances, perhaps accidental, everything that was for-him important, interesting, indispensable, in which he was sincere and did not deceive himself, which comprised the grain of his life, happened secretly from others, and everything that was his lie, his cocoon, in which he hid, in-order to-conceal the-truth, like, for-example, his work in the-bank, the-arguments in the-club, his 'lower race' [presumably a reference to jokes about women], going with the-wife to a-celebration, — all this was open. And according to himself [= in his own terms] he judged others, did not believe that which he saw, and always supposed that every person under the-cover of-a-secret, like under the-cover of-night, passes his real, most interesting life. Every personal existence holds-itself on a-secret, and, perhaps, partly consequently a-cultivated/civilized person so nervously fusses about that in-order-that [his]-personal secret was-respected.

Having accompanied his daughter to school, Gurov set-off to the 'Slavianskii bazar'. He took-off his fur coat downstairs, went upstairs [lit. 'rose upstairs'] and softly knocked on the-door. Anna Sergeevna, dressed in his favourite grey dress, exhausted by-the-journey and waiting, looked at him and did not smile, and scarcely he entered, that she already fell to his breast. As they had not seen each other about two years [inversion = approximation], their kiss was long, lengthy.

'Well, how do-you-live there?' he asked. 'What's new?'

'Wait, I'll-say immediately... I can't.'

She couldn't speak, as [she]-was-weeping. She turned-away from him and pressed a-handkerchief to the-eyes.

'Well, let [her] have-a-little-cry, and I for-the-time-being 'll-have-a-little-sit-down.' he thought and sat-down in an-armchair.

Then he rang and said in-order-that [they] brought to-him some-tea; and then, when he-was-drinking the-tea, she all-the-time was-standing, having-turned-away to the-window... She wept from emotion/excitement, from the-doleful awareness, that their life had-taken-shape so sadly; they see-each-other only secretly, they-hide-themselves from people, like thieves! [Is] their life really not broken?

'Well, stop!' he said.

So much is said, so much left unsaid. You've just read almost a tenth of one of the best stories in Russian literature.

2. Tempus fugit — Вре́мябежи́т

You're not going to get far if you can't locate things and people in time as well as in place, so here goes with a *very* few examples:

B/Ha + prepositional (one exception here)		
в про́шлом in the past	в настоя́щее вре́мя at present	в бу́дущем in the future
в нача́ле at the beginning	в середи́не in the middle	в конце́ at the end
в де́тстве in childhood	в мо́лодости in youth	в ста́рости in old age

B/Ha + accusative
в пе́рвый / сле́дующий / друго́й / после́дний раз for the first / next / last time
раз в неде́лю   на э́тот раз once a week   on this occasion
в э́то у́тро / в э́тот ве́чер / в э́ту ночь / в э́ту секу́нду / в э́ту мину́ту / в э́тот час this morning,...

Instrumental		
у́тром in the morning	ве́чером in the evening	но́чью during the night
ра́но у́тром ра́нним у́тром early in the morning	по́здно ве́чером по́здним ве́чером late in the evening	по́здно но́чью по́здней но́чью late at night

Дни неде́ли — The days of the week	
name Како́й э́то день?	*when? (в + accusative)* В како́й день?
воскресе́нье	в воскресе́нье
понеде́льник	в понеде́льник
вто́рник	во вто́рник
среда́	в сре́ду
четве́рг	в четве́рг
пя́тница	в пя́тницу
суббо́та	в суббо́ту

when? (на + prepositional)
На какóй недéле?
на прóшлой / э́той / бу́дущей недéле
but note
в пéрвую / послéднюю / ближáйшую / мину́вшую недéлю октября́

Мéсяцы гóда — The months of the year

name	*when? (в + prep.)*
Какóй э́то мéсяц?	В какóм мéсяце?
Прóшлый мéсяц	В прóшлом мéсяце
Э́тот мéсяц	В э́том мéсяце
Бу́дущий мéсяц	В бу́дущем мéсяце
январь	в январé
феврáль	в февралé
март	в мáрте
апрéль	в апрéле
май	в мáе
ию́нь	в ию́не
ию́ль	в ию́ле
áвгуст	в áвгусте
сентя́брь	в сентябрé
октя́брь	в октябрé
ноя́брь	в ноябрé
декáбрь	в декабрé

Временá гóда — The seasons
(Instrumental)

name	*when?*	*this, last, next...*	*early/late...*
весна́	весно́й	весно́й э́того гóда	рáнней весно́й
лéто	лéтом	лéтом прóшлого гóда	пóздним лéтом
óсень	óсенью	óсенью бу́дущего гóда	пóздней óсенью
зима́	зимо́й	э́той зимо́й	рáнней зимо́й

Гóды — Years
(в + prepositional)

name	*when?*
Какóй э́то год?	В какóм году́?
Прóшлый год	В прóшлом году́
Э́тот год	В э́том году́
Бу́дущий	В бу́дущем году́
Девянóстые гóды	В девянóстых годáх

1984 год
тысяча девятьсот восемьдесят четвёртый год
в 1984 году
в тысяча девятьсот восемьдесят четвёртом году

Века — Centuries	
which?	*when? (в + prepositional)*
Какой век?/Какое столетие?	В каком веке/столетии?
Двадцатый век	В двадцатом веке
but special	
Средние века	В средние века

Числа —Dates	
which? what?	*when? (genitive)*
Какое (сегодня) число?	Какого числа?
(Сегодня) 4/II	
Четвёртое февраля	Четвёртого февраля

Какое вчера было/завтра будет число? — Вчера было.../Завтра будет...

8/XI.1997 (*name + on*)
Восьмое ноября тысяча девятьсот девяносто седьмого года
Восьмого ноября тысяча девятьсот девяносто седьмого года

11/X.1980 (*name + on*)
Одиннадцатое октября тысяча девятьсот восьмидесятого года
Одиннадцатого октября тысяча девятьсот восьмидесятого года

Среда, 17/VI.1856 (*name + on*)
Среда, семнадцатого июня тысяча восемьсот пятьдесят шестого года
В среду, семнадцатого июня тысяча восемьсот пятьдесят шестого года

If you're speaking Russian and unsure which construction to use to express 'when', try в течение ⊢ gen. 'during (lit. "in the course of")', which covers many eventualities. Во время + gen. is similar, but not normally used with cardinal numerals. 'During' a meal is за + instr.: за завтраком, за обедом, за ужином. If you want to say someone finished something *in*, *within* a certain time, then try за + acc., almost always with a perfective verb. If you want to refer to something coming, e.g. 'in, from now, later', then через and спустя with the accusative are the ones — спустя comes after or before the accusative and is used with the past: спустя неде́лю / неде́лю спустя 'a week later', немно́го спустя 'soon after; a little later' (the order is fixed in this last expression).

And what if you want to refer to something later than the tense of the verb: I went/am going/will go there *for* five days? Here you use на plus the accusative (most common with verbs of motion). If it's 'for' *without* that reference, e.g. 'I was there [for] five days/the whole time', etc., then it's the accusative all on its own. Compare Я прие́ду на два дня 'I'll come for two days' and Я бу́ду там два дня 'I'll be there [for] two days'. For 'after', use по́сле + gen. or, if you mean 'immediately after', use по + prep.; for 'since', use с(о) + gen. 'Before' will be до + gen., but 'immediately before' is пе́ред + instr. or, also with the sense 'towards', под + acc. 'By' is к(о) + dat., and 'about' is о́коло + gen. A few examples:

Он прочита́л кни́гу стихо́в за два часа́.
'He read the book of poetry in two hours.'
Че́рез три часа́ Та́ня бу́дет там. 'Tania will be there in three hours.'
Неде́лю спустя они́ прие́хали. 'They arrived a week later.'
Ве́ня пое́хал/е́дет/пое́дет в Москву́ на ме́сяц.
'Venia went/is going/will go to Moscow for a month.'
По́сле съе́зда 'After the congress' — По прибы́тии 'Straight after [his] arrival'
С нача́ла уче́бного го́да 'Since the beginning of the academic year'
До конца́ уро́ка 'Before the end of the lesson' — Пе́ред экза́меном 'Just before the exam'
Под ве́чер 'Towards evening' — К четвергу́ 'By Thursday'
О́коло двух неде́ль 'About two weeks'

---

3. То́чно — On the dot

Now, what about the clock? You can do it just as in English 'one fifteen', 'eleven forty-five', 'thirteen hundred' — the last gives it away: it's used in stations, etc. and uses the twenty-four-hour clock. For 'at' you just use в + acc. (i.e. nothing changes),. But you will do well to learn how it's really done, and for this you have to know genitives and how numerals work. Here we go:

Кото́рый час? *or* Ско́лько вре́мени? 'What time is it?'

Now, for 'when, at what time?' there are:

Когда́? *or* В кото́ром часу́? *or* Во ско́лько? 'When?/At what time?'

Note the locative of час; the selection of this case, rather than the accusative, to convey 'at...' is restricted to this and to the expression for 'at

(half-past)' (see below). If you want to say 'Until when?', use До
скольки́х?, i.e. use the appropriate preposition and required form of
ско́лько. Or use До каки́х пор? For 'Since when?' use С каки́х пор?
How about 'on the hour'?

Ча́с.	'It's one o'clock.'
Два́/Три́/Четы́ре часа́.	'It's two/three/four o'clock.'
Пя́ть... часо́в.	'It's five... o'clock.'

There's nothing else to learn — just know those numeral constructions. But
if you use the 24-hour clock, note the compounds:

Два́дцать оди́н ча́с.	'It's 2100.'
Два́дцать два́/три́/четы́ре часа́.	'It's 2200/2300/2400.'

And ча́с 'o'clock' may be replaced by но́ль но́ль, thus:

Два́дцать два́ но́ль но́ль.	'It's 2200.'

In the 12-hour system 'a.m.' and 'p.m.' are expressed by the addition of the
following 'adverbs' (the time ranges are approximate):

но́чи	'12:01 a.m. - 6:00 a.m.' (lit. 'of night')
утра́	'6:01 a.m. - 12:00 a.m.' (lit. 'of morning')
дня	'12:01 p.m. - 6:00 p.m.' (lit. 'of day')
ве́чера	'6:01 p.m. - 12:00 p.m.' (lit. 'of evening')

Thus: Два́ часа́ но́чи '2:00 a.m.'

To express 'at (hour)', use the preposition в. To tell time on the hour it is
followed by the *accusative*, which here is identical with the nominative. So
no special form needs to be thought of, in spite of the expression в
кото́ром часу́, with the locative! Thus:

В кото́ром часу́ о́н до́ма?	В ше́сть часо́в.
'At what time is he at home?'	'At six o'clock.'

To do 'past the hour' in the traditional way, you need the following:

(i)   The word мину́та 'minute' and its genitive singular мину́ты and genitive
       plural мину́т.
(ii)   The words че́тверть 'quarter' (feminine) and полови́на 'half', often
       abbreviated to indeclinable по́л.

145

(iii)   The genitive singular (masculine, agreeing with absent чáса) of the ordinals
you need, viz. '1st - 24th'.

For immediate reference, here are those ordinal forms now:

пéрвого	девя́того	семнáдцатого
вторóго	деся́того	восемнáдцатого
трéтьего	одúннадцатого	девятнáдцатого
четвёртого	двенáдцатого	двадцáтого
пя́того	тринáдцатого	двáдцать пéрвого
шестóго	четы́рнадцатого	двáдцать вторóго
седьмóго	пятнáдцатого	двáдцать трéтьего
восьмóго	шестнáдцатого	двáдцать четвёртого

The construction is 'so many minutes of the hour in progress' (you might
find it easier to visualize 'hour in progress' as the next o'clock). Thus:

Сейчáс пя́ть минýт пя́того.	'It's now 4:05.'
Скóро двáдцать четы́ре минýты седьмóго.	'Soon it's 6:24.'
Ужé чéтверть девя́того.	'It's already 8:15.'

To convey 'at (*past*-hour)', в again, but now followed by the *prepositional*
for the 'half hour' (unless you use the indeclinable пóл). Thus:

(В) чéтверть трéтьего.	'At 2:15.'	
В половúне деся́того.	'At 9:30'	*or*
В полдеся́того.	'At 9:30.'	
(В) дéсять минýт двенáдцатого.	'At 11:10.'	

Except for в половúне, в is actually usually omitted, but the accusative
must be retained, visible only in однý and двáдцать однý.

The 24-hour clock may be used. It is, word-for-word, the English 'ten
fifteen', etc. Thus:

Онú приéхали в дéсять трúдцать.	'They arrived at 10:30.'

For 'to the hour', following the traditional system, there is no difference
between a statement of the time ('It's...'), and a statement of time 'at (*to*-
hour)'. Take the preposition без, follow it with the genitive of the number
of minutes or of чéтверть, viz. чéтверти, and then add the cardinal for
the *approaching* hour. Normally you express a form of минýта when the
numeral is or ends in '1, 2, 3, 4'. Thus:

> Уже́ без пяти́ (мину́т) семь.　　'It's already ten to seven.'
> Без четырёх минут три будет концерт.
> '*At* four minutes to three there'll be a concert.'

So it's important to know the genitives of the numbers. They are без + ...

одно́й	оди́ннадцати	двадцати́ одно́й
дву́х	двена́дцати	двадцати́ дву́х
трёх	трина́дцати	двадцати́ трёх
четырёх	четы́рнадцати	двадцати́ четырёх
пяти́	пятна́дцати	двадцати́ пяти́
шести́	шестна́дцати	двадцати́ шести́
семи́	семна́дцати	двадцати́ семи́
восьми́	восемна́дцати	двадцати́ восьми́
девяти́	девятна́дцати	двадцати́ девяти́

'1' and '11' will be followed by мину́ты (genitive singular) while all the others will be followed by мину́т (gcnitive plural). Note that 'thirty-five minutes past' may go either with *past* the hour or *to* the hour.

The 24-hour clock system may be used, word-for-word as in English 'ten forty-five', etc. Here you insert в + accusative 'at...' if appropriate.

> Ро́вно в де́сять три́дцать пя́ть мы бу́дем на вокза́ле.
> 'We'll be at the station at ten thirty-five sharp.'

Useful accompanying adverbs or prepositions include:

ро́вно, то́чно	precisely
приме́рно, приблизи́тельно	approximately
о́коло + genitive	around
до + genitive	before
по́сле + genitive	after
с + genitive	since

Another means of expressing approximation is inversion:

> Уже́ часа́ два́.　'It's already about two o'clock.'
> Часо́в в де́сять.　'At about ten o'clock.'

Keep the preposition in front of the numeral. Certain of these prepositions, of course, involve your having mastered the numeral system:

Óколо десятú часóв.	'Around ten o'clock.'
До двух часóв.	'Before two o'clock.'
Óколо чáса.	'Around one o'clock.'
пóсле четырёх часóв.	'After four o'clock.'
До половúны трéтьего.	'Before two thirty.'
До чáсу.	'Until/Before one.'
С чáса.	'Since one.'

For 'before' and 'after' you can use рáньше or рáнее and пóзже or позднée plus the genitive, resp. 'earlier than...' and 'later than...' (put не in front if you want to say 'not earlier/later than...') — see Chapter 18.

And note the forms which чáс 'one o'clock' takes. There are, of course, set expressions too, e.g. чáс óт часу 'with every passing hour', с чáсу на чáс 'any time now', чáс пробúл' the hour has struck' (compare пробúло чáс 'it has struck one').

Finally, if you want just to say 'half an hour', the word is полчасá.

Wordplay

Taking liberties!

One might say that that's what Gurov was taking. However, over the chapters we've come across many a verb which includes 'take' in its meaning, and we know that the basic pair is брать, берý, берёшь, perf. взять, возьмý, возьмёшь.

Брать is identical with English *bear* 'carry' — and note the related брéмя 'burden' and берéменная 'pregnant'. Give it a prefix and it acquires new meanings (and is perfective). Here are a few examples, and *do* remember I can never give all the meanings; not even dictionaries can do that, but they do have more space than me.

взобрáться	to climb (up onto)
выбрать	to select, choose
добрáться (до + gen.)	to get (somewhere)
набрáть	to gather, collect (+ acc. or gen.); pick up height/speed (высотý, скóрость)
набрáться	to assemble, gather (with gen.; often impers.) (набрáться хрáбрости to pluck up courage)
перебрáть	to sort out, look through; go over (in one's mind)
перебрáться	to get over (e.g. a river); to move (house)
прибрáть	to clear up; tidy away (with к рукáм = to take someone in hand or to get one's hands on)
разобрáть	to take apart; investigate; get to the bottom of, understand
разобрáться (в + prep.)	to get to the bottom of, know a lot about

собра́ть	to collect, gather
собра́ться	to collect, gather, meet; be about to, intend (собра́ться с ду́хом to buck up, cf. па́дать, пасть (паду́, падёшь) ду́хом to become disheartened)
убра́ть	to take away; harvest; tidy up (+ acc.) (убра́ть со стола́ to clear the table)

All the imperfectives are in -бира́ть, and the italicized *o* disappears in the non-past and the imperfective, in other words whenever -бр- becomes -бер-or -бир-. It 'ought' to happen in собра́ть too, but doesn't: соберу́, соберёшь,...

And what of взять? Well, вз- looks like a prefix, and so it is. If we substitute the prefix (sometimes an -н- appears in between), we obtain other verbs. But all these are perfectives. The imperfectives are mainly in -има́ть, that -м- reflecting the -м- in возьму́. Note вы́нуть , which seems to have lost its 'take' component, but still hangs on to its 'take' meaning. So:

снять, сниму́, сни́мешь — снима́ть	to take off, remove; take (a photo)
поня́ть, пойму́, поймёшь — понима́ть	to understand
заня́ть, займу́, займёшь — занима́ть	to occupy
заня́ться...	to study, be busy with (+ instr.)
приня́ть, приму́, при́мешь — принима́ть	to receive, accept
отня́ть, отниму́, отни́мешь — отнима́ть	to take away, remove
доня́ть, дойму́, доймёшь — донима́ть	to exasperate
вы́нуть, вы́ну, вы́нешь — вынима́ть	to take out

The verb ять doesn't occur. It is there in pristine form in Lithuanian *imti* 'to take', and, if you take Lithuanian *imtas* 'taken' and imagine that whenever everything is taken from something, that thing is *empty*, then there you have it! And think of *redeem* and *redemption*. Some people might argue, but it's still fun.

CHAPTER 15

А теперь медленно, но верно

'Now slowly but surely'. Consolidation after the despotism — the old story! It's not quite either Gogol's смех сквозь слёзы 'laughter through tears' or Dostoevsky's очищение через страдание 'purification through suffering', but you must now know a little of what learning Russian is about. You'll be getting that love-hate feeling. And particularly try to make sense of, hate, and discard my versions of texts.

1. It wasn't all politics and economics

It wasn't all writers either. Would Chekhov have persevered with the theatre if it hadn't been for Станиславский Stanislavskii and Немирович-Данченко Nemirovich-Danchenko?

Modern Russian music might have taken shape like the language: Russian folklore — songs relating to the seasons and laments, the influence of the East, and church music. More recently borrowed, in the eighteenth century, would have been elements from Italian music, although French influence followed soon after. Instruments included bells (колокол, pl. колокола, probably going back to a sense of 'noise' and tantalizingly similar to the church word глагол 'verb', formerly 'word'), the gusli or psaltery (гусли, gen. гуслей — pl.-only), and the balalaika балалайка, another closeness between music and talk arising in the idiom бесструнная балалайка 'windbag, chatterbox (lit. "stringless balalaika")' — in case you were wondering, both men *and* women. At one point all instruments but bells were banned. The first great names in modern Russian music would be Aliab'ev Алябьев (1802-1852), mainly for his popular songs and ballads, Dargomyzhskii Даргомыжский (1813-1869), influenced by French comic opera and basing operas on Pushkin's work: Русалка *The Mermaid* (1856) and, posthumously, Каменный гость *The Stone Guest* (1872), and particularly Glinka Михаил Иванович Глинка (1804-1857), creator of the Russian national opera: Жизнь за царя *A Life for the Tsar* (1836; now Иван Сусанин), at one time providing the national anthem, Руслан и Людмила *Ruslan and Liudmila* (1842), based on Pushkin's поэма, and much else, including church music.

At this point one should mention Russian oral heroic poems, the *byliny* былины (pl. of былина) and oral religious poems, the *dukhovnye stikhi* духовные стихи, which have provided much of the inspiration for modern Russian culture. Important, too, are the ballads — many Russians still carry round with them a real knowledge of traditional songs. In Morderer/Petrovskii 1997 there are lots of song-book песенник covers and postcards почтовая открытка with extracts from ballads of the turn of the nineteenth-twentieth centuries. Lots of the phrases are fun — again, on the whole I give a rough translation so you can work it out for yourself and get more of a feel for them (vary them for your own use!):

Не уходи. Побудь со мной.	'Don't go-away. Spend-a-little-time with me.'
Ах, ты бедная, бедная швейка.	'Oh, you poor, poor seamstress.'
Зачем я тебя полюбила!.	'Why did I fall-in-love-with you!'

Она таяла вся	'She melted completely
От любовных речей;	From speeches of-love;
А он глаз не сводил	But he his-eyes did not lower
С её карих очей.	From her brown eyes.'

Звени, звени, гитара,	'Ring-out, ring-out, guitar,
Звени, не умолкай!	Ring-out, do not fall-silent!
Люби, люби, подруга,	Love, love, friend,
Люби, не забывай!	Love, do not forget!'

And my favourite, beneath a slightly distant pretty face on a postcard:

Хоть Вас порой я не терплю,	'Though you at-times I cannot stand,
но всё же, кажется, люблю!	but all the while, it-seems, I-love!'

Coming back to music, a group of committed composers, close in thought to the Populists, were in 1867 nicknamed the 'group of five' by the archeologist and critic Stasov, who the next year wrote on the oriental origins of byliny themes. The five were Balakirev Милий Алексеевич Балакирев (1836-1910), Musorgskii (Mussorgsky) Модест Петрович Мусоргский (1839-1881), celebrated *inter alia* for his opera, based on Pushkin's play, *Борис Годунов* (1874-1896, reworked by Rimskii-Korsakov), Kiui ('Cui') Цезарь Антонович Кюй (1835-1918), by profession a military engineer, Rimskii-Korsakov Николай Андреевич Римский-Корсаков (1844-1908), and finally Borodin Александр Порфирьевич Бородин (1834-1887), a chemist as well as a composer. Later came Glazunov Александр Константинович Глазунов (1865-1936), outstanding pupil of Rimskii-Korsakov and Balakirev.

And Chaikovskii (Tchaikovsky) Пётр Ильич Чайковский (1840-1893) — the operas *Евгений Онегин Eugene Onegin* (1879) and

Пиковая дама The Queen of Spades (1890), and the ballets *Лебединое озеро Swan Lake* (1876), *Спящая красавица The Sleeping Beauty* (1889), and *Щелкунчик The Nutcracker* (1892).

From the pre-Revolutionary period one must mention Skriabin Александр Васильевич Скрябин (1872-1915) and, overlapping the pre- and post-Revolutionary periods, perhaps the last great Russian Romantic, Rachmaninov Сергей Васильевич Рахманинов (1873-1943). Of more recent composers, one has only to mention Stravinsky Игорь Фёдорович Стравинский (1882-1971), though most of his life was spent in the West, Prokof'ev Сергей Сергеевич Прокофьев (1891-1953), and the greatest of them all, Shostakovich Дмитрий Дмитриевич Шостакович (1891-1975).

Exercises 1 to 10

1. Say or write some really simple things about some of the people mentioned above, like when they lived. They're all men, I'm afraid, so родился 'was born' and умер 'died'. Be inventive, imagine a Mrs Tchaikovsky, well, there *was* one: родилась and умерла.

2. Write out the four forms of the past tense of:

1.	брать.	7.	покупать.
2.	быть.	8.	дать.
3.	иметь.	9.	хотеть.
4.	любить.	10.	говорить.
5.	знать.	11.	мочь.
6.	получать.	12.	идти.

3. Write out the present tense of the following reflexive verbs:

1.	раздеваться 'to get undressed'.	4.	сердиться 'to get angry'.
2.	смеяться 'to laugh'.	5.	бриться 'to shave (oneself)'.
3.	мыться 'to wash (oneself)'.	6.	надеяться 'to hope'.

4. Days of the week. Translate into Russian:

1. I'm arriving on Sunday.
2. What are you doing on Thursday?
3. They have breakfast together on Thursdays. (вместе 'together')
4. It's more convenient to arrive in Moscow on Monday. (удобнее 'it's more convenient')
5. Where were you on Wednesday?

CHAPTER 15

5. Time of day. Translate into Russian:

1. What's the time? It is now 9.20 a.m.
2. We arrive at Sheremet'evo at 8.15 p.m.   (Шереме́тьево)
3. It's precisely 10 minutes past six.   (ро́вно 'precisely, on the dot')
4. The concert ends at 9.30 p.m.
5. Where were you at 4 p.m. on Saturday?

6. Years. Translate into Russian:

1. In what year were you born? 1973.
2. When did the last war end? 1945.
3. The war lasted six years, from 1914 to 1918.   (продолжа́ться)
4. He died in October, 1871.

7. Age. Translate into Russian:

1. She is twelve, but her brother is fourteen.
2. He is forty-four.
3. She was twenty when she entered the university.   (поступи́ть в + acc.)
4. Little Tania is only two.
5. How old were you when you learnt how to read?   (научи́ться 'to learn')

'How old are you?' = Ско́лько вам лет? Can you work it out from this?

8. Translate:

1. Они́ улетя́т ме́жду девя́тью и двена́дцатью часа́ми.
2. Мои́ де́ти зараба́тывают бо́льше восьми́ ты́сяч четырёхсо́т сорока́ фу́нтов в ме́сяц.
3. В э́том кни́жном магази́не есть кни́ги на тридцати́ трёх языка́х.

9. Read, and write out, the following numerals in Russian:

1. По́сле (5) часо́в. (After 5 o'clock.)
2. Я дал а́дрес (23) учителя́м. (I gave the address to 23 teachers.)
3. Вчера́ я был на (8) ле́кциях. (Yesterday I was at 8 lectures.)
4. Я с (2) друзья́ми. (I'm with 2 friends.)

10. Put the numerals/quantity words into the correct form and translate:

1. Мой оте́ц рабо́тал в 5 стра́нах.
2. Во (мно́го) магази́нах продаётся вино́.
3. Мы бу́дем в институ́те с 2 до 3 часо́в дня.
4. Она́ дала́ игру́шки (о́ба) ма́льчикам. (игру́шка 'toy')
5. Вы разгова́ривали о (не́сколько) собы́тиях. (разгова́ривать 'converse'; собы́тие 'event')

3. Il'f and Petrov, and Marchenko

First, here's an extract from one of Il'f and Petrov's (Илья́ Ильф (Илья́
Арно́льдович Фа́йнзильберг), Евге́ний Петро́в (Евге́ний
Петро́вич Ката́ев)) two celebrated satirical novels, built around the
adventures of the arch-fixer Оста́п Бе́ндер Ostap Bender, highly topical
in its day and still of considerable human relevance. The other one is
Двена́дцать сту́льев The Twelve Chairs (1928). This one is *Золото́й
телёнок The Golden Calf* (1931).

Пешехо́дов на́до люби́ть. Пешехо́ды составля́ют бо́льшую часть
челове́чества, лу́чшую его́ часть. Пешехо́ды со́зда́ли мир. Э́то
они́ постро́или города́, возвели́ многоэта́жные зда́ния, провели́
канализа́цию и водопрово́д, замости́ли у́лицы и освети́ли их
электри́ческими ла́мпами. Э́то они́ распространи́ли культу́ру
по всему́ све́ту, изобрели́ книгопеча́тание, вы́думали по́рох,
перебро́сили мосты́ че́рез ре́ки, расшифрова́ли еги́петские
иеро́глифы, ввели́ в употребле́ние безопа́сную бри́тву,
уничто́жили торго́влю раба́ми и установи́ли, что из бобо́в со́и
мо́жно изгото́вить 114 вку́сных пита́тельных блюд.

И когда́ всё бы́ло гото́во, когда́ родна́я плане́та приняла́
благоустро́енный вид, появи́лись автомобили́сты.

На́до заме́тить, что автомоби́ль то́же был изобретён
пешехо́дами, но автомобили́сты об э́том ка́к-то сра́зу забы́ли.
Кро́тких и у́мных пешехо́дов ста́ли дави́ть. У́лицы, со́зданные
пешехо́дами, перешли́ во вла́сть автомобили́стов. Мостовы́е
ста́ли вдво́е ши́ре, тротуа́ры су́зились до разме́ра таба́чной
бандеро́ли. И пешехо́ды ста́ли испу́ганно жа́ться к дома́м.

В больши́х города́х пешехо́ды веду́т му́ченическую жизнь.
Им разреша́ют переходи́ть у́лицу то́лько на перекрёстках, то́
есть и́менно в тех места́х, где движе́ние сильне́е всего́ и где
волосо́к, на кото́ром обы́чно виси́т жизнь пешехо́да, ле́гче
всего́ оборва́ть.

...И то́лько в ма́леньких ру́сских города́х пешехо́да ещё
уважа́ют и лю́бят. Там он ещё явля́ется хозя́ином у́лиц,
беззабо́тно бро́дит по мостово́й и пересека́ет её в любо́м
направле́нии.

Pedestrians (= object of verb) it-is-necessary to-love. Pedestrians make-up the-
greater part of-humanity, its better part. Pedestrians created the-world. It's they built
the-towns, erected the-multi-storey buildings, laid the-sewerage and water-supply-
systems, paved the-streets and lit them with-electric lamps. It's they spread culture
through the-whole world, invented book-printing, thought-up gunpowder, threw-
over bridges over rivers, deciphered the-Egyptian hieroglyphs, introduced

into use the-safety razor, annihilated the-trade with-slaves and established that out-of beans of-soya it-is-possible to-prepare 114 nourishing dishes.

And when everything was ready, when the-native planet had-taken-on a-well-ordered aspect, the-automobilists made-their-appearance.

It-is-necessary to-remark that the-automobile also had-been-invented by-pedestrians, but the-automobilists somehow forgot about this at-once. The-meek and intelligent pedestrians [people]-began to-knock-down. The-streets, created by-pedestrians, went-over into the-power of-the-automobilists. The-roadways became twice wider, the-pavements narrowed to the-dimension of-a-tobacco paper. And the-pedestrians began to-squeeze-themselves in-fright to the-houses.

In the-big towns pedestrians lead a-martyr's life. Them [people]-permitted to-cross the-street only at crossroads, that is precisely in those places where the-traffic [is] stronger than anything and where the-little-hair on which the-life of-the-pedestrian usually hangs it-is-easier than anything to-snap.

...And only in the-little Russian towns still [people]-respect and love the-pedestrian. There he still appears as-the-master of-the-streets, nonchalantly wanders along the-roadway and intersects it in any direction.

The second extract отры́вок is from the dignified account of Soviet concentration-camp life by Анато́лий Ти́хонович Ма́рченко Anatolii Marchenko (1938-1986): *Мой показа́ния My Testimony* (1968?). It is one of the few references I shall make to the Soviet period in this book — so much is written about it, it was a momentous eighty years in the history of Russia, but it was a dreadfully wrong turning, one of the many through Russian history. Some good things happened in the early days after 1917, but there was utter horror and increasing по́шлость in the sequence of Ле́нин, Ста́лин, Хрущёв, Бре́жнев — it is less easy to be critical of Андро́пов and Черне́нко (they didn't last), then there was the real hope offered by Горбачёв and perhaps in a horrific way helped on by Черно́быль, after which...

Когда́ я сиде́л во Влади́мирской тюрьме́, меня́ не ра́з охва́тывало отча́яние. Го́лод, боле́знь, а гла́вное, бесси́лие, невозмо́жность боро́ться со зло́м доводи́ли до того́, что я гото́в был ки́нуться на свои́х тюре́мщиков с еди́нственной це́лью, чтобы поги́бнуть. Йли други́м спо́собом поко́нчить с собо́й. Йли искале́чить себя́, как э́то де́лали други́е у меня́ на глаза́х.

Меня́ одно́ остана́вливало, одно́ дава́ло мне си́лы жить в э́том кошма́ре: наде́жда, что я вы́йду и расскажу́ всем о то́м, что сам ви́дел и пе́режи́л. Я дал себе́ сло́во ра́ди э́той це́ли вы́нести и вы́терпеть всё. Я обеща́л э́то свои́м това́рищам, кото́рые ещё на го́ды оста́лись за решёткой, за колю́чей про́волокой.

Я ду́мал о то́м, как мне вы́полнить э́ту зада́чу. Мне каза́лось, что в на́шей стране́, в усло́виях жесто́кой цензу́ры и контро́ля

КГБ за ка́ждым ска́занным сло́вом, э́то невозмо́жно. Да и бесце́льно: до того́ все зада́влены стра́хом и порабощены́ тя́жким бы́том, что никто́ и не хо́чет знать пра́вду. Поэ́тому, ду́мал я, мне придётся бежа́ть за грани́цу, что́бы оста́вить своё свиде́тельство хотя́ бы как докуме́нт, как материа́л для исто́рии.

Год наза́д мой срок ко́нчился. Я вы́шел на свобо́ду. Я по́нял, что был непра́в, что мой показа́ния нужны́ всему́ наро́ду. Лю́ди хотя́т знать пра́вду.

Гла́вная цель мойх запи́сок — рассказа́ть пра́вду о сего́дняшних лагеря́х и тю́рьмах для политзаключённых, рассказа́ть её тем, кто хо́чет услы́шать. Я убеждён, что гла́сность — еди́нственное де́йственное сре́дство борьбы́ с творя́щимся сего́дня злом и беззако́нием.

When I was-['sitting'] in Vladimir prison, me not once [= many a time] seized despair. Hunger, illness, and the-main-thing, the-powerlessness, the-impossibility to-struggle with evil led to the-fact that I was ready to-throw-myself onto my gaolers with the single aim in-order to-perish. Or by-another fashion to-finish with myself. Or to-maim-myself, as others did this at me on the-eyes [= before my eyes].

One-thing stopped me, one-thing gave to-me the-strength[s] to-live in this nightmare: the-hope that I-shall-come-out and tell everyone about that which I had-seen myself and experienced. I gave to-myself the-word for-the-sake of-this aim to-bear and endure everything. I promised this to-my-friends, who still for years remained behind the-bars, behind the-barbed wire.

I thought about-that how for-me to-realize this task. It-seemed to-me that in our country, in conditions of-the-cruel censorship and control of-the-KGB over every uttered word, this [is] impossible. And indeed aimless: as-far-as-that all are-crushed by-fear and enslaved by-the-hard life, that no-one even wants to-know the-truth. Consequently, I thought, to-me it-will-befall [= I shall have] to-flee abroad, in-order to-leave my testimony although if-only as a-document, as material for history.

A-year back my term ended. I came-out to freedom. I understood that [I]-had-been wrong, that my testimony is [lit. are] necessary to-the-whole people. People wish to-know the-truth.

The-main aim of-my notes [is] to-tell the-truth about today's camps and prisons for political-prisoners, to-tell it to-those who wish to-hear. I [am] convinced that openness [glasnost'] [is] the-only effective means of-struggle with the being-created today evil and lawlessness.

CHAPTER 16

1. Стихи серебряного века Poetry of the Silver Age

The Golden Age of Russian poetry, otherwise known as the Age of Pushkin, was unique. The first third of the twentieth century, and extending beyond then, was a more diverse Age, and there was no Pushkin, but this Silver Age was truly a *second* Golden Age. Much of the impetus for this renaissance derives from Владимир Сергеевич Соловьёв Solov'ёv (1853-1900). Poets of this Age, and the list omits so many marvellous ones, include Зинаида Нколаевна Гиппиус Hippius (1869-1945), probably the second Russian woman writer of real stature after Каролина Карловна Павлова Pavlova (1807-1893), Фёдор Кузмич Сологуб Sologub (1863-1927), author of the most extraordinary, distasteful yet compelling, study of paranoia, *Мелкий бес The Petty Demon* (1908), Андрей Белый Belyi (1880-1934), Вячеслав Иванович Иванов Ivanov (1866-1949), Александр Александрович Блок Blok (1881-1921), the magnificent Иннокентий Фёдорович Анненский Annenskii (1856-1909), Владимир Владимирович Маяковский Maiakovskii (1893-1930), the marvellous Велимир Владимирович Хлебников Khlebnikov (1885-1922), Сергей Александрович Есенин Esenin (1895-1925), the powerful and original Марина Ивановна Цветаева Tsvetaeva (1892-1941), Борис Леонидович Пастернак Pasternak (1890-1960), the apparently cold and yet anguished Николай Степанович Гумилёв Gumilёv (1886-1921), the brilliantly concise Владислав Фелицианович Ходасевич Khodasevich (1886-1939), then perhaps the greatest of them all, Осип Эмильевич Мандельштам Mandel'shtam (1891-1938), and the legendary Анна Андреевна Ахматова Akhmatova (1889-1966).

Here I want just to give just one example, from Mandel'shtam.

> Дано мне тело — что мне делать с ним,
> Таким единым и таким моим?
>
> За радость тихую дышать и жить,
> Кого, скажите, мне благодарить?
>
> Я и садовник, я же и цветок,
> В темнице мира я не одинок.

На стёкла вечности ужё легло
Моё дыхание, моё тепло.

Запечатлеется на нём узор,
Неузнаваемый с недавних пор.

Пускай мгновения стекает муть —
Узора милого не зачеркнуть.

1909

Given to-me a-body, what for-me to-do with it, / So single and so mine? / For the-peaceful joy to-breathe and to-live, / Whom, tell, for-me to-thank? / I [am] both the-gardener and the-flower as-well, / In the-dungeon of-the-world I [am] not alone. / Onto the-panes of-eternity already has-lain / My breath, my warmth. / A-pattern will-be-etched on it [= breathing], / Unrecognized from recent times / Let the-mist of-the-moment flow-away — / The-dear pattern is-not to-[be]-efface[d].

If you want to read about him and his times, one of the truly outstanding works of twentieth-century Russian literature is provided by the memoirs of his wife, Надёжда Яковлевна Мандельштам (1899-1980).

2. Adverbially yours

From adverbs to adverbial clauses. We already met conditional sentences, in Chapter 9, so here let's look at the others. This isn't too tall an order, because they all share a similar structure; and I'll introduce you to a really neat way of dealing with many of them. The big rule is: in writing insert a comma between the two clauses:

> Я обрадовался, *когда* он наконёц приёхал *or* Когда он наконёц приёхал, я обрадовался
> 'I was overjoyed *when* he finally arrived'

This sentence has an adverbial clause of *time*; it's pretty straightforward: you use the question word. Here's a short list of others:

after	после того как
as	по мере того как
as soon as	как только
before	перед тем как / прежде чем / до того как
hardly	едва (только)..., как... / лишь (только)..., как...
since	с тех пор как
until	пока (не)
while	в то время как / между тем как / пока / когда

Note how forms of the demonstrative тот 'that' may be used to create these compound conjunctions, much as you use it for 'he who' тот, кто, and 'that which' то, что. You might replace когда above with any of these — would you replace perfective обрадовался   with imperfective радовался in any of them?

As a rule, with compound conjunctions ending in как you can place the comma immediately before как; this either slightly emphasizes the time sense, or reflects an actual pause.

The conjunction 'while' in Russian, as in English, can have a sense of 'whereas'; here you can use в то время как and между тем как, plus тогда как. In в то время как the comma before как may be included when the conjunction is temporal, and excluded when it has the 'whereas' sense. For 'whenever' you can have когда with an imperfective, supported or not by some adverb such as всегда 'always' in the main clause, or preceded by каждый раз,... or всякий раз,... 'every time'.

Place, like time, is quite a risk-free area: start the adverbial clause with whichever is appropriate from где 'where; in/at which place', куда 'where; to which place', or откуда 'from which place; whence'. If you strand your prepositions at the end of the sentence in English, e.g. 'I don't know where he comes *from*', don't try to do this in Russian! It just doesn't work. You may — you will be getting used to this — balance the conjunction with an adverb in the main clause: там, туда, and оттуда neatly balance где, куда, and откуда, respectively, though you can mix them, e.g. Он всё ещё жил *там, откуда* она уехала много лет тому назад 'He still lived there, whence she moved many years ago'. Apart from this, you will often find an adverb of place in the main clause: справа/слева 'on the right/left', направо/налево 'on/to the right/left', везде/всюду 'everywhere', or a prepositional phrase with в, etc., etc.

As for *purpose*, i.e. 'in order to/that', you've already encountered the possibility of doing this with чтобы, followed by the past tense or, where the subjects of the clauses are identical, by the infinitive. As with time, you can expand the conjunction; here we find greater explicitness built in, so the comma *remains* immediately before чтобы: для того, чтобы — с тем, чтобы — за тем, чтобы. When it's a case of an infinitive, however, there are times you *don't* use чтобы: first, when the main verb is a verb of motion (except for those in до- and об-) чтобы is optional unless the infinitive is negated (unless the negated infinitive is contrasted with a non-negated infinitive, when you don't have чтобы). And you don't have чтобы after взять, дать, лечь, остаться, and сесть . Oh dear, we really need examples!

Она поступила в университет (для того), чтобы изучать физику.
'She went up to University to study physics.'

159

> Она́ прие́хала в Ло́ндон ((для того́), что́бы) есть пельме́ни.
> 'She came to London to eat pel'meni.' (optional)
>
> Она́ прие́хала в Ло́ндон, что́бы не есть пельме́ни.
> 'She came to London not to eat pel'meni.' (negated)
>
> Она́ прие́хала в Ло́ндон не есть пельме́ни, а есть шпро́ты.
> 'She came to London not to eat pel'meni, but to eat sprats.' (negated, contrasted)
>
> Она́ се́ла в кре́сло отдохну́ть и сказа́ла: «Дай пое́сть!»
> 'She sat down in the armchair to have a rest and said: "Give me something to eat".'
> (near-auxiliary)

Reason, i.e. 'because', has many manifestations. The most universal is потому́ что, with the comma coming in between when the cause is being stressed. И́бо means the same, but is rather bookish, something like 'for'. Very useful are поско́льку 'insofar as' and так как 'since, as, because', which can also come first in the sentence.

> У нас бы́ло мно́го госте́й, потому́ что был пра́здник.
> 'We had lots of guests because it was a holiday.'
>
> Так как она́ сего́дня не рабо́тает, мы бу́дем смотре́ть телеви́зор.
> 'Since she's not working today, we'll watch TV.'

For *result*, i.e. 'in such a way that', one uses так что.

> Я забы́л докуме́нты до́ма, так что на́до бы́ло верну́ться за ни́ми.
> 'I left the documents at home, so [that] I had to go back for them.'

For *manner*, i.e. 'in such a way that/as if', one often has так 'thus' in the main clause, and either как 'as' or one of the words or expressions for 'as if', e.g. (как) бу́дто, бу́дто бы, сло́вно, то́чно, как е́сли бы (those with бы require the past tense) introducing the subordinate clause. One has also to think of such clauses as having a sense 'in such a way that'; here one uses так, что, for a sense of result, and так, что́бы for a sense of purpose (так cannot be omitted).

> Он э́то де́лает так, как на́до.
> 'He does this as it should be done.'
>
> Я люблю́ её так, как бу́дто она́ мне родна́я до́чь.
> 'I love her as if she was my own [natural] daughter.'
>   (lit. 'she to-me natural daughter'

Degree or *measure* sentences will tend to be done rather literally: in the main clause there will be a sense of 'so (near, etc.)', 'as much/many', 'too'. That sense will tend to determine the conjunction:

so X	стóль/настóлько/так/до тогó	+	that	что
as much/many (X)	стóлько	+	as	скóлько
as X	настóлько/так	+	as	наскóлько/как
too X	слúшком/чересчýр	+	to	чтóбы
sufficiently X	достáточно	+	to	чтóбы
not sufficiently X	не настóлько	+	to	чтóбы

> Мы до тогó устáли, что решúли переночевáть там же.
> 'We were so tired that we decided to spend the night right there.'

And for 'concession', i.e. 'although; in spite of the fact that', here the typical conjunctions are хотя́ 'although' and несмотря́ на тó, что 'in spite of the fact that'.

> Хотя́ наступúла лéто, всё ещё стоя́ла хóлодная погóда.
> 'Although summer had come, the weather was still cold.'

A similar sort of meaning may come across in English 'no matter how (much)...', 'however (hard)...'; these too can be dealt with by хотя́ and несмотря́ на тó, что. But there is another construction, and something to look out for in it is the use of ни, e.g.

> Кто ни приéдет, любóй хвáлит гóрод.
> 'Whoever comes [any person] praises the town.'

> Кудá ни поéдешь, вездé живýт люди.
> 'Wherever you go, people live everywhere.'

Note also the use of пусть/пускáй, как ни, and скóлько ни:

> Пусть онá прекрáсно говорúт по-итальянски, но граммáтики онá совсéм не знáет.
> 'However beautifully she speaks Italian, she doesn't know the grammar at all.'
>
> Скóлько ни старáлись онú достáть билéты на óперу, им не удалóсь это сдéлать.
> 'Try though they did to get tickets for the opera, they didn't manage to [do it].'
>
> Как это ни жаль, но мне порá идтú.
> 'Sorry as I am, it's time for me to go.'

> Как ни приятно у вас, (но) мне надо идти.
> 'However pleasant it is with you, I have to go.'

Пусть is used when there's a contrast between a positive and a negative clause; as сколько 'how much' might suggest, you find it with imperfective verbs with an emphasis on repetition without result; and как is used with verbs of trying and 'it's...' adjectival forms suggesting difficulty, e.g. трудно and тяжело 'it's difficult'.

You can expand the ни construction to many question words. The verb here goes in whatever finite form seems appropriate. One may even find the imperative (and it doesn't have to mean 'you'). Alternatively, and safely, insert бы after the question word and put the verb in the past! Note that a couple of the examples use the Russian for 'nothing' and 'no one', which you'll meet in Chapter 19.

> Что он ни видел, ничто ему не нравилось.
> 'Whatever he saw, nothing pleased him.
>
> С кем он ни говорит, никто его не слушает.
> 'Whoever he talks to, no one listens to him.'
>
> Что бы он ни захотел, у него всегда на это были деньги.
> Whatever he wanted, he always had money for it.'
>
> Что ни говори, она всегда готова помочь.
> 'Whatever one might say, she's always ready to help.'

I've said both too little and too much.

3. Having risen from the table, and without smiling, I resorted to a gerund

Here's the neat alternative: the gerund. It's reckoned to be quite bookish, but you need to know it. No conjunction is expressed, so the meaning emerges from the context. The one limitation is that the understood subject of the gerund has to be identical with the expressed, nominative, subject of the main verb (there are 'subtleties' because of Russian 'subjects'). If it isn't, you have to use those conjunctions! Note too 'without smiling' — that's just a negative gerund — don't use без!

How do you form it? Well, first, it's not 'it', there are two. Some people refer to the present and past gerunds, but it can be more helpful to refer to them as the imperfective and perfective gerunds. The former refers to an action overlapping with that of the main verb, and the latter to an action normally totally preceding that of the main verb: 'doing' — 'having done'.

The imperfective gerund is formed from imperfective verbs (mentioning that just in case!) and, setting aside a few special forms, has just one ending, -я, which spelling rules may force into the shape -a. To get it, take the 'they' form of the non-past (don't include -ся) and replace the last two letters with -я (if it's a second-conjugation verb, just drop the -т). The stress will be that of the 'I' form. For a reflexive verb, add -сь:

читáть — читáю — читáют	gives	читáя
смотрéть — смотрю — смóтрят	gives	смотря
садúться — сажýсь — садя́тся	gives	садя́сь

Lots of verbs don't have imperfective gerunds. As for verbs in -авáть, retain the -вá- in the gerund: давáть 'to give', онú даю́т, but давáя. Most of the exceptions are gerunds which have become something else, usually adverbs; some of these end in -чи (an old, and very 'Russian', form), e.g. бýдучи 'being' (still a gerund); adverbs include крáдучись 'stealthily', умéючи 'skilfully (lit. "knowingly")'. Some acquire oddities, often to do with stress — крáдучись was an example, as is мóлча 'silently, without speaking' (instead of крадýчись and молчá). Also сúдя 'in a sitting position', лёжа 'in a lying position', стóя 'in a standing position', сýдя по + dat. 'judging by' (you expect ending-stress in them all), and благодаря́ + dat. 'thanks to' (the *gerund* means 'thanking' and takes the accusative, like the verb!). But the form can remain unchanged, e.g. хотя́ 'wishing' and 'although' — but note the adverb нéхотя 'unwillingly'.

The perfective gerund is formed from perfective verbs! Basically, replace the -л of the past with -в (if the verb is reflexive, insert -ши-, thus -вшись):

прочитáть — прочитáл	gives	прочитáв
посмотрéть — посмотрéл	gives	посмотрéв
купúть — купúл	gives	купúв
одéться — одéлся	gives	одéвшись

You may come across non-reflexive -вши, e.g. in the idiom несóлоно хлебáвши 'empty-handed, disappointed' — but such forms are just something to recognize. And if there's no -л, just add -ши, e.g. принёс 'brought' — принёсши 'having brought'

A few perfectives, usually optionally, have the same ending as the imperfective — they're mainly verbs of motion plus a few you just have to learn: вы́йдя 'having come out' (or вы́шед(ши) from вы́шел), простя́сь 'having said goodbye', увúдя 'having seen', замéтя 'having

LEARN RUSSIAN

noticed', возвратя́сь 'having come back' (or возврати́вшись or верну́вшись), встре́тя 'having met' (or встре́тив).

Exercises 1 to 3

1. Translate and recast without a gerund:

1. Переходя́ че́рез у́лицу, она́ уви́дела мать.
2. Не рабо́тая усе́рдно, ты никогда́ не бу́дешь свобо́дно говори́ть по-ру́сски. (усе́рдно 'diligently, conscientiously')
3. Входя́ в ко́мнату, Воло́дя упа́л.
4. Открыва́я письмо́, То́ля не́рвничал. (не́рвничать 'to be nervous')
5. Си́дя на дива́не, Ва́ля споко́йно чита́л журна́л.

2. Translate and recast without a gerund:

1. Ко́нчив рабо́ту, Ва́ня пошёл в бар.
2. Написа́в все пи́сьма, Ко́ля засну́л.
3. Войдя́ в ку́хню, ма́ма се́ла.
4. Отдохну́в немно́жко, мы опя́ть взя́лись за рабо́ту.
5. Придя́ на ры́нок, он бы́стро купи́л всё необходи́мое.

3. Translate the words in brackets:

1. (Not having received) письма́, Вади́м не знал, что де́лать. (получи́ть, imperf. получа́ть 'to receive')
2. (After eating) блины́, А́ня пошла́ поспа́ть. (съесть, imperf. есть 'to eat')
3. (Without having said) ни сло́ва, Анто́ния вы́бежала из столо́вой. (ни 'not a')
4. (Having walked past) ми́мо вокза́ла, Дави́д вспо́мнил, что у него́ нет де́нег. (пройти́ 'to walk past')

4. Же́нщина в ру́сском о́бществе Woman in Russian Society

In Chapter 3 we met Ol'ga, standing in for her murdered man in the ninth century. Russian society has been a man's society, ruled by the two-headed monster of authority власть (fem.) and alcohol алкого́ль (masc.). Woman has supported her man — admittedly, as a power in the background. But somehow never *really*; even in the Soviet period, for all its declared equality, the woman bore her domestic and childbearing duty, to support her husband and keep industry well supplied with workers. Even since the sensation of *Неде́ля как неде́ля A Week like Any Other* (1969), by Ната́лья Влади́мировна Бара́нская Baranskaia (1908-), change has been slow — but change can be made up of such little jolts. The story is, too, a considerable work of literature: its narrative structure, the absence of preaching, and the fact that О́льга Воронко́ва, the housewife scientist with a good lifestyle yet struggling to survive, on the whole accepts much of her lot — just as her husband assumes that certain things in the flat he does not do and that his career comes first.

There are now many more women writers; of them I might mention Лидия Корнеевна Чуковская Chukovskaia (1907-1996), Людмила Стефановна Петрушевская Petrushevskaia (1938-), Виктория Самойловна Токарева Tokareva (1937-), and Татьяна Никитична Толстая Tolstaia (1951-). And it's not all writing — think of magnificent artists like Гончарова, Экстер, Удальцова, Попова, and many others.

But let's have an extract from Baranskaia's story, just after the family gets home from a nice walk on the Sunday, the last day of her week.

Возвращаемся домой заснеженные, голодные, весёлые. Пусть уж Дима сначала поест, потом поедет. Варю макароны, подогреваю суп и котлеты. Ребята сразу же уселись за стол и смотрят на огонь под кастрюлями.

После прогулки я очень повеселела. Уложив детей и отправив Диму в овощной рейс, я берусь сразу за всё — бросаю в таз детское бельё, мою посуду, стелю на стол одеяло и достаю утюг. И вдруг решаю — подкорочу-ка я эту свою юбку. Что я хожу, как старуха, с наполовину закрытыми колёнками! Я быстро отпарываю подпушку, прикидываю, сколько загнуть, остальное отрезаю. За этим делом и застаёт меня Дима, притащивший полный рюкзак.

— Видишь, Олька, как тебе полезно гулять.

Конечно, полезно. И, кончив приметку, я надеваю юбку. Дима хмыкает, оглядев меня, и смеётся:

— Завтра будет минус двадцать, будешь обратно пришивать. А в общем, ножки у тебя славные.

Я включаю утюг — загладить подол. Потом подошью, и готово!

— Погладь мне заодно брюки, — просит Дима.

— Дим, ну пожалуйста, погладь сам, я хочу кончить юбку.

— Ты же всё равно гладишь.

— Дим, совсем это не «всё равно», я тебя прошу, дай мне кончить. Мне ещё ребячье стирать, вчерашнее гладить.

— Так зачем же ты занимаешься ерундой?

— Дим, давай не будем обсуждать это, прошу тебя, погладь сегодня свои брюки сам, мне надо дошить.

— А куда ты завтра собираешься? — спрашивает он с подозрением.

— Ну, куда?! На бал!

We-return home covered-in-snow, hungry, happy. Now let Dima first eat-something, then he-'ll-go-off. I-boil macaroni, warm-up the-soup and meat-balls. The-children at-once settled-down at-the-table and look at the-fire under the-pans.

After the-walk I have-become-happy very. Having-put-to-bed the-children and sent-off Dima on the-vegetable run, I at-once get-down to everything — I-throw the-children's underwear into the-basin, wash the-dishes, spread the-blanket on the-table and get the-iron. And suddenly I-decide — I-think-I'll-shorten this skirt of-mine. That I go-about, like an-old-woman, with half covered knees! I quickly tear-off the-fur-lined-hem, estimate how-much to-turn-up, cut-off the rest. On this affair Dima catches me, who's-brought a-full rucksack.

'You see, Ol'ka, how for-you it's-useful to-take-a-walk.'

Of-course, useful. And, having-finished the-tacking, I put-on the-skirt. Dima goes-'hm', having-inspected me, and laughs:

'Tomorrow it'll-be minus 20, you'll sew [it] back. But in general, you've got splendid legs.'

I plug-in the iron — to-iron the-hem. Then I'll-sew-[it]-on, and it's-ready!

'Iron for-me the-trousers at-the-same-time,' Dima asks.

'Dima, please, iron-[them] yourself, I want to-finish the-skirt.'

'But you all-the-same iron-[them].'

'Dima, it isn't all-the-same at all, I-beg you, let me to-finish. For-me still the-children's to-wash, yesterday's to-iron.'

'So why you get-involved in-nonsense?'

'Dima, let's not discuss this, I-beg you, today iron your trousers yourself, to-me it's-necessary to-finish-sewing.'

'And where are you planning-[to go] tomorrow?' he asks with suspicion.

'Well, where?! To the/a-ball!'

CHAPTER 17

1. And it's not all poetry

The best Russian poetry is utterly beautiful; knowing it or about it is crucial; at the same time it's insulting to link it with 'learning the language' — it's life, it's that *other* reality you're drawn to. Even if the poet has taken a bit of poetic licence, it's still, perhaps even more, part of the knowledge of the language which you should appreciate. Particularly useful can be the help it gives with stresses, though in the correct recital of Russian poetry, and in connected speech, stress is less linked to the individual word. And remember: the public recital of poetry in Russia remains extremely popular.

Though the Soviet period was something of a literary wasteland, particularly once the régime was well-established, there were writers of real substance. Let's just list a few, including some post-Soviet writers, in no particular order: Исаáк Эммануи́лович Бáбель (1894-1940), Юрий Кáрлович Олéша (1899-1960), Михаи́л Афанáсьевич Булгáков (1891-1940), Бори́с Леони́дович Пастернáк (1890-1960), Фази́ль Абдýлович Искандéр (1929-), Алексáндр Исáевич Солжени́цын (1918-), Дани́ил Хармс (1905-1942), Евгéний Львóвич Шварц (1896-1958), Ви́ктор Олéгович Пелéвин (1962-), Васи́лий Семёнович Грóссман (1905-1964), Евгéния Семёновна Гинзбýрг (1904-1977), Андрéй Платóнович Платóнов (1899-1951), Андрéй Донáтович Синя́вский (Абрáм Терц) (1925-1977), Евгéний Ивáнович Замя́тин (1884-1937), Михаи́л Михáйлович Зóщенко (1895-1958), Венеди́кт Васи́льевич Ерофéев (1938-1990), Сергéй Донáтович Довлáтов (1941-1990), and Влади́мир Николáевич Войнóвич (1932-). I hope you've realized by now that I also give you these lists for practice in reading Russian!

Let's have one short extract here, from Olesha's memoirs *Ни дня без строчки Not a Day without a Line*. As a novelist Olesha is perhaps most famous for this and for his novel *Зáвисть Envy* (1927), a complex and prophetic modernist portrayal of the clash between the old and the new.

Рýсскому языкý и арифмéтике меня́ учи́ла бáбушка. Вспоминáя об э́том сейчáс, я не могý поня́ть, почемý обстоя́тельства сложи́лись так, что в семьé, где бы́ли мать и отéц, заня́тия со мнóй в связи́ с предполагáвшимся мои́м поступлением в приготовительный класс гимназии были поручены именно бабушке, старой женщине, да ещё польке и не совсем грамотной в русской речи, путавшей русские ударения.

Я переписывал из книги, писал диктовку, учился четырём правилам арифметики. Я не помню, как проходили уроки, сохранились только воспоминания о деталях — о том, что я сижу за обеденным столом лицом к окну и балконной двери, о виске бабушки с сухими, уходящими за ухо волосами...

Держать вступительный экзамен в приготовительный класс одесской Ришельевской гимназии привела меня бабушка. Помню, как мы стояли во дворе под деревьями, с которых падали листья. Они плавали в воздухе, эти жёлто-красные осенние листья, казалось, поскрипывали, проплывая мимо нас...

Кроме меня, ещё многих мальчиков привели держать экзамен. Они распределились на группы: кто тоже, как и мы с бабушкой, под деревьями, почти прислонясь к стволам, кто на скамейках и вокруг них, кто... обязательно эти три примера! Хорошо, пусть три — кто прогуливался по двору со старшими — взрослыми братьями или отцами, — маленькие, умные мальчики в очках, полных сверкающих микроотражений осени, сада, города.

Grandmother taught me the-Russian language and arithmetic. Recalling about this now, I can't understand why circumstances came-together in-such-a-way that in a-family where were a-mother and father, studies with me in connection with my proposed entry into the-preparatory class of-the-Gymnasium were entrusted precisely to grandmother, an-old woman, and on-top-of-it a-Pole and not quite literate in Russian speech, mixing-up Russian stresses.

I copied from the-book, wrote dictation, learned the-four rules of-arithmetic. I don't remember how the-lessons went, only memories about details have-been-preserved — about the-fact that I sit at the-lunch table face to the-window and balcony door, against the-temple [= close up to] of-grandmother with [her]-dry, going-away behind the ear hair...

Grandmother took me to-sit the-entrance exam to-the-preparatory class of-the-Odessa Richelieu Gymnasium. I-remember how we stood in-the-courtyard under the-trees, from which leaves were-falling. They swam in the-air, these yellow-red autumn leaves, it-seemed, they-creaked-now-and-then, sailing past us...

Apart-from me, yet many boys [people]-had-brought to-sit the-exam. They had-been-distributed into three groups: some also, like me and grandmother [note the use of мы], under the-trees, almost having-leant against the-trunks, others on little-forms and around them, others... obligatorily these three examples! Well, let-it-be three — others were-walking-around around the-courtyard with older-people — grown-up brothers or fathers, — little, clever boys in spectacles, full of-gleaming micro-reflections of-autumn, the-garden, the-town.

2. Getting vaguer — did someone say something?

In English the difference between 'somebody' and 'anybody' comes so naturally, until you have to explain it. Russian is rather tricky too. Basically, you do things to question-words. Interesting, actually, question words. If you're asking about something, you don't know something; in other words, a question word is indefinite: Он дал мне чем писа́ть 'He gave me *something* to write with', lit. 'with-what to-write'.

First, there's the particle -то, used when talking of something (a person, thing, or circumstance) which is indefinite for the speaker but really exists and may be definite for other people. In Кто́-то стуча́л в дверь 'Someone knocked at the door', Что́-то с шу́мом упа́ло на тротуа́р 'Something fell onto the pavement with a noise', and Я где́-то встреча́л э́того челове́ка 'I've met that person somewhere', we don't know who knocked at the door at the moment of speaking (but other people might), something definitely fell, and that person was definitely met somewhere. This particle is used in narratives, when a fact is being stated.

The particle -нибудь is used in reference to something indefinite (and singular, though if attached to, say, како́й, one can have the plural for agreement) for everyone concerned. In Позови́те кого́-нибудь из студе́нтов 'Call any [one] of the students', Да́йте мне что́-нибудь почита́ть 'Give me something to read', and Éсли кто́-нибудь придёт, позови́те меня́ 'If someone comes, call me', reference is to absolutely any student available, any old book, and whoever comes. You find -нибудь in particular construction types, e.g. using the future tense, and where there's a strong modal meaning (something indispensable, desirable, possible: на́до, ну́жно, жела́тельно, необходи́мо, сле́дует, хо́чет, хо́чется...), i.e. getting remoter!:

> Когда́-нибудь я расскажу́ вам э́ту замеча́тельную исто́рию.
> 'Someday I'll tell you that remarkable story.'
>
> Мне хо́чется сде́лать вам что́-нибудь прия́тное.
> 'I feel like doing something pleasant for you.'

Or if there's reference to something happening frequently or regularly in the present or past — frequency makes things less specific, i.e. remoter:

> В выходны́е дни мы всегда́ смо́трим каки́е-нибудь переда́чи.
> 'On our days off we would always watch certain programmes.'
>
> Когда́ кто́-нибудь входи́л, дверь ти́хо скрипе́ла.
> 'Whenever someone came in, the door slightly creaked.'

And, remote again, it's the indefinite normally used in questions:

> В э́том журна́ле есть что́-нибудь интере́сное?
> 'Is there anything interesting in this magazine?'
>
> Серге́й уже́ сдал како́й-нибудь экза́мен?
> 'Has Sergei already passed any exam?'
>
> Мари́я е́здила куда́-нибудь ле́том?
> 'Did Mariia go anywhere this summer?'
>
> Вы когда́-нибудь отдыха́ли в гора́х ле́том?
> 'Have you ever holidayed in the mountains in summer?'

and in imperatives:

> Ма́ша, купи́ каки́х-нибудь фру́ктов.
> 'Masha, buy some fruit (= "pieces of fruit").'
>
> О́льга Ива́новна, вы то́лько что верну́лись из командиро́вки. Расскажи́те нам что́-нибудь.
> 'Ol'ga Ivanovna, you've just got back from a business trip. Tell us something [about it].'
>
> Бори́с, дава́й пое́дем куда́-нибудь в воскресе́нье.
> 'Boris, let's go for a trip somewhere on Sunday.'
>
> Пусть кто́-нибудь схо́дит за кни́гой в библио́теку. — Уже́ кто́-то пошел.
> 'Get someone to go to the library for the book' — 'Someone's already gone there.'

and often in sentences expressing conditions, suppositions, uncertainty, and doubt:

> Я вы́полню э́ту зада́чу, е́сли мне кто́-нибудь помо́жет.
> 'I'll sort this problem out if someone helps me.'
>
> Я не уве́рен, зна́ет ли кто́-нибудь о моём прие́зде.
> 'I'm not sure whether anyone knows I've arrived.'
>
> Я не зна́ю, купи́л ли он что́-нибудь к ча́ю.
> 'I don't know whether he's bought anything for tea.'
>
> Я не зна́ю, пое́дет ли он ле́том куда́-нибудь.
> 'I don't know whether he'll go off anywhere this summer.'

The particle -либо is used mainly in bookish language, and is generally synonymous with -нибудь. However, as mentioned, in the case of -нибудь there is a sense of the singular, whereas with -либо there may be a sense of an indefinite number.

> Я не хочу обидеть кого-либо этими словами.
> 'I don't want to offend anyone with these words.'

The particle кое- is used when the speaker refers to something he to some extent knows about, but does not name and so keeps from other people — note how a preposition splits it.

> Кто-нибудь знает о твоём отъезде? — Да. Кое-кто знает.
> 'Does anyone know you've gone?' — 'Yes. Someone knows.'
>
> Я хочу рассказать тебе кое о чём.
> 'I'd like to tell you something.'

And it is also used when talking of a general, but not listed, number of people or things, etc., in which case it may be synonymous with некоторые 'certain...'. Thus:

> Кое-кто из учеников пошёл на лекцию.
> 'Some of the pupils went to the lecture.'
>
> Лекция была интересной, но я кое-что не понял.
> 'The lecture was interesting, but there were some things I didn't understand.'
>
> Из письма я узнал кое-какие подробности.
> 'From the letter I learned certain details.'

As usual, it can be a question of reading and making full use of a dictionary, as some of these pronouns and adverbs have special, unpredictable, meanings, как-то 'once, one day', кое-где 'here and there', почему-то 'for some reason', когда-нибудь 'ever, at any time (not negative)', кое-как 'with difficulty, with great effort; carelessly, in a slipshod manner, anyhow'. Thus:

> Как-то вечером зашёл я в гости к своим друзьям посмотреть фотографии.
> 'One evening I paid a visit to my friends to take a look at their photos.'
>
> Этот редкий цветок ещё встречается кое-где в горах.
> 'This rare flower is still encountered here and there in the mountains.'

171

Ко́е-ка́к удало́сь вы́браться из ле́са.
'Somehow he managed to get out of the forest.'

Учени́к вы́полнил дома́шнее зада́ние на́спех, ко́е-ка́к.
'The pupil did his homework hastily, in a careless fashion.'

Exercise 1

Translate the words in brackets, then translate the sentences:

1. Вы чита́ли (ever) Толсто́го?
2. Я нашла́ (something) в маши́не.
3. Дай мне (something).
4. Éсли ты ку́пишь (something), скажи́ ей.
5. Зашла́ ли она́ тебе́ (somewhere) по́сле врабо́ты? (movement: whither?)
6. Ты надéешься в Москве́ найти́ (some sort of) рабо́ту.
7. На приёме я познако́милась с (someone) интере́сным. (приём 'reception')

3. A reluctant word, and immediate exercise, about word order

One thing I've been trying to avoid is the question of word order. But here are two useful hints. First, if there's an expression of time or place, put it first. If there are both, put one of them first and the other later — I was told to favour time! Secondly, Russian may not have 'the' and 'a(n)', but there is a tendency in languages to put *new* information last and *already-known* information first (or you might just leave it out!). So, 'the' is definite and likely to refer to something known; 'a(n)' is indefinite and likely to refer to something new. Now have a go:

Exercise 2

1 A woman sat down at the table.
2 There's an interesting magazine lying on the sofa.
3 Tomorrow I'll be at a lecture about Dostoevsky.
4 I'll send the letter on Friday. (посла́ть, пошлю́, пошлёшь perf. 'to send')
5 There's no water at the dacha. (use на for 'at' with да́ча)

4. And ever more passive

The passive participles are formed from transitive verbs. There are two, the present and the past. The present passive is restricted these days; more often than not it just provides adjectives, e.g. люби́мый 'favourite (lit. "(which) is loved")', неповтори́мый 'unrepeatable', неугаси́мый 'inextinguishable, unquenchable', незабыва́емый 'unforgettable' — the

172

last three indicate that it provides adjectives of the *(un)-X-able* pattern —
любимый can be seen as 'lovable'. The verbs giving -аемый are
imperfective, e.g. неузнаваемый 'unrecognizable'; those in -имый may
be imperfective or perfective (which goes 'against' the *present* name for this
participle, which makes one think).

The simplest strategy for forming it is to take the first person plural, use
the infinitive stress, and add adjectival endings. Verbs in -ести and -чь
(underlying -к-) have -о́мый, e.g. влекомый 'which is dragged' from
влечь, несо́мый '(which) is carried' from нести. Verbs in -авать keep
the -ва-: дава́емый '(which) is given'.

Just to show how it's used as a participle:

> Кни́га, чита́емая все́ми учени́ками, весьма́ интере́сная.
> 'The book being read by all the pupils is very interesting.'

In real life you'd be much more likely to deal with this thought as follows:
Кни́га, кото́рую чита́ют все ученики́, весьма́ интере́сная.

Far more important is the past passive participle. It's used a great deal,
and is a *sine qua non* in its short form, which is the default when
predicative. It's rather more troublesome to create than the others. It
corresponds to English 'made, done, written, seen', expanded as '(which)
is/has been/had been/ done...'. Except for forms which have lost their
participial functions and become adjective or nouns, it is formed
exclusively, these days, from perfective transitive verbs and has two basic
final components, namely -нный (short forms -н, -на, -но, -ны — a
single н!) and -тый (short forms in -т-), corresponding historically to the *n*
and *t/d* in English *written* and *learnt/looked*.

Subject to exceptions, infinitives in -ать will give -анный and bases in
a consonant will add -ённый to the base (unless the endings are never
stressed). What I mean by bases in a consonant are verbs like вести,
бере́чь, печь with an 'I' form in -у́ after a hard consonant: веду́ 'I lead',
берегу́ 'I save', пеку́ 'I bake' — The 'I' form reveals the underlying final
consonant of the base. Once you have a perfective, change к, г, х if they're
there into ж, ч, ш, and add -енный: приведённый, сбережённый,
испечённый. Second conjugation verbs in -ить and -еть will replace
-ить/-еть with -енный, with alternation of the preceding consonant (look
back at Chapter 5). Exceptions are infinitives in -уть, -ыть, -оть,
-ереть, monosyllabic verbs in -ить (i.e. -ить preceded by consonants
only and nothing else, before a perfectivizing prefix is added), and
infinitives in -ать and -ять of verbs which have a nasal appearing in the
non-past. These verbs have -тый. So:

написа́ть — напи́санный	written
привести́ — приведённый	brought
купи́ть — ку́пленный	bought
встре́тить, встре́чу — встре́ченный	met
осуди́ть, осужу́ — осуждённый	condemned
рассмотре́ть — рассмо́тренный	examined, scrutinized
наду́ть - наду́тый	inflated
откры́ть — откры́тый	open(ed)
расколо́ть — раско́лотый	split, cleft
запере́ть — за́пертый	locked-up (note the loss of the e)
вы́пить — вы́питый	drunk (not 'inebriated')
пережи́ть — пе́режитый	experienced, lived-through
нача́ть, начну́ — на́чатый	begun
вы́жать, вы́жму — вы́жатый	wrung-out

Stress tends to retract from the infinitive ending, but it does remain in forms like приведённый, and in forms like that the stress will be on the ending in the short forms.

The long form is used just as you'd expect: attributively and in apposition, and only then, something we couldn't say about adjectives.

Now, most important, as I've already suggested, is that, predicatively, the short form is more or less *de rigueur* and provides the perfective passive. It's *very* common. Here are a few examples — note how the instrumental case is used to convey 'by X'.

> Письмо́ уже́ напи́сано жено́й.
> 'The letter has already been written by my wife.'
>
> Дверь закры́та 'The door is open.' (= 'has been opened')
>
> Рабо́та бу́дет сде́лана сего́дня ве́чером.
> 'The work will be done this evening.' (= 'will have been done')
>
> Реше́ние бы́ло при́нято И́горем четы́ре дня наза́д.
> 'The decision was taken by Igor four days ago.' (= 'had been taken')

5. Resurrecting Sunday

Just a quick, but very useful, note in connection with past passive participles. Formed like them, from verbs, are one of of the most productive types of noun in Russian, the nouns in -ние (just one н) and -тие. They're usually considered 'Church Slavonic'. They also occur in the 'more native' forms -нье and -тье (the stress may be final, in which case

-ё). Moreover, they can be formed from imperfectives as well as from perfectives. So we have взаимопонимáние 'mutual understanding' (взаи́мный 'mutual') and поня́тие 'idea, conception' (from поня́ть, imperf. понимáть 'to understand'). Or compare подражáние 'imitation' from imperfective подражáть + dat. 'to imitate' (it doesn't have a perfective) and выражéние 'expression' from perfective вы́разить 'to express' (imperf. выражáть).

And note воскресéние 'resurrection' contrasting with воскресéнье 'Sunday', both from воскресáть, perf. воскрéснуть 'to rise from the dead' — record the Easter greeting Христóс воскрéс! 'Christ is risen!' and the response Вои́стину воскрéс! 'Verily he is risen!' Compare with воскрешéние 'the raising from the dead', with a consonant alternation, from transitive воскреси́ть, perfective of воскрешáть, also displaying the alternation.

Exercises 3 to 4

Have a go at these. There's no need for a key, and don't bother about the stress.

3. Give the long past passive participles of the following verbs:

1.	пострóить.	11.	исключи́ть.	21.	поки́нуть.
2.	заня́ть.	12.	узнáть.	22.	заключи́ть.
3.	обсуди́ть.	13.	вы́сказать.	23.	собрáть.
4.	удиви́ть.	14.	объяви́ть.	24.	купи́ть.
5.	приобрести́.	15.	найти́.	25.	дать.
6.	включи́ть.	16.	начáть.	26.	вы́тащить.
7.	вы́брать.	17.	показáть.	27.	схвати́ть.
8.	напугáть.	18.	подня́ть.	28.	отдáть.
9.	сдéлать.	19.	вы́нуть.	29.	брóсить.
10.	продáть.	20.	поня́ть.	30.	прости́ть.

4. Give the short past passive participle forms of the following verbs:

1.	написáть.	11.	подня́ть.	21.	вы́пить.
2.	встрéтить.	12.	вы́учить.	22.	брóсить.
3.	обдýмать.	13.	воспитáть.	23.	заверну́ть.
4.	пригласи́ть.	14.	сдéлать.	24.	разыскáть.
5.	заколóть.	15.	прочитáть.	25.	начáть.
6.	откры́ть.	16.	организовáть.	26.	отня́ть.
7.	отвести́.	17.	объяви́ть.	27.	пересели́ть.
8.	пройти́.	18.	забы́ть.	28.	взять.
9.	спасти́.	19.	вы́нудить.	29.	оби́деть.
10.	купи́ть.	20.	показáть.	30.	обсуди́ть.

175

CHAPTER 18

1. Bulgakov's *Мáстер и Маргарúта* *The Master and Margarita* (1928-1940)

We simply have to have an extract from Bulgakov's complex and unputdownable stylistic *tour de force Мáстер и Маргарúта*, combining narratives of Pontius Pilate's dilemma, the life of the Master (who's written a novel about Pontius Pilate) and Margarita in contemporary Moscow, and the fantastic visit of the devil, a benevolent type, and his retinue to Moscow. Bulgakov was the author of numerous novels and plays, not to mention an excellent biography of Molière. His full-length novel *Бéлая гвáрдия The White Guard* (1922-1928), dramatized as *Дни Турбины́х The Days of the Turbins* (1926), is rumoured to have been liked by Stalin and helped Bulgakov, inexorably opposed to the establishment though he was, survive the thirties. Let's have the beginning of *Мáстер и Маргарúта*.

Никогдá не разговáривайте с неизвéстными

В час жáркого весéннего закáта на Патриáрших прудáх появúлось двóе грáждан. Пéрвый из них — приблизúтельно сорокалéтний, одéтый в сéренькую лéтнюю пáру, — был мáленького рóста, темноволóс, упúтан, лыс, свою прилúчную шляпу пирожкóм нёс в рукé, а аккурáтно выбритое лицó его украшáли сверхъестéственных размéров очкú в чёрной роговóй опрáве. Вторóй — плечúстый, рыжевáтый, вихрáстый молодóй человéк в залóмленной на затылок клéтчатой кéпке — был в ковбóйке, жёваных бéлых брюках и чёрных тáпочках.

Пéрвый был не кто инóй, как Михаúл Алексáндрович Берлиóз, редáктор тóлстого худóжественного журнáла и председáтель правлéния однóй из крупнéйших москóвских литератýрных ассоциáций, сокращённо именýемой МАССОЛИ́Т, а молодóй спýтник его — поэт Ивáн Николáевич Понырёв, пишýщий под псевдонúмом Бездóмный.

Попáв в тень чуть зеленéющих лип, писáтели пéрвым дóлгом брóсились к пёстро раскрáшенной бýдочке с нáдписью «Пúво и вóды».

CHAPTER 18

Нам следует отметить первую странность этого страшного майского вечера. Не только у будочки, но и во всей аллее, параллельной Малой Бронной улице, не оказалось ни одного человека. В тот час, когда уже, кажется, и сил не было дышать, когда солнце, раскалив Москву, в сухом тумане валилось куда-то за Садовое кольцо, — никто не пришёл под липы, никто не сел на скамейку, пуста была аллея.

— Дайте нарзану, — попросил Берлиоз.

— Нарзану нету, — ответила женщина в будочке и почему-то обиделась.

— Пиво есть? — сиплым голосом осведомился Бездомный.

— Пиво привезут к вечеру, — ответила женщина.

— А что есть?. — спросил Берлиоз.

— Абрикосовая, только тёплая, — сказала женщина.

— Ну, давайте, давайте, давайте!..

Абрикосовая дала обильную жёлтую пену, и в воздухе запахло парикмахерской. Напившись, литераторы немедленно начали икать, расплатились и уселись на скамейке лицом к пруду и спиной к Бронной.

Never talk with strangers

In the-hour of-a-hot evening sunset at Patriarch's Ponds [there] appeared two citizens. The-first out-of them — approximately forty-years-old, dressed in a-greyish summer suit, — was of-small stature, dark-haired, well-fed, bald, was-carrying his decorous pork-pie hat in the-hand, and spectacles of-supernatural dimensions in a-black horn-rimmed frame adorned his thoroughly/neatly shaven face. The-second — a-broad-shouldered, ruddyish, shaggy young man in a-check cap cocked onto the-back-of-his-head — was in a-checked-shirt [= cowboy shirt], crumpled white trousers and black slippers/shoes.

The-first was not anyone other than Mikhail Aleksandrovich Berlioz, editor of-a-thick artistic journal and president of-the-administration of-one out-of the-biggest Moscow literary associations, abbreviatedly named MASSOLIT, and his young travelling-companion — the poet Ivan Nikolaevich Ponyrëv, writing under the-pseudonym Bezdomnyi ['Homeless'].

Having-got into the-shade of-the- barely -turning-green limes, the-writers as-first duty rushed to a- multicolouredly painted booth with the-inscription 'Beer and waters'.

To-us it-is-appropriate to-note the-first strangeness of-this terrible May evening. Not only at the-booth, but also along the-whole path, parallel to-Malaia Bronnaia Street, [there] turned-out-to-be not a-single person [note the double negative]. At that hour, when already, it-seems, there-was not even any-strength to-breathe, when the-sun, having-seared Moscow, in-the-dry mist was-falling somewhere beyond the-Garden Ring, — no-one came under the-limes, no-one sat on the-form, the-path was empty.

'Give some-Narzan [= a sort of mineral water],' Berlioz asked.

177

'There's-no Narzan,' the-woman in the-booth answered and for-some-reason took-offence.

'Is-there beer?' Bezdomnyi inquired in-a-hoarse voice.

'Beer [people]'ll-bring by evening,' the-woman answered.

'But what is-there?' Berlioz asked.

'Apricot, only warm,' the-woman said.

'Well, give, give, give!' [weak sense of 'give'; more 'let's be having you!']

The-apricot [water] gave an-abundant yellow foam, and in-the-air it-began-to-smell of-a-hairdresser's. Having-drunk-their-fill, the-littérateurs immediately began to-hiccup, settled-up and settled-down on a-form face to-the-pond and with-[their]-back to-the-Bronnaia.

Go through it, use your dictionary, turn it into something comprehensible to you, and note the constructions. There are a few negative constructions — see Chapter 19, though you may well be beginning to get the hang of them. And, as with most of our texts, take a look at a real translation.

2. The last straw — indirect speech

In Russian, the equivalent of English 'I said/promised/hoped/thought heard *that*...' is dealt with by using что preceded by a comma. What's interesting in Russian is what happens after 'that'. Consider the following English sentences:

Indirect	Direct
I said that I would be there	I will be there
You said that I would be there	you will be there (s/he?)
She said that I would be there	s/he will be there (you?)
She said that they would be there	they will be there

What's important here is to note how English has *would* after *said* on the left, but *will* on the right. English has 'indirect speech' — the 'sequence of tenses'. The basic rule in Russian is that you retain the tense of the direct speech, *but* (just as in English) retain the subject pronoun change (if there is one) of the 'indirect speech' — this pronoun change makes sense, as it removes a certain amount of potential ambiguity. Taking one of the sentences above, 'She said that they would be there' becomes Она́ сказа́ла, что они́ бу́дут [*will* be] здесь. These constructions apply to all sentences where the verb before что is one of communication (take this as pretty broadly understood).

And if the direct speech involves an imperative (including пусть) or a real plea, you're likely to use что́бы (that *forces* the 'past tense'). And if you feel ill-at-ease with that, work out some way round it.

> Она́ сказа́ла ему́ что́бы он не забы́л зайти́ за докла́дом.
> 'She told him not to forget to come for the report.'
>
> Direct: «Не забу́дь(те) зайти́ за докла́дом!»

Indirect speech includes indirect questions, and here you have the same thing: original tense, indirect subject pronoun, and the actual question form. First, indirect yes-no questions, wherein English we have 'if' or 'whether' ('if' here must always be interchangeable with 'whether'):

> Она́ спроси́ла меня́, приду́ ли я на ве́чер.
> 'She asked me whether/if I *would* come to the party.'
> (lit. 'She asked me, will I come to the party?')
>
> Она́ спроси́ла его́, придёт ли он на ве́чер.
> 'She asked him whether/if he *would* come to the party.'
> (lit. 'She asked him, will he come to the party?' — direct = 'you')

That's the general rule; the only things to add are that you can put any single stressed component of the indirect question in front of ли, to emphasize it, that you can tag on и́ли нет 'or not', and that you can have a question without ли, just as most often in Russian *direct* questions. But the ли structure is the one to base yourself on here. Of course, those are yes/no questions. If there's a question-word involved, e.g. когда́, где, почему́, then *use* it.

> Она́ спроси́ла его́, когда́ он зайдёт за докла́дом.
> 'She asked him when he *would* come for the report.'

A brain-teaser is where the interrogative particles неуже́ли 'surely *not*' (where the speaker expects an answer 'yes') and ра́зве 'really' (where the speaker expects an answer 'no') are involved in the direct question. Best to start off as if it's a simple yes/no question and insert an appropriate adverb or expression.

> Ра́зве он пошёл за хле́бом? 'Has he really gone for some bread?'
>
> Она́ спроси́ла, пошёл ли он [на са́мом де́ле] за хле́бом?
> 'She asked if he had actually gone for some bread.'

Exercise 1

Transform the following into indirect speech:

1. Ива́н сказа́л: «За́втра они́ бу́дут до́ма».
2. Зинаи́да спроси́ла: «За́втра они́ бу́дут до́ма?».
3. Па́па отве́тил: «Я бу́ду ждать тебя́ в 9 часо́в на ста́нции метро́».
4. А́нна спра́шивает себя́: «Когда́ Ма́ша отпра́вит письмо́?».
5. О́ля позвони́ла и сказа́ла: «У неё нет свобо́дного вре́мени».
6. Ма́льчик сказа́л: «2 часа́ меня́ устра́ивает».
7. Ве́ничка спроси́л: «Ско́лько остано́вок до Петушко́в?».
8. Ба́бушка сказа́ла Юре: «Зако́нчи рабо́ту к 7 часа́м!».
9. Та́ня ду́мала: «Они́ меня́ про́сто не оставля́ют в поко́е». (про́сто 'simply')
10. Дежу́рная улыбну́лась и сказа́ла: «Я о́чень люблю́ свои́х госте́й». (дежу́рная 'floor lady' in a hotel; adjective functioning as a noun)

3. Дела́ иду́т ху́же — нет, лу́чше, куда́ лу́чше,
(Things are getting worse — no, better, much better)

Well, if you believe that,... It's now time to mention the 'comparative' and the 'superlative' of adjectives. Actually, this is all to do with 'comparison', because even the superlative is comparing, unless it's the 'absolute superlative', which is really just '*very* chic', '*a most* interesting thing'.

Well, it's adjectives, so there must be a short form. And there is, but here it's very simple, thank goodness.

First, the long-form comparative and superlative are formed by putting бо́лее and са́мый, respectively, in front of the long-form adjective — the adjective still goes along with its agreements, and са́мый tags along, but бо́лее doesn't change. (There are a few irregular forms — they're the usual ones.)

The short forms are practically the rule in predicative use — when you're reading Russian, you'll occasionally come across short-form adjectives after бо́лее, but just note that. The typical ending for a short-form comparative is -ee (or -ей), affixed to the adjectival stem and stressed if the short-form feminine is stressed; some rather common adjectives have an ending -e (never stressed) *and* alternation of the immediately preceding consonant.

The short-form superlative is the short-form comparative followed by всего́/всех 'than everything/everyone', as appropriate to the context: Тако́й подхо́д к э́тому вопро́су лу́чше всего́ 'Such an approach to this problem is best', Э́тот студе́нт спосо́бнее всех 'This student is the most capable'. From this you note, too, that 'than' is conveyed by the genitive case of what's being used as the basis of the comparison. Alternatively you can use чём (preceded by a comma, as a rule!).

Ивáн сильнéе Макси́ма   — Ивáн сильнéе, чем Макси́м
'Ivan is stronger than Maksim'

Онá талáнтливее, чем он
'She's more talented than him' (Or 'than *he*', if you prefer!)

Чем must be used for 'than him/her/it/them', in order to avoid ambiguity, viz. 'than *his*...'

After a superlative, e.g. 'the oldest of the manuscripts', *of* is conveyed by из + genitive: сáмые дрéвние из рýкописей and в/на + prepositional: сáмый дрéвний в ми́ре 'oldest in the world'. The short-form comparative and superlative (not with всéх) also function as adverbs. Here's an illustrative list:

base form	meaning	adverb	long	short	superlative
хорóший	good	хорошó	лýчший	лýчше	(сáмый) лýчший сáмый хорóший
плохóй	bad	плóхо	хýдший	хýже	(сáмый) хýдший сáмый плохóй
большóй, мнóго	big, much - many	-	бóльший	бóльше	сáмый большóй
мáленький	small	мáло немнóго	мéньший	мéньше	сáмый -нький
высóкий	high	высóко	вы́сший	вы́ше	вы́сший сáмый высóкий
ни́зкий	low	ни́зко	ни́зший	ни́же	ни́зший сáмый ни́зкий
стáрый	old	-	стáрший	стáрше	(сáмый) стáрший сáмый стáрый
молодóй	young	-	млáдший	молóже млáдше	(сáмый) млáдший сáмый молодóй
рáнний	early	рáно	бóлее...	рáньше, ранее	сáмый рáнний
пóздний	late	пóздно	бóлее...	пóзже, позднéе	сáмый пóздний
далёкий	far	далекó	бóлее...	дáльше далее	сáмый далёкий
бли́зкий	near	бли́зко	бóлее...	бли́же	сáмый бли́зкий
широ́кий	wide	широкó	бóлее...	ши́ре	сáмый широ́кий
ýзкий	narrow	ýзко	бóлее...	ýже	сáмый ýзкий
грóмкий	loud	грóмко	бóлее..	грóмче	сáмый грóмкий
ти́хий	soft	ти́хо	бóлее...	ти́ше	сáмый ти́хий
дорогóй	dear	дóрого	бóлее...	дорóже	сáмый дорогóй

base form	meaning	adverb	long	short	superlative
дешёвый	cheap	дёшево	бóлее...	дешéвле	сáмый дешёвый
корóткий	short	кóрóткó	бóлее...	корóче	сáмый корóткий
длúнный	long	длúнно	бóлее...	длиннéе	сáмый длúнный
дóлгий	long	дóлго	бóлее...	дóльше дóлее	сáмый дóлгий
бы́стрый	swift	бы́стро	бóлее	быстрéе	сáмый бы́стрый
скóрый	swift/soon	скóро	-	скорéе	сáмый скóрый
слóжный	complex	слóжно	бóлее..	сложнéе	сáмый слóжный
тóчный	precise	тóчно	бóлее...	точнéе	сáмый тóчный
рéдкий	rare	рéдко	бóлее...	рéже	сáмый рéдкий
чáстый	frequent	чáсто	бóлее...	чáще	сáмый чáстый
лёгкий	light	легкó	бóлее...	лéгче	сáмый лёгкий
тяжёлый	heavy	тяжелó	бóлее...	тяжелéе	сáмый тяжёлый
мя́гкий	soft	мя́гко	бóлее...	мя́гче	сáмый мя́гкий
жёсткий	hard	жёстко	бóлее...	жёстче	сáмый жёсткий
твёрдый	hard	твёрдо	бóлее...	твёрже	сáмый твёрдый
чи́стый	clean	чи́сто	бóлее...	чи́ще	сáмый чи́стый
гря́зный	dirty	гря́зно	бóлее...	грязнéе	сáмый гря́зный

The forms given are all frequent and there are a good number of irregulars interspersed among them. Adjectives which don't have short forms don't have short comparatives/superlatives either. No more detail here, but note alternative forms and check your reference books regarding the first eight.

Useful are the indeclinable or short comparatives prefixed with по-, which can mean 'a little'; they're extremely common. They are usually postposed, can be adverbial, and can *seem* to be almost attributive:

> Говори́ почётче! 'Speak more clearly!' (from чёткий)
>
> Я познакóмилась с ним поблúже.
> 'I got to know him [somewhat] better.'
>
> Я купúла велосипéд подорóже.
> 'I bought a (little) more expensive bicycle.'

The absolute superlative, by the way, can be dealt with by using о́чень very or one of the adverbs with a similar meaning, e.g. весьма́ exceedingly', совсе́м 'quite, very, rather'.

Adjectives which have short comparatives can also have superlatives in -ейший or, after a hushing consonant, -а́йший. These occur in set phrases or with particular adjectives, e.g. поздне́йший 'subsequent' from по́здний 'late'. They may also function as absolute superlatives, viz. интере́снейший челове́к 'a most interesting person'. Кста́ти 'By the way', if you want to say 'less...' use ме́нее just as you would бо́лее.

And if you want to say '*the* bigger *the* better' use чем... тем...: чем бо́льше тем лу́чше. For 'twice as *good*' use вдво́е лу́чше ('three times as' is втро́е...) and for 'more and more boring' use всё скучне́е и скучне́е (you can omit и скучне́е). And last, 'far/much more useful' is куда́/гора́здо/намно́го поле́знее. The last, meaning 'much more' is also used with an appropriate verb, e.g. 'to prefer', although one may do it more 'analytically': она́ гора́здо бо́льше предпочита́ет отдыха́ть на берегу́ Во́лги 'she much prefers to holiday on the bank of the Volga'.

Exercises 2 and 3

2. Translate:

1. Кто говори́т ме́дленнее, Вади́м и́ли Ва́ня?
2. Ната́ша купи́ла бо́лее дешёвое пла́тье.
3. Ко́фе гора́здо вкусне́е ча́я.
4. Во́лга ши́ре Те́мзы и́ли нет?
5. В нго́роде намно́го интере́снее, чем в дере́вне.
6. Проводи́ть вре́мя в кафе́ прия́тнее, чем на уро́ке.
7. Тут холодне́е, чем в А́фрике.
8. Ру́сские де́вушки умне́е, чем ру́сские ма́льчики.
9. Э́та река́ глу́бже той.
10. Мы говори́м свобо́днее по-неме́цки, чем по-ру́сски.
11. «Война́ и мир» Льва Толсто́го коро́че «Да́мы с соба́чкой» Анто́на Че́хова?
12. В Великобрита́нии лу́чше и́ли ху́же, чем во Фра́нции?

3. Translate the words in brackets then translate the sentences:

1. В Эдинбу́рге жизнь (is calmer). (споко́йный 'calm')
2. Ка́тя говори́т (more slowly than me). (ме́дленный 'slow')
3. Я покупа́ю конья́к (more often), чем пи́во (beer).
4. Она́ хо́чет пла́тье ([a bit] longer).
5. Пу́шкин (better known) поэ́т, чем Тю́тчев.

CHAPTER 19

1. Венедикт Ерофеев and *Москва-Петушки* (1973)

One has to have an extract from Venedikt Erofeev's masterpiece, relating the ever more confused journey, or non-journey, of an alcoholic, Venichka Erofeev, from Moscow to Petushki, or is it to the Kremlin he has never seen and to his murder in the entry whence he emerged, hung over, at the beginning of the twenty-four hours? Little was known of Erofeev for many years, and his reputation as an alcoholic, a condition which led to his painful death, overshadowed his brilliance and erudition. *Москва - Петушки* is an immensely rich, complex, and tragic creation, steeped in literary, biblical (he claimed to know all the Bible by heart), political, and folkloric references. He possesses the quality shared by all great writers: he loves his creations, and on top of it is intensely Russian, though he did like Faulkner, Maupassant, Kafka, and the Belarusian writer Vasil' Bykaw [Bykov], and adored Latin. For him the poet Zinaida Gippius, Gogol, the celebrated critic and thinker Nikolai Rozanov, and Vladimir Nabokov are the Russians who have marked his life and writing.

In his own words: Быть русским — лёгкая провинность 'Being Russian is a minor offence'.

Москва. На пути к Курскому вокзалу

Все говорят: Кремль, Кремль. Ото всех я слышу про него, а сам ни разу не видел. Сколько раз уже (тысячу раз), напившись или с похмелюги, проходил по Москве с севера на юг, с запада на восток, из конца в конец, насквозь и как попало — и ни разу не видел Кремля.

Вот и вчера опять не увидел, — а ведь целый вечер крутился вокруг тех мест, и не так чтобы очень пьян был: я, как только вышел на Савёловском, выпил для начала стакан зубровки, потому что по опыту знаю, что в качестве утреннего декохта люди ничего лучшего ещё не придумали.

Так. Стакан зубровки. А потом — на Каляевской — другой стакан, только уже не зубровки, а кориандровой. Один мой знакомый говорил, что кориандровая действует на человека антигуманно, то есть, укрепляя все члены, ослабляет душу. Со мно́ю почему́-то случи́лось наоборо́т, то есть душа́ в вы́сшей сте́пени окре́пла, а чле́ны ослабе́ли, но я согла́сен, что и э́то антигума́нно. Поэ́тому там же, на Каля́евской, я доба́вил ещё две кру́жки жигулёвского пи́ва и из го́рлышка альб-де-дессе́рт.

Вы, коне́чно, спро́сите: а да́льше, Ве́ничка, а да́льше — что́ ты пил? Да я и сам путём не зна́ю, что́ я пил. По́мню — на у́лице Че́хова я вы́пил два стака́на охо́тничьей. Но ведь не мог я пересе́чь Садо́вое кольцо́, ничего́ не вы́пив? Не мог. Зна́чит, я ещё чего́-то вы́пил.

А пото́м я пошёл в центр, потому́ что э́то у меня́ всегда́ так, когда́ я ищу́ Кремль, я неизме́нно попада́ю на Ку́рский вокза́л. Мне ведь, со́бственно, и на́до бы́ло идти́ на Ку́рский вокза́л, а не в центр, а я всё-таки пошёл в центр, что́бы на Кремль хоть раз посмотре́ть: всё равно ведь, ду́маю, никако́го Кремля́ я не уви́жу, а попаду́ пря́мо на Ку́рский вокзал.

Moscow. On the-way to the-Kursk Station

Everyone says: the-Kremlin, the-Kremlin. From everyone I hear about it, and myself not-once have-seen it. How-many times already (a-thousand times), having-drunk-my-fill or from/after a-hangover, have-I-walked through Moscow from north to south, from west to east, from end to end, throughout and anyhow — and not once have-[I]-seen the-Kremlin.

So as-well yesterday again [I] didn't see [it], — and you-know the-whole evening [I]-turned-around around those places, and it's-not that that [I]-was very drunk: I, as soon-as I-came-out on Savelov [station], [I] know that in the-capacity of morning tipple [деко́хт = деко́фт/дико́фт and refers to impecuniousness or being half-starved] people have still not thought up anything better.

So. A-glass of-Zubrovka. And then — on Kaliaevskaia [Street] — another glass, only already not of-Zubrovka, but of-coriander [vodka]. One acquaintance of-mine said that coriander [vodka] acts antihumanely on a-person, that is, strengthening all the-limbs, weakens the-soul. With me for-some-reason it-happened the-other-way-round, that is the-soul in the-greatest degree became-stronger, and the-limbs weakened, but I agree that this too [is] antihumane. Consequently, there too, on Kaliaevskaia, I added yet two tankards of-Zhigulëvskii beer and out-of the-neck [= straight from the bottle] *albe-de-dessert*.

You, of-course, will-ask: and further [= next], Venichka, and further — what did you drink? And I even myself don't properly know what I drank. I-remember — on Chekhov Street I drank-up two glasses of-Okhotnich'ia [hunter's vodka]. But after-all I couldn't cross the-Garden Ring, not having-drunk something? I-couldn't. That-means, I drank something else.

And then I went into the-centre, because it-['s] always like-this with me, when I look-for the-Kremlin, I unfailingly end-up at the-Kursk Station. For-me, you-know, actually, [it] was necessary even to-go to the-Kursk Station, and not into the-centre, and I nonetheless went into the-centre, in-order to-take-a-look at the-

Kremlin at-east once: and, all-the-same, I-think, I won't see any Kremlin, and I-'ll-end-up straight at the-Kursk Station.

For a superb translation of this demanding but brilliant text, as *Moscow Stations*, do see that by Stephen Mulrine, Faber and Faber, 1997. And do not imagine that alcohol is anything but a most dreadful scourge, in Russia as elsewhere.

2. Мы почти кончили (The last lap), but let's not get too negative

I hope you're beginning to accept that the rumours about Russian being difficult is a case of 'Much ado about nothing': Много шума из ничего. In other words, let's get down to negatives — many a teacher of my generation swears by the old *Penguin Russian Course*, the one with the wonderful Ж on the front (I wonder how many converts to Russian that letter made!), and the conviction that, if you got past Lesson 24 (out of thirty) and the presentation of a particular negative construction, you were home and dry. Well, here you meet it in Chapter 19, practically the last!

Negatives and the problems everyone has interpreting them (especially in questions) should help convince you that you have built-in already much of what will make you an effective (or ineffective!) user of a language — so learn the forms and use your intelligence. Of course, one can argue this: don't different languages represent their speakers' different conceptions of the universe, like Inuits and their types of snow and Bretons and the noises their carts make? Well, a lot of that is myth and let's not overdo it: different language communities, different cultures, different drinking habits — it all adds to life, and there is so much more that's shared.

Now, the base of negation in Russian is не, a particle which must attach, from a stress point of view, to a following word; it's usually unstressed itself, but in a few common combinations it itself is stressed: не был, не было. It means 'not' and and negates the following verb, or if you want it to negate something else, then you put it before that instead, e.g, Не я болею от нечего делать 'It's not me who's ill from doing nothing'. Remember that it's also, all on its own, the negative of the present tense of быть 'to be', unless you want to be emphatic and then have не есть: Маша не студентка 'Masha's not a student'.

Whatever you do, don't confuse this with нет, which is either the word for 'no' (or for 'yes', because Russians answer negative questions in surprising ways — *and* get confused) or the word for 'there is not, there are not' relating to absence or unavailability and always constructed with the genitive of what is absent or unavailable: Нет его 'He's not in', Нет хлеба 'There's no bread' (the future and past are не будет and не было, which never change). Just note that the Russian for 'he's not at home' or the like is Его нет дома; Russians may reject Он не дома, though you might feel it's OK if there's an implication of where he *actually* is, or where you might prefer the syntactic balance: Он не дома, он на работе 'He's not at home, he's at work'.

Now, how about emphasizing the negation! Here there are sequences such as вовсе не, нисколько не, никак не, and совсем не 'not at all' (make sure with this last one that you retain the word-order, otherwise, i.e. as не совсем, it means 'not quite, not absolutely'). Note with the second and third that we have ни in front of сколько 'how much, how many' and как 'how'. This is our first glimpse (outside the texts, where you've had it lots of times) of the so-called 'double negative'.

What's important here, according to most books, is that you can create a negative pronoun or adjective or adverb by prefixing ни- and accompanying the verb with не. So: нигде (не) 'nowhere', никуда (не) 'nowhere (movement)', ниоткуда (не) 'from nowhere', никогда (не) 'never'. Negative adjectives are никакой (не) 'no(ne)... (at all)' and the synonymous никой (не); there's also ничей (не) 'no one's', but I'm told that's rare. The most familiar are никто (не) 'no one' and ничто (не) 'nothing'. These both decline like кто and что, though it's worth bearing in mind that ничто, even in what you'd expect to be the nominative, tends to be replaced by the genitive, ничего: Совсем ничего не приходило мне в голову 'Nothing at all came into my head', Ничего не случилось 'Nothing happened' — you can see these have something of the 'impersonal' about them (i.e. no nominative subject). You use the nominative proper when the verb has an animate direct object: *Меня* ничто не удивляет 'Nothing surprises *me*' (though Меня ничего не удивляло is still fine).

Ничего on its own, by the way, is the good all-round response to someone's enquiry as to how things are: 'nothing special, all right, wonderful', just give it whichever intonation and facial expression fits! The accusative proper, of course, is ничто, but it too tends to be ничего, except when it's governed by a preposition which requires the accusative — sorry about dotting all the *i*'s (что ставлю точки над «и»). So: я ни на что не надеюсь 'I have no hopes of anything, I rely on nothing'.

Now, look what happened: the preposition came in between ни and что. This is what has to happen whenever a preposition gets involved: она ни с кем не беседовала 'she wasn't chatting to anyone', мы ничего ни о чьей работе не знаем 'we don't know anything about anyone's work', ни в коем случае 'in no circumstances'. So what about Много шума из ничего? Well, here the split doesn't occur because ничто means 'a nothing, a triviality'; the same will go for никто in the meaning 'a nobody'.

Two other things: first, you'll come across expressions where не is 'missing' — these might be seen as set expressions, e.g. они вернулись ни с чём 'they returned empty-handed'. And secondly, and slightly overlapping, the negative не + verb ни..., ни... 'neither... nor...': я никогда не был ни в Москве, ни в Петербурге 'I've never been either to Moscow or St Petersburg', она не пьёт ни чая, ни пива 'she drinks neither tea nor beer' (remember the genitives after negatives — this is one construction where you really *have* to do it).

A slightly fun area here is how you deal with 'he neither drinks nor smokes' — in a recent and very good grammar I noticed the example он ни пьёт ни ест 'he neither drinks nor eats' (in other words, no не) and immediately ran to two native speakers. They didn't like it, and both suggested он не пьёт и не ест (a bit like what one might recommend in French: *il ne boit et il ne mange (non plus)*, though *il ne boit ni ne mange* seems more natural — interesting (but that's another question) that 'drinking' comes first in Russian and French).

In fact, он ни пьёт ни ест is fine (though there should be a comma before the second ни): in one poem of Pushkin's, *Жених The Bridegroom*, we have at one point Не пьёт, не ест, не служит 'doesn't drink, doesn't eat, doesn't serve', and at another Сидит, молчит, ни ест, ни пьёт 'sits, is silent, doesn't eat, doesn't drink' (eating comes first here — the rhyme *avant toute chose*). Perhaps the essential point here is that ни can be used with almost any part of the sentence and what makes it different from не is that it is more emphatic:

---

object
Я не верю никому: ни ему, ни тебе.
'I don't believe anyone: neither him nor you.'

subject
Ни я, ни он не знали об этом. 'Neither I nor he knew about this.'

predicate
Он ни пьёт, ни ест. 'He neither drinks nor eats.'

simple enumeration, no emphasis
Он не пьёт, не ест. 'He doesn't drink, he doesn't eat.'

Now, after all this, what about от нечего делать 'out of having nothing to do', which I slipped in earlier, to get you thinking, and confused? Well, there is a series of negative forms with не- instead of ни-: некого 'there is no one', нечего 'there is nothing', некогда 'there is no time', негде 'there is nowhere', некуда 'there is nowhere (motion)', неоткуда 'there is "from nowhere"', не́зачем 'there is no reason why'. These are all constructed with the infinitive and a 'subject', if expressed, in the dative: Ему́ не́где сиде́ть 'He's got nowhere to sit', Вам не́куда идти́ 'You've nowhere to go', Ей не́когда 'She's got no time'. (It *is* possible to use the negative of 'to have' instead, e.g. у меня́ нет чем писа́ть 'I've nothing to write with' — this sort of construction is useful when you forget a word: У тебя́ есть... чем писа́ть? 'Do you have a... something to write with?') If a preposition is involved, it splits не́- and whatever case of кого́ and чего́ is required — in the set expression от не́чего де́лать the preposition probably doesn't govern the genitive -чего but the whole не́чего де́лать.

Let's explore a few. First, Мне не́кого спроси́ть 'I've no one to ask' — here one has не́ *кого* because the genitive is the direct object of спроси́ть. And in Мне не́кому дать кни́гу 'I've no one to give the book to' one has не́*кому* in the dative, reflecting the person to whom the book would be given, if there was someone to give the book to — 'there isn't-to-whom for-me to-give the-book'! In Не́кому бы́ло пойти́ на ве́чер 'there was no one to go to the party', one has не́кому as the dative 'subject'. Не́чего is quite important, as it provides some useful set phrases: in не́чего де́лать it means 'there's nothing to be done [about it]', and in general it means 'there's no point in, no need to'. Splitting the pronoun, we get, for example, Им не́ о чем бы́ло говори́ть 'They had nothing to talk about', Ей не́ с кем бу́дет рабо́тать 'She'll have no one to work with'.

And there are three which, it turns out, aren't negative: Не́кий is used with surnames to indicate 'someone by the name...', e.g. не́кий Ивано́в, не́кая Ивано́ва 'a certain Ivanov(a)'; не́кто has the same meaning: не́кто Ивано́в, не́кто Ивано́ва 'a certain Ivanov(a)' (you're unlikely to find plural forms, and this just isn't possible with не́кто anyway). Не́что 'something' also occurs, e.g. не́что кру́глое 'something round'; and there is the useful expression не́что вро́де + gen. 'something like' (вро́де is invaluable in conversation, having the sense 'sort of'!).

Exercises 1 to 4

Once again, no need for a key.

1. Put the nouns into the genitive case and translate:

1. Он в э́том совсе́м не принима́ет (уча́стие). (принима́ть уча́стие в + prep. 'to take part in')
2. Мы не дади́м ему́ (ни одна́ буты́лка во́дки).
3. Я не хочу́ (я́блоко).
4. В шкафу́ (оде́жда) нет. (оде́жда 'clothes (fem.sing. — a collective)')

2. Translate whole sentences into Russian, for a change:

1. I don't know why she didn't buy any milk. (молоко́ 'milk')
2. That's not the book I wanted to read.
3. I'll come not at five but at seven.
4. I won't write a single letter today.
5. She can't help buying grapes. (не мочь не + inf. 'not to be able to help but'; виногра́д 'grapes (masc. sing. (collective)')')

3. Translate the negative words in brackets, then translate the sentences:

1. Я (nothing) зна́ю об э́том.
2. На встре́че (there was/will be nobody) симпати́чного. (встре́ча 'meeting', симпати́чный 'likeable')
3. Мы (nowhere) лети́м.
4. Он не заходи́л (to nobody — use к + dat. in this 'to call on' construction).
5. Ты (never) слу́шаешь того́, что тебе́ говоря́т.
6. Они́ (nothing) интересу́ются. (constructed with the instr.)

4. Translate:

1. Ве́чером не́ с кем бу́дет разгова́ривать.
2. Не́где бы́ло сиде́ть и споко́йно чита́ть.
3. Нам не́ к кому́ заходи́ть.
4. Нам в Ту́ле не́чего де́лать.
5. Нам не́когда серьёзно ду́мать о жи́зни.

3. После́днее сло́во?

When you've understood this chapter, and revisited everything before it (I still revisit my first ever Russian textbooks), the nuts and bolts of Russian are yours, or at least they're a precious loan. It remains for you to build on it by voracious reading of texts and dictionaries and by using a fuller grammar or textbook. I do hope that in this Прогу́лка по ру́сскому языку́ 'Russian Walkaround' I've not only helped you to the basics of the language and culture, but helped confirm in your mind how open-ended and human language is, and how the most precious thing you can bring to learning Russian, or any other language, is your own naturally acquired knowledge of your native language or languages. Studying languages may be the closest you'll come to life-long learning about life. In some possible other words, all this is *about* Russian, it's not Russian. Enjoy the personal enrichment it brings — it really does.

And you've still got Chapter 20, just to show it goes on, and on.

CHAPTER 20

1. Россия и русская душа

The Russians' love for culture and artistic creation is a constant — hardly anyone in the world can be venerated as much as Pushkin, that writer whose genius is so complete and apparently effortless that many of his works seem trite in translation. Russian is 'soul', and for many of us who are not Russian that essence is somehow out of reach. You can count on a Russian, you know where you are with him or her, but don't see this 'reliability' in western terms. In other words, be comfortable with a Russian, and be yourself. Don't 'expect' things, just let yourself go and know that there'll be lots of pain and emotion and excitement. And, of course, there is the odd 'stiff' Russian: Karenin, Anna's husband, Shtol'ts, Oblomov's well-meaning and disciplined but emotionally stunted friend.

Russians are breadth and adaptability, and are immensely kind. And that is the country and the mixture of peoples. The land is painfully immense, and over much of that immensity inhospitable and bleak, not to mention now giving up the dreadful secrets of the Soviet era. And it was not empty. Remember the Russians, like us all, began as a mixture, and through the expansion into Siberia, the North, the Caucasus, and Asia became an even more complex entity.

Breadth, adaptability, complexity — all this richness is reflected, imperfectly of course, in the Russian language, the eye into the Russian soul. A language, any language, reflects our attempt to give shape to deeper things, and learning a language, and that includes learning *about* your native language, the one you acquired naturally, can be one of the most enriching of experiences. Language suffuses everything. I would dare to argue that learning a language such as Russian, with its complex grammar, its complex origins, and its immensely rich literature, is one of the best and most relevant investments any of us can make. Mandel'shtam even expressed the opinion that the organized nature of the Russian language saves the Russians from nihilism and chaos.

And, most important, *listen to* Russian — that's also the soul, and utterly central to many Russians' attitude to their language. Nathalie Sarraute, the French author, was Russian by birth and approved translations of her works into English only once she had heard them read to her — not to mention that she always read her own French out to herself. Come to think of it, any serious language-learner spends hours talking aloud to himself or herself.

LEARN RUSSIAN

2. A few more extracts, to finish

First, another of Kharms's *Случаи Incidences*, *Голубáя тетрáдь №10 Blue Notebook No.10* (1937), splendid for genitives:

Жил одѝн рьʹжий человéк, у котóрого нé было глаз и ушéй. У негó нé было и волóс, так что рьʹжим егó называ́ли услóвно.

Говорѝть он не мог, так как у негó нé было рта. Нóса тóже у негó нé было.

У негó нé было да́же рук и ног. И живота́ у негó нé было, и спиньʹ у негó нé было, и хребта́ у негó нé было, и никакѝх внýтренностей у негó нé было. Ничегó нé было! Так что непоня́тно, о ком идёт речь.

Уж лýчше мы о нём не бýдем бóльше говорѝть.

There-lived a red-haired man, who didn't have eyes and ears. He didn't have hair either, so that [people]-called him red-haired in-theory.

He couldn't speak, as he didn't have a-mouth. He didn't have a-nose either.

He didn't even have arms and legs. And he didn't have a-stomach, and he didn't have a-back, and he didn't have a-spine, and he didn't have any insides. Didn't have anything. So that it's-incomprehensible, about whom goes speech [= who it's a question of]

Already better we won't talk about him any-longer.

Just a little point here: you note the form хребѣа́. It's likely to be genitive. In front of the ending, -a, there are two consonants, so perhaps, in the nominative, if it's masculine, there's a mobile vowel. Look up хребто (in case it's neuter), and хребет and хребот. This is what you can end up doing when learning Russian — at least it's far easier than Celtic languages with their consonants changing at the *beginning* of words.

And now yet another, *Сон The Dream*:

Калýгин заснýл и увѝдел сон, бýдто он сидѝт в куста́х, а мѝмо кустóв прохóдит милиционéр.

Калýгин проснýлся, почеса́л рот и опя́ть заснýл, и опя́ть увѝдел сон, бýдто он идёт мѝмо кустóв, а в куста́х притайлся и сидѝт милиционéр.

Калýгин проснýлся, положѝл пóд голову газéту, чтобы не мочѝть слюнями подýшку, и опя́ть заснýл, и опя́ть увѝдел сон, бýдто он сидѝт в куста́х, а мѝмо кустóв прохóдит милиционéр.

Калýгин проснýлся, переменѝл газéту, лёг и заснýл опя́ть. Заснýл и опя́ть увѝдел сон, бýдто он идёт мѝмо кустóв, а в куста́х сидѝт милиционéр.

Тут Калу́гин проснулся и реши́л бо́льше не спать, но момента́льно засну́л и уви́дел сон, бу́дто он сиди́т за милиционе́ром, а ми́мо прохо́дят кусты́.

Калу́гин закрича́л и замета́лся в крова́ти, но просну́ться уже́ не мог.   .

Калу́гин спал четы́ре дня и четы́ре но́чи подря́д и на пя́тый день просну́лся таки́м то́щим, что сапоги́ пришло́сь подвя́зывать к нога́м верёвочкой, что́бы они́ не сва́ливались. В бу́лочной, где Калу́гин всегда́ покупа́л пшени́чный хлеб, его́ не узна́ли и подсу́нули ему́ полуржано́й.

А санита́рная коми́ссия, ходя́ по кварти́рам и уви́дя Калу́гина, нашла́ его́ антисанита́рным и никуда́ не го́дным и приказа́ла жа́кту вы́кинуть Калу́гина вме́сте с со́ром.

Калу́гина сложи́ли попола́м и вы́кинули его́ как сор.

Kalugin fell-asleep and saw a-dream, as-if he sits in bushes and past the-bushes goes-past a-policeman.

Kalugin woke-up, scratched [his] mouth and again fell-asleep, and again saw a-dream, as-if he walks past bushes, and in the-bushes a-policeman had-hidden and is-sitting.

Kalugin woke-up, put a-newspaper under [his] head, in-order not to-wet the-pillow with-dribble, and again fell-asleep, and again saw a-dream, as-if he is-sitting in bushes and past the-bushes goes-past a-policeman.

Kalugin woke-up, changed the-newspaper, lay-down and fell-asleep again. [He] fell-asleep and again saw a-dream, as-if he walks past bushes, and in the-bushes sits a-policeman.

Here Kalugin woke-up and decided more not to-sleep, but immediately fell-asleep and saw a-dream, as-if he sits behind a-policeman, and past go-past bushes.

Kalugin shouted and began-to-toss-and-turn in [his] bed, but already could not wake-up.

Kalugin slept four days and four night in-a-row and on the-fifth day woke-up so thin [lit. 'as such a thin man'] that [his] boots it-was-necessary to-attach to [his] feets with-string, so-that they didn't fall-off. In the-bakery, where Kalugin always bought [his] wheaten bread, him [people] didn't recognize and palmed-off to-him a-half-rye.

And the-sanitary commission, going around the-flats and having-seen Kalugin, found him antisanitary and suitable to-nowhere [= good for nothing] and ordered the-janitors to-throw-out Kalugin together with the-rubbish.

Kalugin [people]-folded in-half and threw-out as rubbish.

Now an extract from the closing moments of Viktor Pelevin's novel *Омо́н Ра Omon Ra* (1992), dealing with the Soviet space programme. The cosmonaut protagonist, Omon, is woken up by a cleaning woman.

— Эй! Мужчи́на!

Я откры́л глаза́. На́до мной склоня́лась же́нщина в гря́зном се́ром хала́те; на полу́ ря́дом с ней стоя́ло ведро́, а в её руке́ была́ шва́бра.

— Тебе́ пло́хо, что ли? Тебе́ чего́ на́до здесь?

Я перевёл взгляд — пря́мо напро́тив меня́ в стене́ была́ кори́чневая дверь с на́дписью «прове́рить до 14.VII». Ря́дом висе́л календа́рь с большо́й фотогра́фией Земли́ и слова́ми «За ми́рный Ко́смос!». Я лежа́л в коро́тком коридо́ре с си́ними кра́шеными сте́нами; вокру́г бы́ло три и́ли четы́ре две́ри. Я погляде́л вверх и увида́л в стене́ напро́тив календаря́ чёрную ды́ру вентиляцио́нного лю́ка.

— А? — спроси́л я.

— Пья́ный, что ли, говорю́?

Держа́сь за сте́ну, я встал на́ ноги и побрёл по коридо́ру.

— Куда́? — сказа́ла же́нщина и ре́зким движе́нием разверну́ла меня́.

Я пошёл в другу́ю сто́рону. За угло́м начина́лась крута́я и дово́льно высо́кая ле́стница вверх, упира́вшаяся в деревя́нную дверь; из-за две́ри доноси́лся нея́сный шум.

— Дава́й, — подтолкну́ла меня́ же́нщина в спи́ну.

Я подня́лся по ле́стнице, огляну́лся — она́ насторо́женно смотре́ла на меня́ сни́зу, — толкну́л дверь и оказа́лся в полутёмной ни́ше, где стоя́ло не́сколько челове́к в гражда́нском. Они́ не обрати́ли на меня́ осо́бого внима́ния. Издалека́ послы́шался нараста́ющий гул, я погляде́л вбок и прочёл бро́нзовую на́дпись: «БИБЛИОТЕ́КА И́МЕНИ ЛЕ́НИНА».

«Земля́», — вдруг по́нял я.

'Hey, mister!'
I opened [my] eyes. Over me leaned a-woman in a-dirty grey overall; on the-floor next-to her stood a-bucket, and in her hand was a-mop.
'It's-bad to-you [= You don't feel well], is that it? What [it]-is-necessary to-you here?'
I transferred [my] look — directly opposite me in the-wall was a-brown door with an-inscription 'to-check before 14.7'. Next-to-it hung a-calendar with a-big photograph of-the-Earth and the-words 'For a-peaceful Cosmos!' I was-lying in a-short corridor with blue painted walls; around were [lit. 'was'] three or four doors. I looked up and say in-the-wall opposite the-calendar the-black hole of-a-ventilation hatch.
'Eh?' I asked.
'Drunk, is it, I-say?'
Holding-on to the-wall, I got-up onto [my] feet and wandered-off along the-corridor.
'Where?' the-woman said and with-an-abrupt movement swung- me -round.

I set-off in the-other direction. Round the-corner began a-steep and quite high set of steps up, which-leant into a-wooden door; from-behind the-door came an-unclear sound.

'Come-on,' the-woman pushed me in the-back.

I went-up up the-steps, looked-round — she guardedly looked at-me from-below, — pushed the-door and found-myself in a-half-dark niche, where several people in civvies stood. They did not pay special attention to me. From-afar was-heard a-growing rumble, I looked to-the-side and read a-bronze inscription: 'LENIN LIBRARY' [lit. 'Library in-the-name-of Lenin'].

'Earth,' I suddenly understood.

And the end, which one trusts will be a beginning, is with Pushkin. First, because it is so full of the spirit of Russian folklore, so simple and beautiful, and also because it plays quite a rôle in Chekhov's *Три сестры*, we have the prologue to *Руслан и Людмила* (1820) — be careful, your life could so easily become the constant intoning of the first six lines.

У лукомо́рья дуб зелёный;
Злата́я цепь на ду́бе том:
И днём и но́чью кот учёный
Всё хо́дит по́ цепи круго́м;
Идёт напра́во — песнь заво́дит,
Нале́во — ска́зку говори́т.

Там чудеса́: там ле́ший бро́дит,
Руса́лка на ветвя́х сиди́т;
Там на неве́домых доро́жках
Следы́ неви́данных звере́й;
Избу́шка там на ку́рьих но́жках
Стои́т без о́кон, без двере́й;
Там лес и дол виде́ний по́лны;
Там о заре́ прихлы́нут во́лны
На брег песча́ный и пусто́й,
И три́дцать ви́тязей прекра́сных
Чредо́й из вод выхо́дят я́сных,
И с ни́ми дя́дька их морско́й;
Там короле́вич мимохо́дом
Пленя́ет гро́зного царя́;
Там в облака́х перед наро́дом
Через леса́, через моря́
Колду́н несёт богатыря́;
В темни́це там царе́вна ту́жит,
А бу́рый волк ей ве́рно слу́жит;
Там сту́па с Ба́бою Яго́й
Идёт, бредёт сама́ собо́й;

Там царь Каще́й над зла́том ча́хнет;
Там ру́сский дух... там Ру́сью па́хнет!
И там я был, и мёд я пил;
У мо́ря ви́дел дуб зелёный;
Под ним сиде́л, и кот учёный
Свой мне ска́зки говори́л.
Одну́ я по́мню: ска́зку э́ту
Пове́даю тепе́рь я све́ту...

By a-bay [is] a-green oak-tree; / A-golden chain [is] on that oak: / And day and night a-learnèd cat / Constantly walks around on [that] chain; / [It] goes right — strikes-up a-song, / left — tells a-fairy-story. // *There* [are] miracles: there the-wood-demon roams, / A-mermaid sits on branches; / There on unknown paths / [Are] traces of-unseen wild-animals; / A-little-hut there on hen's legs / Stands without windows, without doors; / There a-forest and vale [are] full of-visions; / There at dawn the-waves wash-in / Onto the-sandy and empty shore, / And thirty handsome knights / In-a-line come-out from the-clear waters, / And with them their-sea 'uncle'; / There a-king's-son in-passing / Captures a-dread tsar; / There in clouds before the-people / Through the-forests, over the-seas / A-sorcerer carries a-knight; / There in a-cell a-princess grieves, / And a-brown wolf serves her truly; / There a-mortar with Baba-Yaga / Comes, wanders itself by-itself [all on its own]; / There Tsar Kashchei ails over gold; / There the-Russian spirit... there it-smells of-Rus! / And there I was, and honey I drank; / By the-sea I-saw a-green oak / Under it [I] sat, and a-learnèd cat / Told me its fairy-tales. / One I remember: this fairy-tale / [I]-'ll-make-known now to-the-world...

And now one of Pushkin's most beautiful love poems (1829), a good test for your understanding of Russian cases and a must for learning by heart:

Я вас люби́л: любо́вь ещё, быть мо́жет,
В душе́ мое́й уга́сла не совсе́м;
Но пусть она́ вас бо́льше не трево́жит;
Я не хочу́ печа́лить вас ниче́м.
Я вас люби́л безмо́лвно, безнаде́жно,
То ро́бостью, то ре́вностью томи́м;
Я вас люби́л так и́скренно, так не́жно,
Как дай вам Бог люби́мой быть други́м.

I loved you: love still, perhaps, / In my soul is-extinguished not completely; / But let it worry you no more; / I do not wish to-sadden you by-anything. / I loved you silently, hopelessly, / Tormented now by-meekness, now by-jealously; / I loved you so sincerely, so tenderly, / As may God grant to-you to-be loved by-another.

Where next? Well, it's worth the journey: Счастли́вого пути́!

REFERENCE SECTION

1. Nouns, adjectives, and family names

a. Nouns

The cases are given in the order most familiar to us, but I replace their names with the forms of кто and что and place o before the prepositional, to emphasize that this case is always accompanied by a preposition — well, if you want to argue, you could suggest that it isn't in a phrase such as о большóм здáнии 'concerning the big building' (i.e. not repeated before the prepositional form здáнии).

You should be able to work the cases out, even if you yourself are more familiar with a different order.

I've also inserted the stresses. Again, I've striven not to dwell on stress patterns in this book. What *is* comforting is to know that by *free stress* is simply meant that there is no *overall* rule as to where the stress falls. But you will find that there *are* regularities, and over time you will become familiar with them. As I wrote somewhere else here, in spite of knowing Russian for years I have spent a great deal of time while writing this book checking and rechecking stresses — when you're writing, your most basic assumptions are often called into question, not to mention that I discovered that for years I'd been stressing certain words incorrectly. I also began to suspect that my software was moving some stresses around, as I seemed to make some completely ridiculous mistakes — this might be put down to things being done in the head, not in the text.

A few hints: first, the longer the word, especially if it's got a suffix, *or* if it's a borrowing, the more likely it is to have fixed stress; secondly, quite a few words will have ending-stress restricted to the GDIP plural; thirdly, though zero-endings can't be stressed (because there's nothing there!), if every other ending in the table (or within the singular or plural) is stressed, then, in a sense, the zero-ending *is* stressed, but because there's nothing there the stress has to go onto the *nearest* vowel — you see this in стол 'table' and in quite a few genitive plurals, e.g. волóс 'of the hair', where the DIP have ending-stress: волосáм, волосáми, о волосáх. And there are words where the stress moves around more, or there are alternative stresses — I've indicated the latter in the book by putting two stresses on a few words. Finally, note how some words which you associate with a *ye* vowel, e.g., сестрá 'sister', actually, once that *ye* is stressed, e.g. сёстры (nom.pl.), turn out to have *yo*.

Masculine

case/meaning singular	table	god	knife	museum
кто? что?	стол	бог	нож	музе́й
кого́? что?	стол	бо́га	нож	музе́й
кого́? чего́?	стола́	бо́га	ножа́	музе́я
кому́? чему́?	столу́	бо́гу	ножу́	музе́ю
кем? чем?	столо́м	бо́гом	ножо́м	музе́ем
о ко́м? о чём?	о столе́	о бо́ге	о ноже́	о музе́е

case/meaning plural				
кто? что?	столы́	бо́ги	ножи́	музе́и
кого́? что?	столы́	бого́в	ножи́	музе́и
кого́? чего́?	столо́в	бого́в	ноже́й	музе́ев
кому́? чему́?	стола́м	бога́м	ножа́м	музе́ям
кем? чем?	стола́ми	бога́ми	ножа́ми	музе́ями
о ко́м? о чём?	о стола́х	о бога́х	о ножа́х	о музе́ях

case/meaning singular	servant	person	citizen	father
кто? что?	слуга́	челове́к	граждани́н	оте́ц
кого́? что?	слугу́	челове́ка	граждани́на	отца́
кого́? чего́?	слуги́	челове́ка	граждани́на	отца́
кому́? чему́?	слуге́	челове́ку	граждани́ну	отцу́
кем? чем?	слуго́й	челове́ком	граждани́ном	отцо́м
о ко́м? о чём?	о слуге́	о челове́ке	о граждани́не	об отце́

case/meaning plural				
кто? что?	слу́ги	лю́ди	гра́ждане	отцы́
кого́? что?	слуг	люде́й	гра́ждан	отцо́в
кого́? чего́?	слуг	люде́й	гра́ждан	отцо́в
кому́? чему́?	слу́гам	лю́дям	гра́жданам	отца́м
кем? чем?	слу́гами	людьми́	гра́жданами	отца́ми
о ко́м? о чём?	о слу́гах	о лю́дях	о гра́жданах	об отца́х

case/meaning	brother	husband	way, path	town
singular				
кто? что?	бра́т	му́ж	пу́ть	го́род
кого́? что?	бра́та	му́жа	пу́ть	го́род
кого́? чего́?	бра́та	му́жа	пути́	го́рода
кому́? чему́?	бра́ту	му́жу	пути́	го́роду
кем? чем?	бра́том	му́жем	путём	го́родом
о ко́м? о чём?	о бра́те	о му́же	о пути́	о го́роде
plural				
кто? что?	бра́тья	мужья́	пути́	города́
кого́? что?	бра́тьев	мужéй	пути́	города́
кого́? чего́?	бра́тьев	мужéй	путéй	городо́в
кому́? чему́?	бра́тьям	мужья́м	путя́ми	города́м
кем? чем?	бра́тьями	мужья́ми	путя́ми	города́ми
о ко́м? о чём?	о бра́тьях	о мужья́х	о путя́х	о города́х

Neuter

case/meaning	window	field	building	time
singular				
кто? что?	окно́	по́ле	зда́ние	вре́мя
кого́? что?	окно́	по́ле	зда́ние	вре́мя
кого́? чего́?	окна́	по́ля	зда́ния	вре́мени
кому́? чему́?	окну́	по́лю	зда́нию	вре́мени
кем? чем?	окно́м	по́лем	зда́нием	вре́мени
о ко́м? о чём?	об окне́	о по́ле	о зда́нии	о вре́мени
plural				
кто? что?	о́кна	поля́	зда́ния	времена́
кого́? что?	о́кна	поля́	зда́ния	времена́
кого́? чего́?	о́кон	полéй	зда́ний	времён
кому́? чему́?	о́кнам	поля́м	зда́ниям	времена́м
кем? чем?	о́кнами	поля́ми	зда́ниями	времена́ми
о ко́м? о чём?	об о́кнах	о поля́х	о зда́ниях	о времена́х

Feminine

case/meaning	yacht	hand/arm	land/earth	exercise book
singular				
кто? что?	я́хта	рука́	земля́	тетра́дь
кого́? что?	я́хту	ру́ку	зе́млю	тетра́дь
кого́? чего́?	я́хты	руки́	земли́	тетра́ди
кому́? чему́?	я́хте	руке́	земле́	тетра́ди
кем? чем?	я́хтой	руко́й	землёй	тетра́дью
о ко́м? о чём?	о я́хте	о руке́	о земле́	о тетра́ди
plural				
кто? что?	я́хты	ру́ки	зе́мли	тетра́ди
кого́? что?	я́хты	ру́ки	зе́мли	тетра́ди
кого́? чего́?	яхт	рук	земе́ль	тетра́дей
кому́? чему́?	я́хтам	рука́м	земля́м	тетра́дям
кем? чем?	я́хтами	рука́ми	земля́ми	тетра́дями
о ко́м? о чём?	о я́хтах	о рука́х	о земля́х	тетра́дях

case/meaning	bird	article (written)	guest (fem.)	village
singular				
кто? что?	пти́ца	статья́	го́стья	дере́вня
кого́? что?	пти́цу	статью́	го́стью	дере́вню
кого́? чего́?	пти́цы	статьи́	го́стьи	дере́вни
кому́? чему́?	пти́це	статье́	го́стье	дере́вне
кем? чем?	пти́цей	статьёй	го́стьей	дере́вней
о ко́м? о чём?	о пти́це	о статье́	о го́стье	о дере́вне
plural				
кто? что?	пти́цы	статьи́	го́стьи	дере́вни
кого́? что?	пти́ц	статьи́	го́стий	дере́вни
кого́? чего́?	пти́ц	стате́й	го́стий	дереве́нь
кому́? чему́?	пти́цам	статья́м	го́стьям	деревня́м
кем? чем?	пти́цами	статья́ми	го́стьями	деревня́ми
о ко́м? о чём?	о пти́цах	о статья́х	о го́стьях	о деревня́х

b. Adjectives

бе́л-ый, -ая, -ое, -ые 'white' = hard non-ending-stressed

Masculine	Neuter	Feminine	Plural
бе́лый	бе́лое	бе́лая	бе́лые
бе́лый/бе́лого	бе́лое	бе́лую	бе́лые/бе́лых
бе́лого		бе́лой	бе́лых
бе́лому		бе́лой	бе́лым
бе́лым		бе́лой (бе́лою)	бе́лыми
о бе́лом		о бе́лой	о бе́лых

больн-о́й, -а́я, -о́е, -ы́е 'ill, sick' = hard ending-stressed

Masculine	Neuter	Feminine	Plural
больно́й	больно́е	больна́я	больны́е
больно́й/больно́го	больно́е	больну́ю	больны́е/больны́х
больно́го		больно́й	больны́х
больно́му		больно́й	больны́м
больны́м		больно́й (больно́ю)	больны́ми
о больно́м		о больно́й	о больны́х

бли́зк-ий, -ая, -ое, -ие 'near' = hard non-ending-stressed; -final к/г/х

Masculine	Neuter	Feminine	Plural
бли́зкий	бли́зкое	бли́зкая	бли́зкие
бли́зкий/бли́зкого	бли́зкое	бли́зкую	бли́зкие/бли́зких
бли́зкого		бли́зкой	бли́зких
бли́зкому		бли́зкой	бли́зким
бли́зким		бли́зкой (бли́зкою)	бли́зкими
о бли́зком		о бли́зкой	о бли́зких

сух-о́й, -а́я, -о́е, -и́е 'dry' = hard ending-stressed; final к, г, х

Masculine	Neuter	Feminine	Plural
сухо́й	сухо́е	суха́я	сухи́е
сухо́й/сухо́го	сухо́е	суху́ю	сухи́е/сухи́х
сухо́го		сухо́й	сухи́х
сухо́му		сухо́й	сухи́м
сухи́м		сухо́й (сухо́ю)	сухи́ми
о сухо́м		о сухо́й	о сухи́х

то́щ-ий, -ая, -ее, -ие 'skinny' = hushing non-ending-stressed

Masculine	Neuter	Feminine	Plural
то́щий	то́щее	то́щая	то́щие
то́щий/то́щего	то́щее	то́щую	то́щие/то́щих
то́щего		то́щей	то́щих
то́щему		то́щей	то́щим
то́щим		то́щей (то́щею)	то́щими
о то́щем		о то́щей	о то́щих

больш-о́й, -а́я, -о́е, -и́е 'big' = hushing ending-stressed

Masculine	Neuter	Feminine	Plural
большо́й	большо́е	больша́я	больши́е
большо́й/большо́го	большо́е	большу́ю	больши́е/больши́х
большо́го		большо́й	больши́х
большо́му		большо́й	больши́м
больши́м		большо́й (большо́ю)	больши́ми
о большо́м		о большо́й	о больши́х

зи́мн-ий, -яя, -ее, -ие 'winter's' = soft

Masculine	Neuter	Feminine	Plural
зи́мний	зи́мнее	зи́мняя	зи́мние
зи́мний/зи́мнего	зи́мнее	зи́мнюю	зи́мние/зи́мних
зи́мнего		зи́мней	зи́мних
зи́мнему		зи́мней	зи́мним
зи́мним		зи́мней (зи́мнею)	зи́мними
о зи́мнем		о зи́мней	о зи́мних

во́лч-ий, -ья, -ье, -ьи 'wolf's' (волк 'wolf'); including тре́тий 'third'

Masculine	Neuter	Feminine	Plural
во́лчий	во́лчье	во́лчья	во́лчьи
во́лчий/во́лчьего	во́лчье	во́лчью	во́лчьи/во́лчьих
во́лчьего		во́лчьей	во́лчьих
во́лчьему		во́лчьей	во́лчьим
во́лчьим		во́лчьей (во́лчьею)	во́лчьими
о во́лчьем		о во́лчьей	о во́лчьих

Such adjectives typically have a 'possessive' nuance.

ку́ц-ый, -ая, -ее 'tailless'

Masculine	Neuter	Feminine	Plural
ку́цый	ку́цее	ку́цая	ку́цые
ку́цый/ку́цего	ку́цее	ку́цую	ку́цые/ку́цых
ку́цего		ку́цей	ку́цых
ку́цему		ку́цей	ку́цым
ку́цым		ку́цей (ку́цею)	ку́цыми
о ку́цем		о ку́цей	о ку́цых

Such adjectives are mainly compounds based on -лицо́ 'face', e.g. бледноли́цый 'pale, palefaced'.

длинноше́-ий, -яя, -ее 'long-necked'

Masculine	Neuter	Feminine	Plural
-ше́ий	-ше́ее	-ше́яя	-ше́ие
-ше́ий/-ше́его	-ше́ее	-ше́юю	-ше́ие/-ше́их
-ше́его		-ше́ей	-ше́их
-ше́ему		-ше́ей	-ше́им
-ше́им		-ше́ей (-ше́ею)	-ше́ими
о -ше́ем		о -ше́ей	о -ше́их

Such adjectives are provided by compounds based on ше́я 'neck'.

c. Family Names

Here is a table for family names in -ин, -ын, -ев, -ов, -ёв. The adjectival forms are italicized. Let's have Чáплин 'Chaplin', basically Ukrainian or dialectal, but derived from Russian цáпля 'heron'.

Чáплин	Чáплино	Чáплина	Чáплины
Чáплина	Чáплино	Чáплину	Чáплин*ых*
Чáплина		Чáплин*ой*	Чáплин*ых*
Чáплину		Чáплин*ой*	Чáплин*ым*
Чáплин*ым*		Чáплин*ой*	Чáплин*ыми*
о Чáплине		о Чáплин*ой*	о Чáплин*ых*

2. Abbreviations and a note on the translations-glosses

a. Abbreviations

A, acc.	accusative	lit.	literally
arch.	archaic	loc.	locative
D, dat.	dative	masc.	masculine
emph.	emphatic	N, nom.	nominative
fem.	feminine	neut.	neuter
G, gen.	genitive	P, prep.	prepositional
ger.	gerund	part.	partitive
I, instr.	instrumental	perf.	perfective
imp.	imperative	pl.	plural
imperf.	imperfective	prov.	proverb
inf.	infinitive	sing.	singular
intr.	intransitive	tr.	transitive

b. Note on the translations-glosses

In the translations-glosses, which are approximate and, at times intentionally, inconsistent, I have aimed at achieving a balance between suggesting the meaning — the exact meaning is difficult to achieve at the best of times, and giving some insight into the grammatical structure of the words and phrases. For the latter to have been done properly would have required a quite different book.

3. A few terms, with reference to Russian

agreement
links indicating which words go together, e.g. a singular masculine noun in the accusative case form will require an adjective in the accusative singular masculine. This allows agreeing words not to be next to each other in text, rather useful for poets but also a *real* option in the language.

apposition
the addition of extra information in a sentence, agreeing with the information to which it corresponds, e.g. 'the boy, *young and inexperienced*, smiled nervously'.

aspect
many Russian verbs are considered to occur in aspectual pairs, the difference focussing on the implication or not of a *limitation* on the action/state described by the verb (an alternative, and perhaps initially clearer, generalization, would be *change*). This intersects with *tense*; thus, the imperfective aspect does not imply any limitation on the meaning (e.g. change, beginning, result) and is available to all tenses (present, past, future), while the perfective, which implies a limitation, is generally held not to be available to the present.

attribute
the qualification of a word by another, typically of a noun by an adjective, e.g. 'the *young* girl'.

case
an ending on a word indicating its relationship to other words in the sentence, e.g. subject or object of a verb, agreement with, typically, a noun, government by a verb or preposition. A governed word is usually tied to its position after a governing preposition, but otherwise cases permit a flexible word order. Russian has at least the following cases: nominative, accusative, genitive, dative, instrumental, prepositional.

conditional
in Russian mostly the past tense of the verb accompanied by the particle бы and conveying the sense 'would'. Its functions partly overlap with those of the subjunctive in, say, French.

finite
the tense forms of a verb, basically the non-past, though the past may now be included.

future
overall identical with the non-past, though a special 'compound future' exists for imperfective verbs. See 'non-past'.

gender
classifications for the purpose of agreement. In Russian masculine, feminine, and neuter.

205

gerund   an invariable verbal form corresponding to 'doing' when it means 'when X is/was doing, because X is/was doing', etc. (thus a 'verbal adverb'). This also covers 'without/not doing' (for the negative), 'having done', 'without/not having done'. It is available when X is identical with the subject of the main (finite) verb in the sentence.

government   the requirement by one word of a particular case form in another word, typically after verbs and prepositions. Thus, certain verbs and prepositions 'take' certain cases.

hard   consonants without the characteristic described under 'soft', thus what one might imagine to be the basic sound of a consonant.

imperative   the command form of the verb, e.g, '*Go* home!', *Listen* carefully!' This extends in Russian into wishing ('optative') expressions, e.g. 'let's...', 'let him...'

infinitive   the citation or dictionary form of the verb, corresponding to English '*to* X'. The past tense may be readily formed from it. One needs on the whole to know one or two of the non-past forms to derive everything else.

non-palatalized   see 'hard'.

non-past   the set of endings conveying all English equivalents of the present and future tenses. In Russian a special future form, though with non-past endings (as with perfective 'futures'), exists for быть 'to be'; it is used autonomously and with the imperfective infinitive to provide the imperfective future.

number   the endings words take in order to indicate at least singular and plural.

object   typically part of what the sentence is saying, the new information. Thus, in *Ivan sees Masha*, *Masha* is the object. In English the object comes after the verb; in Russian this is very often the case but, because of the case system, is less obligatory. There may be a division into 'direct object', expressed in the accusative', and 'indirect object', expressed otherwise.

palatalized   see 'soft'.

participle   superficially similar to the gerund, but corresponding to 'who/which is/was doing', etc. and adjectival in form (a 'verbal adjective'), thus having case, gender, and number.

particle	Reflexive -ся/-сь and the imperative -те may be seen as particles, but more important are the 'little words' which may be attached to others and convey contrast and emphasis of various degrees, e.g. же, -то, ведь.
past	gender endings in the singular and a single plural form conveying past time in verbs, going back to an original resultative or perfect participle. Covers most of the English 'past tenses'.
predicate	what the sentence is about, the part which, for example, says something about the subject, e.g. 'Nina *saw the cat*'.
prefix	a component added before the root of a word.
preposition	a word or group of words originally conveying temporal and spatial information, now much wider, and making more explicit the meanings of the cases, e.g. *in, after, before, on, without, thanks to, towards*.
reflexive	a verb form involving action directed to oneself or to 'each other' or used, seemingly arbitrarily, in other verbs. Formally, the attachment of a particle -ся/-сь to the forms of the verb.
root	the basic form of a word without prefixes, suffixes, and endings.
soft	a consonant where the 'basic' articulation is accompanied by a closeness of the tongue to the roof of the mouth (the hard palate) and characterized by what might be heard as a *y*-sound following hard on the consonant but actually integral to the consonant. Thus a soft *l* might seem similar to the sound of Italian *gli* or English *lli* in *million* (provided the *i* is not pronounced fully), and could be contrasted with a 'hard' *l*, as in *look* and in extreme pronunciations almost like *w* (but to be avoided!).
stem	the form of a word to which endings are added, i.e. the root including any prefixes/suffixes.
stress	the pronunciation of one vowel in the word more prominently than the others, in Russian the pronunciation of one vowel 'clearly', which has as consequence a weaker pronunciation of the others. In Russian the stress can occur anywhere and must be learnt.
subject	typically what the sentence is about, grammatically very often conveyed in the nominative case. Russian impersonal sentences (sentences with grammatical subjects) may often be interpreted as having subjects expressed in other ways.

subjunctive   see 'conditional'.
suffix   a component added after the root of a word.
tense   the form of the verb conveying the time of the 'action'. From the point of view of actual forms, Russian has past and non-past (= present and future) tenses, a special future having developed for the imperfective and thus making aspect a formal feature of the grammar.
verb of motion a small group of verbs, some of them very important, which in their simplest form are generally considered to have two imperfectives, one quite particular in time and place ('one-directional') and the other less constrained ('many-directional').
voiced   consonants pronounced with the accompaniment of buzzing of the vocal cords, e.g. *z*, *zh*, *v*, and as such contrasted with voiceless consonants, e.g. *s*, *s h*, *f* respectively, which lack this buzzing.
voiceless   see 'voiced'.

INDEX

END-PIECE

Writing this book has been a real challenge. I owe an immense debt of gratitude to the authors of a mass of books used over the years, from every one of whom I have learnt so much. In the list below I mention a very few books which have spent more time on my desk than others while I was working — one or two of them have 'mistakes' (and mine will too), but every one of them also provided precious information and hints — I think that's how things should be. Constantly in the background were Peter Jones's wonderful *Learn Latin* and *Learn Ancient Greek.*

More important, of course, were the immensely patient people who answered my questions and told me how to express things better. When undertaking a book of this sort one is constantly placed in the most trying situations — the roots of one's at times assumed knowledge are sorely tested, rather specific and difficult issues are constantly cropping up, and there is a dilemma regarding the selection of material and of particular approaches. One thing I *can* say is that every bit of Russian in this book has been approved or is taken from an authentic source, such that nothing has been 'made up' in order to illustrate a point. The other thing is that, while I have tried the impossible, namely to be 'simple', I have felt that such an approach risks being deceptive and condescending — I haven't been intentionally deceptive (though there may have been some self-deception) and I hope I haven't been condescending. So there is a good deal here which some people might consider 'difficult'. All I can say is that there are many approaches to writing a textbook (I'm not sure that I consider this a textbook, by the way), that you don't *have* to use or like this one, and that my own experience (if I may call it that) suggests that there is room for an approach such as the one I've adopted here. And, like every literary author exploited in the chapters, I'm rather fond of my subject, and of languages in general, and if that comes across, wonderful.

Bibliography and References

Morton Benson, *Dictionary of Russian Personal Names*, Cambridge: Cambridge University Press.

F.M. Borras, R.F. Christian, *Russian Syntax. Aspects of Modern Russian Syntax and Vocabulary*, Oxford: Clarendon Press, 1971 (second edition)

Bernard Comrie, Gerald Stone, Maria Polinsky, *The Russian Language in the Twentieth Century*, Oxford: Clarendon Press, 1996.

Roger Comtet, *Grammaire du russe contemporain*, Toulouse: Presses Universitaires du Mirail, 1997.

L.A. Deribas, *Русский язык на курсах и в кружках*, Moscow: Russky Yazyk, 1987. (The transliteration of the name of the publishing house as it appears in English.)

V. Dronov, *Le nouveau russe sans peine*, Chennevières-sur-Marne: Assimil, 1995.

T.F. Efremova, V.G. Kostomarov, *Словарь грамматических трудностей русского языка*, Moscow: Russky Yazyk, 1993.

Francesca Fici Giusti, Lucyna Gebert, Simonetta Signorini, *La lingua russa. Storia, struttura, tipologia*, Roma: La Nuova Italia Scientifica, 1991.

O.I. Glazunova, *Давайте говорить по-русски*, Moscow: Russky Yazyk, 1997.

S. Khavronina, *Russian as we speak it*, Moscow: Russky Yazyk, 1986 (eighth of many editions)

S. Khavronina, A. Shirochenskaya, *Russian in Exercises*, Moscow: Russky Yazyk, 1989.

S. Khavronina, L. Kharlamova, *Русский язык*, Moscow: Russky Yazyk, 1996.

James S. Levine, *Schaum's Outline of Russian Grammar*, New York, etc.: McGraw-Hill, 1999.

Frank J. Miller, *A Handbook of Russian Prepositions*, Newburyport: Focus Texts, 1991.

I. Pulkina, E. Zakhava-Nekrasova, *Russian. A Practical Grammar with Exercises*, Moscow; Russky yazyk, 1994 (sixth edition)

Larissa Ryazanova-Clarke and Terence Wade, *The Russian Language Today*, Routledge: London and New York, 1999.

M.A. Sheliakin, *Справочник по русской грамматике*, Moscow: Russky Yazyk, 1993.

B.O. Unbegaun, *Russian Grammar*, Oxford: Clarendon Press, 1957.

Also the many dictionaries — I don't want to make a recommendation: simply make sure you go for something which gives grammatical and stress information in the entries. For your Russian future, the best specialist dictionary is without doubt A.A. Zalizniak's *Грамматический словарь русского языка* (Moscow: Russky yazyk, 1987), and one which stands out head and shoulders above most modern dictionaries (and is a wonderful read) is Sophia Lubensky's *Random House Russian-English Dictionary of Idioms* (New York: Random House, 1995).

And now for some less linguistic books:

Robert Auty and Dimitri Obolensky (eds), *An Introduction to Russian Language and Literature*, Cambridge: Cambridge University Press, 1977.

James H. Billington, *The Icon and the Axe. An Interpretive History of Russian Culture*, New York: Vintage, 1970.

F.A. Brokgauz and I.A. Efron (compilers), *Малый энциклопедический словарь*, Moscow: Terra, 1997 (reprint of the second edition, 1907).

Archie Brown, Michael Kaser, and Gerald Smith, *The Cambridge Encyclopedia of Russia and the former Soviet Union*, Cambridge: Cambridge University Press, 1994.

Hélène Carrère d'Encausse, *Le malheur russe. Essai sur le meurtre politique*, Paris: Fayard, 1988.

Neil Cornwell (ed.), *Reference Guide to Russian Literature*, London and Chicago: Fitzroy Dearborn Publishers, 1998.

Zita Dabars, with Lilia Vokhmina, *The Russian Way. Aspects of Behavior, Attitudes, and Customs of the Russians*, Lincolnwood: Passport Books, 1996.

K.V. Dushenko, *Словарь современных цитат*, Moscow: Agraf, 1997.

I.P. Eremin and D.S. Likhachëv, *Художественная проза киевской Руси XI-XIII веков*, Moscow: GIZhL, 1957.

J.L.I. Fennell (selection, introduction, prose translations), *Pushkin*, Harmondsworth, etc.: Penguin Books, 1964.

Simon Franklin and Jonathan Shepard, *The Emergence of Rus 750-1200*, London and New York: Longman.

Camilla Gray, *The Russian Experiment in Art 1863-1922*, London: Thames and Hudson, 1962

Genevra Gerhart, *The Russian's World. Life and Language*, New York, etc.: Harcourt Brace Jovanovich, 1974. (The latest edition, which I haven't seen, is apparently very much to be recommended.)

R.I. Iarantsev, *Русская фразеология. Словарь-справочник*, Moscow: Russky Yazyk, 1997.

Daniil Kharms, *Incidences*, London and New York: Serpent's Tail, 1993. (Edited and translated by Neil Cornwell.)

Walther Kirchner, *Russian History*, New York: HarperCollins, 1991 (seventh edition).

Dimitri Obolensky (ed.), *The Penguin Book of Russian Verse*, Harmondsworth: Penguin Books, 1965 (revised edition).

Valentina Morderer and Miron Petrovskii (compilers), *Русский романс на рубеже веков*, Kiev: Oranta Press, 1997.

Anne-Marie Olive, *Guide de civilisation russe*, Paris: Ellipses, 1998. (A very welcome type of work, though certain facts as given, e.g. dates, should be treated with caution.)

Pierre Pascal, *Histoire de la Russie*, Paris: Presses Universitaires de France, 1967 (sixth edition).

Nicholas V. Riasanovsky, *A History of Russia*, New York — Oxford: Oxford University Press, 1993 (fifth edition).

A.D. Stokes (selector), *Хрестоматия по древней русской литературе — Anthology of Early Russian Literature*, Letchworth: Bradda Books Ltd, 1963 (based on N.K. Gudzii, *Хрестоматия по древней русской литературе XI-XVII веков*, Moscow, 1962).

Max Vasmer, *Russisches etymologisches Wörterbuch*, Heidelberg: Carl Winter, 1953-1958 (three volumes).

Excellent editions of texts can be obtained from *Bristol Classical Press*, a member of the Duckworth group.

What next?

I hope this book has maintained the enthusiasm you must have started with; otherwise why did you buy it? Though there is something about the book which means you will come back to it time and again, what you really need now is the establishment of a broader framework, to guarantee you the motivation you get from other enthusiasts. Contact your local, or not so local, adult education institutes, schools, and universities to find out what is available — these days the internet is likely to help you here too. If you can find a Russian, persuade them to let you use their language with them. And feel free to contact me — your comments and requests for help and advice will be most welcome. My e-mail address is:

<jip@st-andrews.ac.uk>